WOMAN IN HINDU LITERATURE

WOMAN
IN
HINDU LITERATURE

R. P. SHARMA

GYAN

GYAN PUBLISHING HOUSE

New Delhi 110 002

"Of All Things Upon Earth That Bleed and Grow,
A Herb Most Bruised is Woman"

—Euripides : Media (431 B.C.)

* * * *

"Modern Society is not a Society of People;
it is Merely a Society of Males"

—Henrik Ibsen : Notes and Jottings (1882)

WOMAN IN HINDU LITERATURE
(Literature, Sociology, Women's Studies)

ISBN : 81-212-0501-8

Published 1995 in India by
Gyan Publishing House
5, Ansari Road,
New Delhi 110 002

Printed at Tarun Offset Press, New Delhi.

PREFACE

The author of a modernist apology for the "synthetic culture" of the Indo-Aryans makes claims which are simply untenable in the light of available material on the early history of India. He says contradictory things in the same breath. On the one hand, for example, he claims that the Indo-Aryan culture is a synthetic product while, on the other, he holds that "it was the highly educated brain and the organizing Aryan genius which played the determinative part in giving that product the shape and direction it is seen to have taken" (Ghose 1988 : iii). He speaks of 'mass conversion ceremonies' (Vratyastoma Yajnas) organized by the Indo-Aryans to Aryanize the non-Aryans and then he claims that the former borrowed many beliefs and customs from the latter. His book is on the whole replete with confused and confusing generalizations on Indo-Aryan literature and culture. But two of his general propositions call for a critical scrutiny. One of these propositions contends that the incoming Aryans did not confront or subdue the pre-Aryan inhabitants of the Indus Valley simply because there was, he believes, an interval of at least a thousand years between the 'catastrophic' disappearance of the Indus Valley Civilization and the advent of the Aryans into the Indus Valley region (cf. p. 241).

Historical opinion on the real cause of the disappearance of the Indus Valley Civilization (or the Harappan Culture) is divided. But a number of historians agree that the advent of the Aryans was the most probable cause of such disappearance. The Aryans came to India with fire, sword, chariot, horse and a radically different culture. It was only natural that they confronted and subdued the native inhabitants (cf. Thapar 1966 : 34, Allchin 1968 : 143, Majumdar *et. al.*, 1978 : 14, Smith 1981 : 32 & Mahajan 1990 : 47). Apologists like Ghose have therefore to be continually reminded that the history of Hinduism derives its identity from the systematic Aryanization of the non-Aryans as much as from the firm institutionalization of Aryan customs, beliefs and manners. There seems to be little doubt that those who established Hinduism as a system of faith and a way of socio-political behaviour were the tall, fair-skinned, long-nosed, 'handsome' and powerful Aryans who took excessive pride in their cultural advancement, intellectual maturity and physical superiority and who intensely feared and hated the relatively shorter, dark-skinned, snub-nosed and less sophisticated inhabitants of pre-Aryan India. The Aryans and the pre-Aryans represented the polarities of a human population. They differed from one another in so many ways and to such an extent as there was hardly anything common between them. Pre-Aryan customs, beliefs and institutions were treated with contempt by the invading Aryans. It was just a quirk of fate that the pre-Aryan inhabitants could not cope with the superior arms and fighting strategies of the incoming Aryans and history took a turn that it did. Now, looking back over the millenia, no academic should try to ambiguate or cover up a fact of history that so pointedly stares us in the face today.

The ethnic composition of the pre-Aryan inhabitants of India was probably some sort of a mixture that we might call 'Afro-Dravidian' (cf. Thapar 1966 : 26, Allchin 1968 : 137, Majumdar *et. al.*, 1978 : 14, Mahajan 1990 : 47 and Date 1993). It is probable that India has been inhabited for hundreds of thousands of years. The original natives, however, may have been very primitive tribes scattered over vast tracts of land and divided into small pockets. At some time, may be, thousands of years ago, waves of Afro-Dravidians began to pour in to conquer the natives and to spread all over the country. And then towards the middle of the second millenia the Aryans began to stream in. With the advent of large groups of Aryans, the Afro-Dravidians were conquered and converted into an order that has existed since. These successive invasions and conquests changed the demographic composition of India. It is likely that a large number of inhabitants were simply destroyed in course of these invasions, conquests and conversions. As Majumdar *et. al.*, put it : "Many must have perished, and many more, reduced to subjection, formed the lowest strata in the community of the conquerors, while a few bands were saved from a similar fate by the shelter offered by fastnesses and jungles. This last category alone has preserved, to a certain extent, the physical features, the languages, the habits of their remote ancestors, offering us a fair glimpse of the sort of life they must have led in times long gone by" (1978 : 14). Nevertheless, by the time of the Epics, Aryan ascendancy over the Dasas, Dasyus or Shudras was complete (cf. Thapar 1966 : 37-38).

Ghose's second proposition is more dangerous and misleading than his first proposition. It needs to be immediately pointed out that nothing can be farther from the truth than a proposition which seeks to prove that the doctrine of Hindu castes is "non-Aryan in origin" (1988 : 154). The caste-system is the differentia of the Brahmanic socio-religious philosophy. When the Aryans came to India, they encountered the natives who were radically different from them in terms of physical features, complexion, beliefs, customs and manners. The Aryan perception of the "self" in relation to the "other" was crucially determined by the colour of the skin and this led to the rigid separation between the conqueror and the conquered in terms of caste. As the most vital principle of Brahmanic Hinduism, the doctrine of caste (first a binary division between the Aryan and the non-Aryan and then expanded to a four-fold division into Brahmanas, Kshatriyas, Vaishyas, and Shudras) had to be recognized as one of the directive principles of the socio-religious organization that was going to take shape in the wake of the Aryan conquest of India. It was probably owing to "a fear of the Dasas and even greater fear that assimilation with them would lead to a loss of Aryan identity" that the founders of Brahmanic Hinduism considered it expedient to divide the whole population into four castes in order that the non-Aryan could become part of the Aryan fold and yet remain outside the Aryan pale (cf. Thapar 1966 : 38. Smith 1981 : 61 and Mahajan 1990 : 86-87). The Sanskrit words for caste, *varna* and *jati,* mean `colour' and `birth' (cf. Thapar 1966 : 38 and Majumdar 1990 : 86). The twin components of colour and birth came to be emphasized throughout the Vedic period. Relevant sections in the *Rig-Veda* and the *Yajur-Veda* make it quite explicit that the four castes have to be arranged in a descending order with reference to colour and heredity. The Vedic definition of caste leaves no room for interpretation. It is so simple and clear. The first three castes, although arranged in order of decreasing fairness and of the decreasing prestige of the accompanying occupation, have a common ground: they are all **dvijas** (the twice born) while the fourth one is the non-Aryan outcast caste.

Close on the heels of Ghose's naive apology, comes the postmodernist defence of the Hindu caste system offered by an eminent scholar in a recent but otherwise excellent paper on the Diasporic Hindu. It is baffling that in his reasoned 'reflections' on the status of the Diasporic Hindu, Bhikhu Parekh comes up with an untenable and sweeping generalization. He is of the view that the *Ramayana* is "a relatively casteless text. Valmiki, its author, belonged to a primitive tribe. Kamban, who rendered it in Tamil and popularized it, was also from a lower caste. Tulasidasa, whose rendering of it is highly popular, was a Brahmin, but belonged to a castefree and devotionally oriented bhakti movement. ... The message of the epic is largely non-casteist" (1993).

A couple of remarks by way of clarification are in order here. Parekh, to say the least, has got the whole thing upside down. He should know that one does not have to be an emperor to support or propagate imperialism. Likewise, it is not obligatory for one to be a Brahmana in order that one may subscribe to or popularize the doctrine of Brahmanism or Brahmanization. It is not required of a thinker or writer to be an orthodox or 'pure' Brahmana to sing the praise of Brahmanhood. Apart from this, it is not an incontrovertible fact of history that Valmiki belonged to a primitive tribe or that Kamban was of a lower caste. For all we know, Kamban was perhaps a non-Brahmana priest and a protege' of a princely mentor. Tulasidasa appears to have been an orthodox Brahmana both by birth and training. As regards Valmiki's lineage, it is not certain that he was a non-Brahmana. On the contrary, he was perhaps a Brahmana of a very illustrious line. He says in the last verse of the epic (VII, 111.11) that he is the son of Pracheta who is traditionally reckoned as one of the great sages (Prajapatis or Maharshis cf Roy & Gidwani 1986 : 244). The doctrine of the four castes and the four stages (Varnashrama dharma) forms the core of Vedic or Brahmanic Hinduism. It is, therefore, impossible for a Hindu text, not to speak of a Hindu classic, to be casteless, castefree or noncasteist. With the single example of the Samvuka-episode in its concluding part, Valmiki's *Ramayana* deserves to be seen as a thoroughly caste-conscious, caste-sensitive or casteist Hindu classic. In view of such doctrinal constraints of the *Ramayana*, Parekh's generalization sounds preposterous and indefensible.

With the successful consolidation of their position in India, the Aryans established, once for all, a socio-religious system which divided people into high and low, master and slave, superior and inferior on the basis of their colour, occupation and sex, and assigned their hereditary roles and functions accordingly. Within a paradigm like this the woman and the Shudra (a term which gradually replaced 'Dasa', 'Dasyu' or 'Anarya') were lumped together and assigned the roles and functions of slaves and servants. The Aryan or Indo-Aryan framework presents a rigidly defined social hierarchy in which woman and Shudra were placed at the bottom. The only way of survival for such 'lowly' people within this framework was to serve and please their masters. Any one who resisted or tried to rebel was liable to be eliminated. The history of Brahmanic Hinduism has, therefore, been the history of the Aryan indoctrination of women and Shudras. Hinduism was codified in the Vedas and re-inforced in the Upanishadas, Puranas, Smritis, Epics and other sacred books. It was codified and re-inforced by Brahmanas or Brahmanizers in the interest of the Aryans/Indo-Aryans. Hinduism thus became a synonym for Vedism, Aryanism and Brahmanism, in spite of the plethora of euphemisms used in literature, whether secular or sacred. It is no wonder that the entire corpus of secular and sacred literature of the Hindus seeks to rationalize the colour-based and gender-based division of society and put the target people in their place as a matter of their destiny. From the earliest Vedism to the postmodernist Brahmanism, the pillars of Hindu society have been unanimous in their choral apotheosis of the establishment known as Hinduism. Hindus are perhaps the only community on earth who have not yet faced any systematic resistance (despite Draupadi, Razia Sultan, Lakshmi Bai, Indira Gandhi and the like) to their continued hold on the socio-religious structure of their power game. And the main reason for their unchallenged and continuing supremacy has been that men (except the handful of Tantriks or Shaktas) have not yet defined femininity as a viable concept nor have educated or powerful women yet made it a class issue to unsex men or to oblige them to unsay what they have been saying for ages.

Hindu writers do not, perhaps cannot, conceptualize characters like Clytemnestra or Nora or even Helene Alving. The king of kings and the Commander-in-chief of the Greek army, Agamemnon sacrifices his daughter for success in war and turns to other women to have nice time during his long absence from home. The Trojan

War is successfully completed and Agamemnon returns home. As soon as he arrives at the Palace, he is taken in, trapped in a net and stabbed to death by his wife, Clytemnestra. She kills him because he killed her daughter without her permission; she kills him because he associated himself with other women; but most importantly, she kills him because she cannot put up with his 'manly' position; she kills him not only out of vengeance but also as a means of achieving her independence of him as a human being. His murder is her salvation. Aeschylus makes this point so clear in his masterpiece named after his hero, who is, by all standards, such a great warrior and conqueror but who is outmanned by the terrific Clytemnestra. Ibsen's Nora has been a faithful and loving wife to Helmer for eight years and has borne him three children. Something happens and Helmer fails to take her blame on him and Nora suddenly makes up her mind to get out of wedlock. Helmer invokes religion, morality and the laws of society to dissuade her. Nora says she does not know what religion or morality is; as for the laws of society, she tells Helmer, "when a wife leaves her husband's house, as I am doing now, he is absolved by law of all responsibility for her. I can at any rate free you from all responsibility. You must not feel in any way bound, any more than I shall. There must be full freedom on both sides. Look, here's your ring back. Give me mine" (Ibsen 1970 : 193). Helene Alving is not Nora. She runs away from her debauched husband, no doubt, but she is persuaded to return home only to be rewarded with the birth of a syphilitic son, premature widowhood, the son's painful death by the softening of the brain and the destruction by fire of her husband's expensive memorial. But self-critical Helene soon realizes that her life has been a farce. She dives deep into seeing for herself the meaning of wifehood and motherhood and ultimately discovers a mere 'nothingness' but she can at least be proud of her discovery. It is nothing less than a discovery that she can see life so clearly. In a mood of enlightened vision, she tells Pastor Manders : "we are all ghosts, Pastor Manders, every one of us. It's all kinds of old defunct theories, all sorts of old defunct beliefs, and things like that. It's not that they actually *live* on in us; they are simply lodged there, and we cannot get rid of them. I've only to pick up a newspaper and I seem to see ghosts gliding between the lines. Over the whole country there must be ghosts, as numerous as the sands of the sea. And here we are, all of us, abysmally afraid of the light" (Ibsen 1970 : 232). Ibsen wrote *Ghosts* and *A Doll's House* more than a hundred years ago. Compare a heroine in a Hindu masterpiece and see how shadowy and inauthentic she looks beside Ibsen's. The greatest woman of Sanskrit drama is a mere shadow beside even a weakling like Helene. What does Shakuntala achieve after all her sufferings and humiliations? Can she see even a ray of light? Can she see that she cannot see the light? Abandoned by her parents, brought up by a poor mendicant, picked up, used and left off by a middle-aged powerful seducer, she is a pitiable young pregnant girl with no hopes for the future. She goes to the ruthless one-time seducer who rejects her just out of hand. And then she has to wait for years to end up as a captive for life in the harem of a doddering, hopeless ruler. This Shakuntala is projected as the greatest heroine of Sanskrit drama without any qualms of conscience on the part of educated readers and learned critics.

Teaching a course on drama for the first time in my NEHU career in 1985, I became interested in the literary representation of women characters, particularly in Hindu literature. I started reading books on Hindu literature but soon began to realize that I could only collect a long list of stereotypes. As I was reading more and more books on the subject, the NEHU Centre for Literary and Cultural Studies organized a two-day National Seminar on 'Women in Literature' on 4-5 August 1986. I attended all the sessions. Then came the last session, part of which was devoted to comments and questions and answers. As I had not asked any question, the Convener of the Seminar asked me to comment on my understanding of the proceedings of the Seminar. I felt quite disappointed with what had been presented at the paper-reading sessions and so I made a remark by way of my comments. Addressing myself to the learned participants, I said: "Either you do not mean what you have been saying or you have been deliberately trying to take the audience for a ride". Two of the participants told me after the Seminar that they had never examined literary portrayals of women characters from women's point of view. They had never in fact questioned the concepts on which literary character-sketches of women characters are based. The papers had therefore turned out to be a truckload of readymade stuff in so-called 'women's studies'. Now, papers presented at a Seminar organized by a women's college in Bangalore and published under the title *The Image of Woman in Indian Literature* (cf. Yashoda Bhat 1993) do not show a state of affairs any better than the one shown by the 1986 NEHU Seminar. The 'image' volume raises questions like : Who is the real woman? What is her real entity? Has she an identity of her own? but does not seem to make any conscious and critical effort to answer even one of them. Besides, it includes a patronizing Foreword by Narasimaiah and a dismissive and pejorative article by Krishnamoorthy, in addition to other trite and hackneyed write-ups on women.

A majority of workshops, seminars, papers and books on women do not convince sceptical students of women's studies for the simple reason that they do not want to take the bull by the horns or to call a spade a spade. They do not do what is expected of them. "Some of them", to borrow a remark of Richards (though made in quite another context), "many of them indeed, are profitable starting-points for reflection, but neither together, nor singly, nor in any combination do they give what is required" (1960 : 2). I fail to understand why women writers, writers who are committed to the cause of women, cannot explode the myth of the so-called Hindu philosophy of man-woman equality. It is unfortunate that even intelligent and educated women should fail to identify and expose the basis of such myths. Woman cannot be emancipated unless the entire thinking about femininity is wholly revolutionalized. This can be done, needless to add, only by woman herself. Unless woman totally rejects male definitions of her roles and functions and salvation, she cannot achieve true liberation. It is only woman who can and must decide what is proper and necessary for her. It is only woman who can and must identify and stabilize the true meaning of femininity. It is only woman who can and must define and defend her autonomy.

However, in spite of all that I say in this study, I do acknowledge (turning Eliot's famous remark about Shakespare to suit the present context cf. 1951:126) that about anything so bulky and complex as Hindu literature, " it is probable that we can never be right; and if we can never be right, it is better that we should from time to time change our way of being wrong. Whether Truth ultimately prevails is doubtful and has never been proved; but it is certain that nothing is more effective in driving out error than a new error ". One can only hope that if serious and concerted efforts are made to bring about a radical change in the traditional paradigm of femininity, things will definitely become better, both for academic perceptions as well as for the assignment of gender roles in society. It must be made absolutely clear to everyone that women can no longer be cajoled, swindled, patronized or ignored.

Personally speaking, I would like to clarify that my understanding of womanhood is primarily based on my knowledge of two women-Chandrakala and Meera—(my wife and daughter, respectively) for more than three decades now. I have tried to analyze my behaviour both in and out of my psyche and have come to the conclusion that my reading of masculinism is in fact a reading of my own self in relation to them. This study should therefore be seen as an exercise in self-criticism. I am the vicious and hypocritical Hindu male. I am the *pater familias.* I am the demanding husband and the commanding father. My description of the masculinist image is actually a description of my own image. However, I may indulge in a little amount of self-glorification by reclaiming I A Richards' apology for his historic book published exactly seven decades ago (cf. Richards 1960). My book, I fear, will seem to many sadly lacking in condiments which have come to be expected in writings on women in literature, particularly on women in Hindu literature.

I would take this opportunity to express my profound sense of gratitude to Dr. B. Pakem, Professor of Political Science and Vice-Chancellor, NEHU, Shillong for the Introduction. I would also like to thank my friend Sri R.C. Pandey, CIEFL, Regional Centre, Shillong for his generous library support and Dr. N.P. Goel, Department of Geography, NEHU, Shillong for proof-reading the final typescript. It gives me a great sense of satisfaction to place on record that Om Prakash, my son, has been so consistently and critically helpful to me in finalizing my manuscript. My thanks are also due to my friends, colleagues and students who have helped me in many ways.

R.P. SHARMA

Department of English
NEHU, Shillong
01 January 1995.

Introduction

I consider it a great privilege to have been able to go through the manuscript of Dr. R.P. Sharma, Department of English, North-Eastern Hill University, Shillong, on his serious literary work *Woman in Hindu Literature.* I also consider it my professional duty to gladly accept his request to write an introduction to this very important work. The reason for assigning me this task is the author's decision, since I do not claim to be an authority on Women's Studies in general nor on Hindu women in particular. Though I am a resident of India (Bharat) and an Indian (Bharatiya) by birth, the task is much more difficult for me in view of the fact that, by birth in the periphery of the great Indian tradition, I am a non-Hindu by faith, belonging to a non-patrilineal society and professionally trained in a discipline other than literature. However, this does not deter me from trying to understand the problem of Hindu women as depicted in the present volume as I am a part, perhaps, of what is called Indianness (Bharatiyata). It is with this conviction that with great pleasure I am writing the following few words on the literary work of Sharma who professes himself to be a Hindu.

Women's studies occupy an important place in the curricula of so many educational institutions in our country. For centuries women, all over the world, including India, have been an oppressed lot. After India's independence, our Constitution makers had pledged themselves in the Preamble to the Constitution of India "to secure to all citizens ... equality of status". But so far there has been no remarkable achievement in the direction of the actual improvement of the status of women. True, after 1956, some legislative enactments were made for improving the lot of Indian women, particularly in the field of property-ownership. There were also attempts to improve their conditions in the fields of education and employment. However, whatever improvement was achieved was by and large the outcome of the general processes of social change or evolution in the country rather than through state legislation. That was why the Government of India thought it necessary to constitute a Committee on the status of women by a resolution of the then Ministry of Education and Social Welfare on September 22, 1971 to examine all questions relating to the rights and status of women and to recommend useful guidelines for the formulation of social policies regarding women. The Report of the Committee which was ready by December 1974 was presented to the Government of India in 1975 coinciding with the celebration of the International Women's Year. The International Women's Year was later on extended to the International Women's Decade (1975-1985). Ever since that time there has been a spurt of activities in studying the status of women in our country. I only hope that our International Women's Year and International Women's Decade will not turn into an International Women's Century.

In the Preface, Sharma refers to some studies on women carried on in the country. It is the casual nature of such women's studies which really irritates him. These studies fail to raise relevant questions such as : Who is the real woman? What is her real entity? Has she an identity of her own? In the absence of such relevance, the problems of women in India have not been critically examined. There are no doubt some studies of a serious nature on the specific question of the status of Hindu women but he questions their validity too. It appears to me that he takes a stand between the modernist apology of the "synthetic culture" of the Indo-Aryans and the post-modernist defence of the Hindu caste system. In order to take up this difficult position he has to indulge himself in an exercise of self-criticism too. It is to his credit that he has been able to do so as the following pages of this book would indicate.

The first chapter of the book deals with the aim and the central theme of the subject matter under study. The aim of Sharma in his study is to give "an account of the age-old and consistent discrimination against woman in Hindu history in the aftermath of the Aryan invasion and conquest of India". From a binary classification of people into Aryavarna and Dasavarna, there developed a four-fold classification of the first three castes for the Aryans and the fourth for the non-Aryans, the Shudras who were regarded as non-caste. This classification was duly supported by the principle of divine origin of placing the first three groups each under a god and the fourth one with no god at all, resulting in the division of labour for the four varnas. All this is quite familiar to the students of the history and civilization of the Indian people. But what has not been overtly emphasized, as Sharma does, is to be found in the central theme of this book in which he excludes the non-Aryan Hindus or non-Hindu Aryans since all Hindus are not Aryans and all Aryans are not Hindus. The central theme of *Woman in Hindu Literature* is to examine the nature of the oppression of Hindu women due to the constructs of Aryanization. Sharma writes : "Aryanization creates a hiatus between the Aryan male on the one hand and the Aryan female, the non-Aryan male and the non-Aryan female on the other. It idolizes the Aryan male and denounces the Aryan female and the Shudra". Further, he is of the opinion that the Aryan female is in fact equated with the Shudra ideologically by saying that : "To be a Shudra is bad, to be a woman is worse, to be a Shudra woman ... is worst", and reaches a crescendo with the words : "Hindu literature cannot be regarded as a literature that respects or supports male-female equality".

While writing on Hindu women, Sharma does not lose sight of the practices prevailing in other parts of the world. He is quite aware of the low status of women elsewhere and is intrigued by the fact that women are treated in all sorts of ways in literature. He is very clear in his mind that their sufferings are not due to their faults or vices but are created by men. Being a man of literature, he could have a peep into the thought process or world view of Western women when he ponders over the view expressed by Ismene in *Antigone* that it is by "nature" rather than by man-made convention that women "do not attempt" to rival men. He, therefore, wonders why women, despite some "exceptional women", have not yet made it a class issue to "unsex man". It is in this context that he compares the *Iliad* and the *Ramayana* where the struggle is not really because of a woman but because of a politico-economic war.

It is also interesting to note that Sharma refers to the egalitarian society of the pre-Aryans which was replaced by the hierarchical and fragmented society of the Aryans. In the pre-Aryan agricultural society the Mother Goddess (Shakti) was worshipped; in the Harappan civilization there was also the practice of mother worship and matriarchate existed as in ancient Greece; and the importance of woman prevailed in pre-Vedic Tantrik (Shakta) doctrine. In this connection I would like to point out that since time immemorial people all over the world have practised and followed the matrilineal structure. Gradually, the matrilineal system was affected due to the advent of different religious philosophies and agricultural practices, new systems of trade and commerce and the development of science and technology. The effect was so much that a large number of such societies disappeared and gave way to patrilineal systems. However, in some pockets of the world as among the African, South-East Asian and Oceanic tribal communities, where the processes of social change were very slow, the remnants of the system still continue to exist. In India too, it is held by many scholars that matriliny existed in pre-Aryan days and later on the Aryan system of patriliny was superimposed upon it. The fact that the Mother Goddess is still worshipped with attention and respect in various forms as a benevolent mother as well as a destroyer of evils and demons is attributed to the matrilineal base of Indian culture. We still have traces of such matrilineal societies in some parts of Kerala, Karnataka and Madhya Pradesh. In North-East India, the remnant of the matrilineal society is now confined only to the state of Meghalaya, though in the recent past we had such a society among the Rabhas and the Tiwas of Assam too.

"Politics of Discrimination", the second chapter of the book, raises a number of theoretical issues regarding the position of women in society. What Plato, as pointed out by the author, says in the *Laws* ("the origin of society was patriarchal") may not be universal in time and space. We do have examples of matrilineal societies as old as, if not older than, Plato. In addition to what has been referred to above, in China Taoism allowed women-priests and in North-East China there was, as early as 5000 BC, the practice of the worship of female figurines and Mother Earth or the Goddess of Mery called *Guanyin* in Chinese and *Kannon* in Japanese. In spite of this fact, the contention of Sharma is sustainable in that women may reign but they do not rule. To prove his point further he also refers to the

Biblical story of Eve as the "helpmeet" of Adam. But it is contended by present-day women theologians (in John S. Pobee, *Women, Culture and Theology*, Delhi, 1994) that the idea of a "helpmate" suggests that a woman, like God, "helps those who acknowledge their weakness and inferiority". In other words, the woman must be superior to man if we read two Biblical creation stories instead of one only. Further, both in the Old Testament (Gen 2:24) and in the New Testament (Mark 10:4-6) there are references to a matrilocal system in that the man is required to leave his parents and to live in his wife's family. But Sharma has his point in that, in practice, Christians in general follow the Jewish society where women occupy a lower position. Even in African matrilineal society where human beings have been earlier designated either as "male-man" or "female-man", now a woman has to "borrow" her husband's name. But this does not change the basic foundation of man-woman relationship just as in the case of a Filipino woman whether she is a *mujer indigena* or a *mujer cristiana* which made an American Governor-General to remark : "In the Philippines, the best man is the Filipino woman". It is, therefore, difficult to absolutize the culture in which the Bible was written.

The plight of Muslim women under the orthodox Muslim Law has also been highlighted by Sharma. Here, too, it is true that for non-Muslims, Islam is basically anti-woman. But women theologians again argue that on the contrary Islam was the first religion to "liberate" and "emancipate" woman. It is contended that cultural practice rather than Islam is responsible for the deplorable condition of Muslim women. Hence, the crux of the problem is the relationship between religion and culture. It so happened that Islam tended to expand into cultures and cultures have absorbed Islam and has reached such a point where it is really very difficult to differentiate between what is culture and what is Islam. The Quran (4:4) says : "And give the women (on marriage) their dower". But Sharma again scores a point in that Muslims do the contrary and collect the dowry from the woman instead. Stated differently, the Muslim Laws have been interpreted to suit male interests because the same verse adds : "but if they (the women), of their own good pleasure, remit any part of it (the dower), take it and enjoy it with right good cheer".

This "ambivalent attitude" of males to women in different societies is to be seen in the ambivalent attitude of Hindu males to women also. Sharma asserts that on the one hand Hindu texts eulogize some women but on the other hand they do not bear witness to the Hindu claim on gender equality. It is in such a situation of duplicity that in exasperation he cries out : "Perhaps no patriarchal people are as discriminatory against women as Hindu Law-makers are". He aptly calls his second chapter "Politics of Discrimination". The next three chapters deal with what Sharma calls `Ritualization of Marriage', `Strategies of Exploitation' and `Saga of Sexualization'. While idealizing matricentric or contract marriage, Sharma strongly denounces patricentric marriage (among Hindus) which pretends to be a religious marriage only to invoke God's help to undermine women. The treatment of Helen of Sparta and Sita of Ayodhya by their respective husbands after the war has been ably shown by him as a study in contrast. After the war against Troy, "Helen is recovered and brought to Sparta with honour". On the other hand, Rama goes to war against Lanka and "Sita is recovered only to be continually insulted and harassed till such time as she terminates her life". But it is not clearly stated why this difference exists between the *Iliad* and the *Ramayana* in view of the fact that the two marriages were patricentric. Sharma only says that in the case of Helen, Menalaus owes his kingship to his marriage with her, while Rama does not owe his kingship to his marriage with Sita. Rama fights the war only "to defend the honour and reputation of his great family" and not for the honour of Sita who by then is treated as "a bleeding ulcer".

In Hindu literature another contradictory practice in the ritualization of marriage is that while polygyny is acceptable, polyandry is regarded as prostitution, though the same literature has to rationalize the case of Draupadi who is the soul of the *Mahabharata*. In the matter of prostitution too while courtesans are respected and the devadasees are acceptable, the common prostitute is frowned upon. In spite of this classification Sharma has very rightly pointed out that the whole system of prostitution is an example of "chronic self-deception". Similarly, he terms child-marriage, which is encouraged by Hindu literature, as "sadistic paedophilia" and laments that, "we fail to criticize our heritage" in spite of legislations against such practice since 1929. On widow-burning which he terms a "notorious custom" and a "heinous practice", he says that while in other societies it was "part of their pre-history", in the case of Hindus it was "part of their post-Vedic history", meaning thereby that Vedic Hindus did not burn their widows as even the *Arthashastra* mentions "widow-marriage". Sharma has revealed illuminatingly that this takes place because of the replacement in Hindu literature of the Rig-Vedic expression "to the altar (*agre*)" by the post-Vedic Brahmanic expression "widow-burning (*agne*)". Though it was abolished in 1829, there has been no amelioration of the condition of Hindu widows.

After giving a full exposition of Hindu literature ranging from the sacred to the secular (which is later on regarded as religious) Sharma comes to the conclusion that : "The entire corpus of Hindu literature from the *Rig-Veda* to the *Kamasutra* should be seen as a careful stockpiling of strategies to convert a woman into a machine which can be used or abused at the pleasure of the male and without any regard for her working capacity". Sharma also asserts that the *Ramacharitamanasa*, the Bible of the Hindi-speaking Hindus, contains elements of "obscurantism regarding wifely duties" duly matched by the "ruthlessness of its denigration of women". Comparing Hindu women with Western women, Sharma refers to the former's condition by drawing attention to the "abjectness of their plight ... work without end, without rest, without remuneration and without appreciation". Not only that, they are also subjected to indiscriminate sexuality and violence. Again, compared to Western wife-batterers, some Hindu males resort to "bride-burning" (or dowry-killing) in spite of the fact that it was made a culpable offence in 1961. It does not end there. One form of violence leads to another. Apart from wife-battering and bride-burning, violent acts of rape have recently been replaced by violent acts of gang-rape which often lead to the murder of the innocent victim. No wonder then that the sex ratio of women in India has been on the decline. The unfavourable sex ratio for women was 972/1000 in 1901 and fell down to 929/1000 in 1991 (*IASSI Quarterly*, New Delhi, July-December, 1993). It may fall even more in future. Some other causes like female infanticide may be added to the reasons mentioned by Sharma above. Yet, as opined by him, the Hindu male justifies all this by raising a masculinist slogan that "woman is the enemy of woman". It does really sound like a gospel of male wisdom which, in fact, it is not. In comparing the status of Indian women with Western women it should also be noted that in addition to the burden of housekeeping and job attending, Indian women have also to carry the burden of tradition, society and religion.

In support of his critique on the saga of sexualization, Sharma quotes Basham who says: "The literature of Hindu India, both religious and secular, is full of sexual allusions, sexual symbolism and passages of frank eroticism" which is why Sharma opines that: "In Hindu thought the dividing line between eroticism and spiritualism is blurred". He also questions the divided loyalities of Hindu males who adore the *Upanishadas* and love the *Kamasutra* at a time. Sharma does not spare even Vatsyayana and criticizes those who have showered praise on his *Kamasutra* by saying : "It is amazing that his work despite such glaring deficiencies should have appealed to generations of religious thinkers and creative artists". He is quite convinced that : "It appeals to the general readers and to the pious mainly because it offers pornography through so-called spiritualism". The end result of all these literary masterpieces on sexualization is reducing woman to the status of a mere sex object. Like Vatsyayana, Kalidasa, who has been regarded as the Shakespeare of India, has also been severely criticized by Sharma for the "offensively sexual descriptions" in his poetic masterpiece the *Kumarasamabhava*. "A modern Hindu", says Sharma, "surveying religious literature in Sanskrit, gets the shock of his life and loses all sense of literary pride". He further adds : "He finds in his literature an obsessive concern with the criminalization of theology or the theologization of criminality and comes to the conclusion that it is high time such duplicity was exposed and rejected once and for all".

"Horrors of Denigration", the sixth chapter, sums up the nature of Hindu male thinking on the status of women. In the various Hindu literary texts, a woman has been looked down upon as an agent of the devil, fickle-minded, unreliable, impure, unchaste, irreligious, crooked, envious, disdainful, instructable, unclean, untruthful, undesirable, stupid and what have you. In the *Kamasutra*, there is a report about the people of Saurasena who justify their kissing the mouths of women since there is nothing wrong with this "indecent practice" as "women are naturally unclean". Sharma rightly calls it a "perverse nature" indeed. Even a good woman is ranked below a bad man according to the *Taittiriya Samhita*. It really amounts to distorting the feminine image and condemning the innocent woman as reflected in the sub-titles of the two sections of the chapter.

Upto this stage, it appears that Sharma has tried his best to demolish the myth of male superiority over women as sanctioned by Hindu literature. However, in defence of Hindu literature so far as the portions relating to women are concerned he has referred to the five greatest examples of the glorified ideal of womanhood in Hindu history. He mentions the names of Mandodari, Tara, Savitri, Draupadi, and Sita. But he has limited the greater part of his discussion only to Draupadi and Sita. In the conventional sense, Draupadi, according to Sharma's analysis is neither a wife nor a prostitute. She is somewhere in between the two and perhaps "wife-sharing" may be an appropriate term for her actual status. Whatever may be her status, Sharma looks at her as a "rebellious heroine" who is also "invincible, taintless and immortal". On the other hand, Sita is young, beautiful, innocent and devoted to marital fidelity, and unlike Draupadi she is a "silent sufferer". She has suffered so much that her tragedy is viewed by Rajagopalachari as "the voiceless and endless suffering of our women folk" and the present author with indignation regards "Sita's fire-ordeal, banishment and self-destruction as the most shameful chapters in the Indo-Aryan treatment of women". Personally too, I have always been baffled by such a tragedy and other similar tragedies of women in our present-day society notwithstanding the contention of G.B. Kanuga in his *Immortal Love of Rama*, (New Delhi, 1993) that Sita was never abandoned by "Rama, the Righteous".

The concluding chapter has, therefore, reached a climax in the sense that in between the two concepts of a "rebellious heroine" and a "silent sufferer", there lies a remedy for women through the theology of liberation. However, the problem as perceived by the author is that "there are women who abet men in committing crimes against women and sometimes against themselves". At the same time they want to be liberated. But the sad part of it, as Sharma puts it succinctly, is that women "want new opportunities but old security, new freedom but old protection". Hence, there is a need for a "new ideology" where not only some women are in a position to take up even national or governmental leadership but in the improvement of the position of women in general. True, tradition-bound Hindus may find it difficult to "adopt a new philosophy which would demand a radical departure from a repressive past to a liberal future". Hence, Sharma thinks even of "feminine insurgency", if all else fails.

The terms "new ideology", "new philosophy" and "feminine insurgency" in Sharma's work have prompted me to look at them from the perspective of post-modernism of Modern European Philosophy contained in Stephen K White, *Political Theory and Post Modernism* (1992). In the sixties and seventies of the present century the traditional relationship between man and woman came under unprecedented attack from feminists. The feminist politics of post-modernism has emphasized the concept of "difference feminism" coupled with the issue of "care" versus "justice". In some ways, post-modernism in society and politics and for that matter in philosophy is connected with post-structuralism. The structuralist analysis takes into account the logical working of "binary oppositions" like man-woman opposition. In the present context, post-structuralism means the displacement of the status of foundational opposition. Jacques Derridar's idea of "deconstruction", for example, refers to such kind of opposition. Or take Michel Foucault who deconstructs hiearchical distinctions. In doing that his intention is "to show how social institutions give practical force to such discursive distinctions and how such discursive distinctions are reconstituted in radically different ways in different historical periods". To my mind, post-structuralism and deconstruction emphasize the importance of "responsibility to otherness" rather than "responsibility to act". Hence, in the case of man-woman opposition in the patriarchal society the moral dimension of the "responsibility to otherness" is clearly evident, and much more so, when the 'other' attended to is a woman.

I am now coming to a close. Any social movement including feminist movement will have, therefore, to contain an element of intellectual thrust. We are fortunate enough in not lacking such intellectual materials from our Hindu literature. In fact, Sharma refers to such source materials when he says that women may take the help of the tradition of scholarship variously known as the Shakta cult, Shaktism and Tantrism where women are respected by men. Even in the post-Aryan history there were memoirs of some men who could see and appreciate women, though in mainstream Hinduism, those men could not wield any authority. Those traditions and memoirs, says Sharma, "would not allow any pejorative reference to women". The *Mahanirvana Tantra* and *Brihada Samhita* texts may bear testimony to this fact. Sharma believes that "Shaktism is a unique extant gift of the Afro-Dravidian matriarchy that probably existed in India till it was replaced by Indo-Aryan patriarchy". Of course, here is not a place for me to discuss the other problems of women even in matrilineal societies. Suffice it to say that though Sharma's conclusion is so beautiful, he still apprehends that "this study may be disputed". I would then say that such a dispute would only confirm the fact that the book has served its purpose and hope that the dreams of Mahatma Gandhi and Pandit Jawaharlal

Nehru would come true. Gandhi once said : "By sheer force of a vicious custom, even the most ignorant and worthless men have been enjoying a superiority over women which they do not deserve and ought not to have", and Nehru once wrote : "The future of India will probably depend ultimately more upon women than men" (IASSI Quarterly, July-December, 1993).

It is really a pleasure to read the book *Woman in Hindu literature* by Sharma which has been written in a lucid literary style. His expressions and interpretations are very clear and concise. It goes to his credit that he has been able to present a remarkably comprehensive and scholarly survey of the various aspects of the subject matter under study. His book should greatly help the study and understanding of this vital issue confronting our Indian society in general and women in particular.

B. PAKEM

NEHU, Shillong
28 January 1995.

CONTENTS

1

Constructs of Aryanization

> "It is difficult for a woman to define her feelings in language which is chiefly made by men to express theirs"
>
> --*Hardy : Far from the Madding Crowd*

Our life is full of blatant contradictions. Surrounded by despair and death, we stick to life and harbour hopes for unending prosperity. Steeped in ignorance, treachery and corruption, we brag about our unflinching commitment to sublime knowledge, ultimate truth and sky-high morals. Irredeemable atheists though we are, we keep trumpeting our faith in God and religion, at times, with an acute awareness that we are lying to one another. True to our genetic inheritance, we continue to be cut-throat liers and pretenders, despite our claim that we have achieved enormous advances in sanity and self-knowledge. Born and brought up in the world of contradictions and falsehoods, each of us ends up as a bundle of lies and distortions.

Far more helpless and dependent than his contemporaries in other parts of the animal kingdom, the human child is obliged by the contingencies of his birth to pass through a series of gruelling tests and experiences to make sufficient sense of his having taken the human form. He has to learn to sit up and crawl, walk and run, eat and sleep, laugh and cry, speak and listen, love and hate, and work and pray, just as his elders do in order that he may qualify for the membership of the human community he happens to be in. In addition to these exercises, he has to learn a language, partake of a culture, subscribe to a theology, develop a way of placing himself in relation to others and accept a form of polity so that he may become a *bona-fide* member of a community that his protectors, providers and parents have already structured for him. He is required to take part in all the prescribed and pre-determined activities, processes and ceremonies without question and resentment. He has to do all these not because he likes to do some or all of these but simply because the accidents of his birth and form make it mandatory for him to follow the dictates of his self-appointed masters. He can neither confront the heartless griffins that constantly surround him nor can he escape the army of meaningless rituals that queue up to invade him like the myriad forms of a pestilence.

The progress of a human child into an adult and useful member of a community depends, according to the custodians of communal identity, upon the quality and extent of his initiation into the ceremonies and rituals that constitute civilized existence. The human child is, in fact, dehumanized to become 'human' and yet he is obliged, in adult life, to testify under oath that the whole process of his dehumanization had to be planned and executed as a necessary condition of his humanizing development into a fully civilized being. Traditional ways of humanizing or civilizing a child into a social, political, moral and religious adult must be viewed as the most barbaric aspect of human civilization and development. The child is never allowed to act or grow with dignity in any significant sphere of life. He cannot eat and sleep, laugh and cry, act and play or love and hate the way he would like to. He is not only bullied into joining others in the infinite variety of forms and activities; in all these, he is obliged to do his part slavishly or mechanically and yet to pretend that he is doing everything on his own and for his own benefit. He has neither the freedom of choice nor the freedom of modality. His progress from infancy to adulthood consists in constructing a habit of doing and a habit of thinking which enable him only to conform to the demands of his community and yet to declare that he is ever doing fine.

Under circumstances like these, it is only inevitable that a conscientious adult—one in millions though—at some stage in life begins to view the story of his progress from infancy to manhood as an epic of pretentions and lies. An emerging awareness of this type gradually takes the form of an honest and individual scepticism and the adult starts to ask questions about a number of things that concern him most—about social and political institutions, religious rituals and practices, personal relationships and their mutual incompatibilities. Some of his questions may be : What is an individual? Who is he? Where does he come from? Where does he belong to? Does he belong to another individual? Does he belong to his community? Why does he do what he does? Why should he do what he does? Should he believe in a reigning deity? Does he really believe in what he says he believes in? Is he true to himself? Is he true to the others around him? Is it possible to be true to oneself as well as to others at a time? What is more important—the individual or the crowd? Can the individual, at times at least, rise above the crowd? Can the individual ever change the crowd's way of thinking or of doing? What is, above all, the meaning of existence?

Questions like these obviously point to the various forms of communal vis-a-vis individual identity—some of the forms being language, culture, race, religion, nationality, gender, class and occupation. We may, without much difficulty or confusion, discuss individual and communal identity with reference to one, some or all of these forms or markers and hope to formulate some tentative generalizations about the human situation as it obtains at a specific point of time in a specific milieu. We may choose whatever markers we like and then try to relate what an individual or a community does to why he or it does so without passing a judgement on the relative merit of the marker or markers in question. However, we may easily arrange these markers into a sequence with a view to showing that one marker is prior to another. It is in this sense that the present study attempts to examine its subject matter with reference to race and religion as the two fundamental markers of Hindu identity. Many Hindus believe that their ancestors descended from a certain ethnic stock originally known as "The Indo-Aryan" and that these Indo-Aryans developed a system of faith which is ideally monotheistic, though it entertains a large variety of gods and goddesses at the lower levels of the hierarchy.

Racial identity is generally sought to be established in terms of physical features like the colour of the skin, the colour and type of hair, the shape of the head, nose and eyes, the size of the body, the breadth of the chest, the length of the arms and the length and size of the thighs and legs, etc. The degree of intellectual development and the type of spiritual vision are often associated with physical features to define the full meaning of the racial identity. Similarly, religious identity is defined with reference to the nature of assumptions about the supreme deity, his relation to man, forms of rituals and prayers, rules of initiation and ostracization and the administrative structure of the sacred establishment. Every human community belongs to a religious fraternity as well as to a racial group. But as race and religion do not always correlate with each other, it is possible that people of one ethnic stock adhere to different systems of faith and people of one religious fraternity trace their origin to different ethnic stocks, including the Indo-Aryan, as Indo-Aryans are divided into different religious fraternities.

Race and religion are indeed very powerful markers of communal identity and it is often difficult to decide which of the two is more significant from the point of view of the community. But if we treat them as two discreet units of a sequence, we may find that race is prior to religion. It may be expedient for people sharing a system of faith, irrespective of their diverse ethnic histories, to stand together on most occasions in life but it does not therefore prove that ethnic kinship is less powerful than shared religiosity as a cohesive force. We have to have the correct perspective to judge which of these two is more basic to human consciousness of identity. Race and religion seem to operate on two different levels of human consciousness. Religious cohesiveness is directly visible whereas racial kinship operates on much deeper and subtler levels. It is true that inter-religious clashes are more frequent than inter-ethnic clashes but it needs to be emphasized here that the former are also far more superficial and momentary than the latter. Religious clashes may shed more blood than ethnic clashes but we must note that the latter cause much deeper wounds than the former. We must look beneath the surface to know that a shared system of faith may not bind different groups of people into a coherent and abiding brotherhood as a shared ethnic origin may. People sharing a common ethnic origin are often found drawn to one another spontaneously, irrespective of their mutual separation in terms of nationality or religion. Racial unity may be far more natural and intimate to human perception of oneness. Religious unity may be secondary, exterior and artificial to human consciousness of fraternity. Racially divided people may not ever succeed in forming a well-knit and stable fraternity. They may adhere to a common form of worship and yet may not develop a shared outlook. They may perform the same rituals and yet may not expect a shared benefit for all. They may go to the same place of worship and yet may scoff at one another. They may read the same scripture and yet may not make a shared response.

Since 'religion' is going to be used very frequently in the following pages, it is desirable that a clear distinction be drawn, for the purpose of this study, between the two meanings of this word. Religion is both a feeling and a thought, a spontaneity and a deliberation, a poetry and a planning, a vision and a manouvre, a revelation and a strategy, a personal response to the mysteries of life and a collective demand to run an organization, an acknowledgement of the unique blessings of life and a complex of rituals and schemes to maintain an establishment, an inspired perception of the ultimate truth and an organized system of thought to rule other minds. An established or institutionalized form of religion is a complex of rituals, a system of thought, a network of strategies and an organization of vested interests. Religion in the sense of a creativity, a vision or a revelation is something unique to individual consciousness. It is only an individual who feels and thinks about why and how life matters to him, about why and how he is what he is. It is only an individual who is a true philosopher, a poet, a sage, a seer or a prophet, although it is probable that several individuals separated in time and space feel and think about a particular phenomenon in identical or in closely similar ways. The collection of visions and revelations that forms the body of sacred literature across cultures should by itself demonstrate that a number of inspired individuals have felt about and responded to a certain set of phenomena as if they belonged to the same family. The eternal poetry of these wonderful visions fascinates us as nothing else can, for this type of poetry flows from those sublime heights of spiritual perception where man is only man. In this sense, religion comes to man as a perennial orchestra of universal and ageless prophets and invites him to join the divine music of the human heart. There is no rule or system in this orchestra. The only rule or system is its eternal music.

Such music of the immortal heart of man can never be labelled or categorized. Any attempt to systematize or classify such prophetic visions or inspired songs is unnecessary and wicked, parochial and selfish. No ritualism or systematization can ever be spontaneous or spiritual for an individual who feels and communicates the mysteries of being and the ecstasies of becoming. The moment an attempt is made to impose an order or system on these mysteries and ecstasies, they disappear and there remain only the dry , sterile , cold and empty words and phrases. As soon as an attempt is made to formulate a set of rules or strategies for these visions and revelations, a divine gift is converted into a social liability and a political commitment. No one can force a human soul and mind to feel and think about God or about the mysteries of life in a routine or academic manner. As soon as a sacred vision is reduced to a ritual, the vision becomes a text which can only be prescribed but can never be enjoyed or celebrated. Institutionalization of visions and revelations destroys the virginity of spiritual perception and offers instead a set of constructs which cannot move or inspire a sensitive human being.

Institutionalization converts poetry into politics and then we have religion which is only politics. As a matter of fact, we have by now reached a stage of human civilization where we cannot separate religion from politics or politics from religion. We have now religion in political forums and politics in places of worship. Our politics is *religious* as our religion is *political*. The synonymity between religion and politics is simply intriguing. So is their interdependence. Humanity has already suffered irreparable damages due to its political religion or religious politics. The politics of religion and the religion of politics have already done a greater harm than has any other human construct and yet we continue to cling to our politico-religious and religio-political leaders in the hope of ushering in an era of peace and prosperity for our kind. Our religion has failed us and we cannot expect it to help us move forward with peace and sanity unless we denied all its labels, classifications and establishments.

Perhaps never in its history has institutionalized religion offered any succour to mankind. It is no accident that religion has shed more blood than any other single human institution has. Is it not a miracle that such a divisive and violent institution should survive for such a long span of time? How does it continue? Who does it benefit? As soon as we raise such questions, we begin to identify the beneficiaries of organized religion and the devices that keep it going. We can easily point to the beneficiaries of the religious establishment. The leaders of the establishment are archetypal figures: they are ubiquitous and phoenix-like: they rise from their ashes. Replete with duplicity and deceit, these noisy members are there in places of worship as well as outside to attract and mesmerize a crowd. The crowd gathers around them because they raise hopes and point out short-cuts to prosperity and happiness. The crowd needs children, money, jobs, and above all, passports to bliss. It turns to leaders for making everything available. Once hypnotized by its leaders, the crowd begins to dance to their tune. If some wakeful soul ever tries to shock the crowd out of its illusions, it turns violent and destructive. An average conscientious individual can only look around to realize the utter hopelessness of the human predicament and feel sorry for the majority. Unless there is a Socrates in every home, the conscientious individual cannot visualize the freedom of the crowd from religious exploitation.

1.1 Genesis of Aryanization

> "A Brahmanȧ must be revered, though he be devoid of goodness or virtue; but a Shudra never, however virtuous or learned"
>
> —*Ramacharitamanasa*

Defined as a story of invasions and conquests, the history of India manifests three crucial turning points in its long and chequered career: the Aryan invasion and conquest, the Perso-Arabic invasion and conquest, and the British invasion and conquest. Each invasion and conquest brought to India the conqueror's language and theology. The Aryans brought with them the Sanskrit language and Vedism, the Perso-Arabs the Persian and Arabic languages and Islam, and the British the English language and Christianity. These invasions and conquests differ from one another in period, language and theology. But it is astonishing that their mutual differences in these three dimensions notwithstanding, all these invasions and conquests should share the same socio-political philosophy as well as the same structure of religious establishments. Each of them sought to impose a socio-political philosophy and a religious establishment intended to justify and perpetuate the superiority of the conqueror to the subject people. Everything about the conqueror, the subject people were coerced into believing, was unique and faultless, and hence worthy of emulation. The conqueror was born to rule and the conquered were destined to obey. It was the will of God that the conqueror should show his subjects the way in every walk of life.

There could be no common ground, the conqueror believed, between the ruler and the ruled, except their master-slave relationship.

Another interesting dimension of agreement among these invading-conquering tribes lay in their shared attitude to the position of woman in the various areas of the socio-political and religious life of the community. With the arrival of the invading-conquering tribes in the subject territory, there had to be two kinds of women: the conqueror's woman and the subject woman. The subject woman was to be viewed as a part of the subject crowd. But the conqueror's woman became a dubious character. She was neither wholly on the conqueror's side nor wholly on the subject's side. The personality of the conqueror's woman came to be split into two parts: on the one hand, she was part of the conqueror's baggage while, on the other hand, she became part of the subject race. As far as her duties and obligations were concerned, she was just a private slave of her master, even though she could distinguish herself from the large battalion of the subject-slaves. But she could claim her distinction from the subject-slaves only in respect of her physical proximity with the master. She could still be called daughter, wife and mother, no doubt, but she could not find the right niche for herself in the power-politics of her master because she remained woman and as such was fit only to be ordered about. Her master was convinced, more than ever, that all authority—whether social, political or sacramental—must emanate from and vest in man. The present study is intended to account for the age-old and consistent discrimination against woman in Hindu history in the aftermath of the Aryan invasion and conquest of India.

Modern Hindu society is, no doubt, a complex blend of people drawn from diverse ethnic stocks but the people whose socio-political ideology and religious theory established and institutionalized Hinduism as a stable system were the Aryans who came from outside, spoke Sanskrit and composed the scripture. It is due to these supremely intelligent, far-sighted and powerful people that Hinduism even today, at least notionally, remains essentially Indo-Aryan in its form and philosophy. Most caste Hindus still believe in their Indo-Aryan descent even though they have lost much of the colour of their skin and the sharpness of their features. The Aryan conquest of India may be viewed as not only the earliest and the most massive event in Indian history; it may also be seen as the most decisive historical development which determined the shape that future India was going to take for ever. The Indo-Aryans changed almost everything—from the family to the State—and established instead their own power units and social institutions, political ideology and centres of authority, economic order and measures of public welfare, scales of judgement and norms of ideal conduct, religious theory and beliefs, structures of thought and standards of intellectual excellence, moral values and perspectives of life here and hereafter. The extent and quality of the Aryan grip on the intellectual history of India may be gauged from a very simple fact: the Aryans destroyed almost everything pre-Aryan so that the history of India was to become the history of the Indo-Aryans. How little we know today about pre-Aryan India! Invading Aryans came to India, conquered India and gave India their own name. Post-Aryan India came to be known as "the land of the Aryans" *(Aryavarta)* or "the land of the gods" *(devabhumi)* as their language was to be known as "the language of the gods" *(devabhasha)*.

As we all know, all Hindus are not Aryans nor are all Aryans Hindus but Hinduism is even today predominantly Aryan in all its forms and functions. One could possibly trace certain developments in Hinduism to non-Aryan sources but most of such developments have been rather marginal. Non-Aryan influences do not seem to have ever been a decisive part of mainstream Hinduism which is just another term for Aryanism. The history of Hinduism has been the history of Aryanism in India, the history of Aryanism or Indo-Aryanism (to be more precise) has been the development of Vedism which, in turn, has been a euphemism for Brahmanism. It is for this reason that terms like 'Aryanism', 'Hinduism', 'Vedism' and 'Brahmanism' are used here as synonyms. Since this study is mainly concerned with Indo-Aryan Hindus, it will not include non-Aryan Hindus or non-Hindu Aryans in its definition of Hinduism in India. The two basic assumptions of this study are:

(1) that Aryans migrated to India from some other parts of the world, and

(2) that Aryan Hindus manifest a sense of greater spiritual affinity for non-Hindu Aryans everywhere than they do for non-Aryan Hindus in India mainly because their racial identity is far dearer to them than their linguistic, territorial, cultural or even religious identity. An Aryan is, first and last, an Aryan. He may speak any language;

> he may belong to any part of the world; he may have any culture or he may subscribe to any faith but his basic or decisive identity is his racial identity. An Aryan can transcend the barriers of religion, language, or culture but he cannot transcend the limits of his raciality. An Aryan is characterized by an unshakable faith in the innate superiority of his race to any other race as well as by his consistent perception of the non-Aryan as different and inferior. We read in the *Rig-Veda* (X:XX:8): "we are surrounded on all sides by Dasyu tribes ... their rites are different: they are not men! O destroyer of foes! kill them. Destroy the Dasa (Dasyu) race". The Aryan's impatience with the indigenous population was emphasized in an article in *The Statesman* not many years ago: "The Aryans were savagely hostile to the black aborigins, the children of the soil, when they were not ready to be their bonded slaves" (Dasgupta 1990).

Aryanism is an ideology that seeks to formulate and justify arbitrary definitions of racial superiority to the 'other' in terms of certain physical features as well as in terms of certain norms or forms of intellectual development. By Aryan standards white or fair skin, long and pointed nose, big blue eyes, broad chest and shoulders, long arms and legs, round and sloping thighs, slim waist and thin reddish lips are some of the necessary criteria of physical beauty. Any one who does not fulfil these criteria deserves to be dismissed as physically inferior. Similarly, Aryan norms and forms of religion, politics, science, literature and culture are some of the necessary criteria of intellectual excellence. Any community that does not possess these Aryan norms and forms of 'civilization' must be considered intellectually inferior. The Aryan equates difference with inferiority: the 'other' is inferior because it is different. But the Aryan never cares to ascertain the validity of his criteria of excellence or superiority. Why should white or fair skin be considered superior to dark or black skin? In what sense is a pointed nose more agreeable than a snub nose? How does a He-God become more adorable than a She-Goddess? Or why should a layered society be more civilized or civilizing than an egalitarian society? The absolutism of the Aryan norms and forms of superiority is mind-boggling. The Aryan just believes in the natural superiority of his notions, theories and constructs, and wants the other to take them on faith. The fact that the

Aryan race has so far been more manipulative and successful than others in a number of ways does not by itself prove that it is superior to other races in an absolute sense. The Aryan race has certainly accumulated, over the millenia, several 'firsts' to its credit. It has the most systematically documented history, religion, science, literature, social philosophy, and political theory and institutions. It claims the largest number of 'prestige' languages and territories and the greatest share of recorded human 'achievements'. But the accidents of history can never be taken as proof of its innate superiority to others.

It is sometimes contended that 'Arya' or 'Aryan' is never used in the ethnic sense in Vedic or post-Vedic texts and that it is used only to mean 'freeman' or 'master' as opposed to 'slave' or 'servant' (cf. Chanda 1976 : 245, Roy & Gidwani 1983 : 119). The view taken in this study, however, is that 'Arya' or 'Aryan' is almost invariably used in the ethnic sense in all texts, including the Vedas and the Epics. The degree of intensity with which 'Arya' or 'Aryan' is opposed to terms like 'Dasa', 'Dasyu', 'Ghor', 'Mlechcha', 'Shudra', 'Asura', 'Nishachara', 'Rakshasa', 'Nishada', and 'Anarya' provides incontrovertible evidence of its semantic fixity in ancient Hindu texts. The Indo-Aryans are described as a self-conscious, domineering, blessed and proud race even in recent books on Hindu history. The author of *The History of Aryan Rule in India,* for example, describes the Indo-Aryans as a 'dominant' and 'masterful' race (Havell 1972 : 3-4). He argues that according to ethnographic investigations the Indo-Aryans described in the Hindu epics were "a tall, fair-complexioned, long-headed race with narrow, prominent noses, broad shoulders, long arms, slim waists like the lion and thin legs like the deer" (p 32). The non-Aryans who were gradually subdued by the "superior arms and superior intellect" of the Aryans are referred to with "horror and disgust" and are described as Rakshasas or demons in Hindu epics (p. 13). The Aryans who came to India and made it their home, bequeathed to us, says Bader, their songs and epic poems which are "the oldest monuments of our race and the souvenirs of its origin" (1964 : 3). "The white Aryans", Bader adds, "were proud of the purity of their race, their delicacy of feeling, their religious instincts" and hence they despised the 'Dasyus' (p. 23). According to Sengupta, the Indo-Aryans were" a virile and hearty race, "a fair-skinned, tall, stalwart people", "who despised the snub-nosed, dark-skinned, phallus-worshiping Dasas or Dasyus" (1974 : 26, 27 & 28). Returning to the same point a few pages later,

Sengupta remarks "from the first conquest of the earlier civilization, the Aryans, a fair-skinned race, looked down upon the original Indians of a darker race and caste actually began with colour difference of the conqueror looking down upon and disparaging the vanquished" (p. 59). In an article in the *Encyclopedia Britannica*, Goetz tells us that the indigenous non-Aryan inhabitants of India, generally styled `Dasyus' (*i.e.*, people to be tamed) were "profoundly hated .... by the Aryan settlers" (1980). An Indian anthropologist observes: "We get some evidence in the Vedic literature of conflicts between the Aryans or the civilized people and the forest-dwelling communities. The aboriginal inhabitants with whom the Aryans came into contact have been described as `Ghor' which means 'dark'; they are `noseless' (Bose 1975 : 108). An eminent Indian scientist propounded the view at the Indian History Congress in Mysore in 1993 that the earliest peopling of India began with large-scale migrations from Africa about fifty to sixty thousand years ago. Based on genetic techniques of demographic studies, this view holds that the influx of dark-skinned Africans into India continued for thousands of years and that the waves of fair-skinned Aryans from Central Asia began around six thousand years ago (Date 1993). The Africans who came from the South and the Aryans who came from the North in course of time composed the demographic structure of the land which was to be known as India in later times. These two groups of migrants differed from each other in almost all respects: in place of origin, in period of arrival, in number, in colour of skin, in physical features, in language, in politics and in theology. It was only inevitable that they had mutual distrust and dislike for each other. It was just a quirk of fate that the populous and early migrants were over-powered by the later and smaller tribes of settlers. An Indologist of the fame of B.N. Pande remarks: "It is hard to believe that the Aryans were indigenous to India" (Kalidas 1993).

There appears to be no valid reason to support the view that Aryans did not come from outside or that terms like 'Aryan' and 'Dasyu' were ever used in non-ethnic, neutral senses. These terms have always been racist terms and they themselves prove that their coiners were people who came to India from outside and who had to put up with Indians who were already there. One could refer to several extracts in *The Indo-Aryan Races* which provide, contrary to the intentions of the author, sufficient ground for the conclusion that the history of India is very largely a manipulation of the Aryan rulers. In the opening lines of the book the author says that the hymns of the *Rig-Veda* "reveal two hostile peoples ... the deva-worshipping Aryas and the deva-less and rite-less Dasyus or Dasas" (Chanda 1976 : 1). A few pages later, he observes: "the conception that the difference between the different groups of people is congenital and not artificial was founded on the fact that the earliest social groups known to the Aryans ... actually differed ... in colour (varna) and other prominent physical characters.... Colour and race differences, real or fancied, together with hereditary function, gave birth to the caste-system" (pp. 35-36). Towards the end of the book, the author says that in the early Vedic age "the noseless aborigins, who opposed the Aryas, were called Dasyus or Dasas. In the later Vedic literature, the Shudra, instead of the Dasyu or Dasa, is contrasted with the Arya" (p. 245). The claim of Dr. S.R. Rao of the National Institute of Oceanography on the "Indianness" of the early Aryans and their language Sanskrit (cf. Kanchan 1987) sounds, in the light of available material—which points to their "foreignness"—both unnecessary and spurious. The children of Buddha and Gandhi need no apologies for talking about embarrassing hometruths. The view that the Aryans came to India from outside is accepted by a whole host of scholars (cf. Bader 1964 : 3, Havell 1972 : 4-5, Sengupta 1974 : 28, Baig 1976 : 4-6, Chanda 1976 : 26, Goetz 1980 & Lal 1980 : 375-376).

Scholars widely agree that the Aryans streamed into India through the North-Western passes of the Himalayas, that they gradually conquered the whole of India and monopolized every significant aspect of the socio-politico-religious life in India through their superior arms, intellectual power and organizational skill, that they always distinguished themselves from the indigenous people because they were different in the colour of skin and physical features and that they did everything possible to keep the majority subject population constantly under their control. According to Goetz, the people who brought with them "the horse and the chariot and the Sanskrit language ... are generally known as Aryans, the name by which they referred to themselves. They were a branch of related group of nomadic and semi-nomadic peoples originally inhibiting the steppe country of Southern Russia and Central Asia. Other branches of these peoples penetrated in Europe bringing with them Indo-European languages that developed into the chief language groups now spoken there" (1980). "The Aryan people", writes Havell, "who gradually imposed their civilization upon the whole of India were closely related, that masterful race ... their entry into India was chiefly through the North-Western gateways of the Himalayan mountain wall" (1972 : 4). Havell goes on to say, "The pioneers of Indo-European civilization, like their fellow Aryans in Southern Europe, won their way more by their superior intellectual qualities than by their fighting strength. Though for many centuries holding themselves aloof from the non-Aryan races and jealously guarding their spiritual inheritance from profanation by the uninitiated, their laws, political institutions and religious ideas gradually became for the vast majority of the people the warp and weft of Indian life, even for the millions in whose veins no Aryan blood can now be traced" (p. 9). Likewise an Indian scholar of Vedic India holds that "the Aryans of the entire Indo-European stock followed the same customs and practices" (Shastri 1969 : 32). The universal unity of the Aryan spirit which transcends the boundaries of language, culture, religion and nationality may be expressed in a single sentence if we borrow what Elvin writes in another context: "They do not worship different Gods; they all worship the same God in different ways" (1961).

It is probable that Aryans originally lived in surroundings where life was not so easy nor was Nature so benign as it was elsewhere. Food and shelter were perhaps scarce. Light, fire, water and vegetation were perhaps rarities. Fertile agricultural land and plentiful fruit gardens were perhaps not available. The climate and the topography perhaps did not much change from month to month, year to year. Perhaps it was all white, dull and icy. Such endless monotony and hardship may have led the inhabitants to surmise that their life and surroundings were created and controlled by an all-powerful and unchanging God. Primitive and ice-bound Aryans perhaps imagined a divine order which was an unconscious extension or a psychological parallel of their real physical world. Their perpetual cravings for light, fire, water and vegetation may have led them to imagine Gods of those who were headed, of course, by One God, the Supreme Deity, the Brahma, the Lord of creation, preservation and salvation. Such scarcity of food and the daily cycle of hardships may have turned the early Aryans into professional hunters and food gatherers. Their circumstances may have obliged them to kill in order to live. They could not afford to be non-violent and vegetarian. Besides, their surroundings may have compelled them to keep their women and children inside the caves. They had to be protected from wild beasts and the hazards of Nature. They could not be allowed to accompany men on hunting expeditions. Circumstances like these may have made it expedient for adult males to assume the role of providers and protectors of their women and children. It was no linguistic accident that the Vedic word for 'husband' or 'brother' came to mean 'the protector' (Bharta/Bhrata) and that for 'wife' or 'sister', 'the protected' (Bharya/Bhagini). It was no act of blasphemy that early Aryans "ate meat and drank intoxicating liquors" (Havell 1972 : 13). The sages of the *Brihadaranyaka Upanishada* did not find it embarrassing to prescribe: "In case one wishes that a son, learned, famed, a frequenter of council-assemblies, a speaker of discourses desired to be heard, be born, that he be able to repeat all the Vedas, that he attain the full length of life—then the (man and woman) should have rice boiled with meat and should eat it prepared with ghee. The two are likely to beget (him) with meat, either veal or beef" (VI : IV : 18, Hume 1949 : 171).

In *The Aryan Ecliptic Cycle* H.S. Spencer hypothesizes that Aryans originally lived in the North polar region and that they were compelled to leave their original habitat due to the onset of the Ice-Age and to migrate southwards around 10,000 B C (1965 : 15-16). On the authority of the *Avesta* he tells us that the Aryan paradise was located "in a region where the sun shone but once a year" (p. 22). "Even those migrating Aryans had by then developed such a high state of civilization and culture that they were able to face and conquer the other races in course of time to establish their sway over the whole of Asia and Europe" (pp. 15-16 & 28-31).

According to Spencer, Aryans had long been a very powerful people but their most important achievement had been in the realm of religious theory. They believed in and adored deities representing the various aspects of the natural phenomena, no doubt, but above all, they subscribed to a system of religious meditation which may be described as "stellar worship" (p. 18). As the first prophet of the Aryan race, Zarathushtra taught the vibration theory of creation which explained the origin of the universe in terms of the Laws of Vibration and radiation. The Prophet showed that Light and Fire were indissolubly united in the process of creation and that they had to be taken as the basic manifestation of the Law of Vibration (p. 24)

Hymns of adoration to the gods of Light and Fire that we find in Vedic literature do definitely seem to suggest that Vedic Aryans, like their Zorostrian predecessors, believed in stellar worship as well as in the supremacy of the theory of radiation and vibration. It is not for nothing that the Indo-Aryans ultimately selected Vishnu to be their highest God, the Absolute. Vishnu comes to us as the personification of the sun which in turn combines the twin powers of heat and light in the creation and preservation of life. Light and Fire gave the Vedic Aryans not only a viable explanation of the mystery of creation and preservation of life but also what they had always wished to have in abundance. As had been their wont, the Aryans established in India a divine pantheon which accorded maximum prominence to the powers of light and fire. In the *Rig-Veda* some sages are introduced as the "Sons of Agni", while mankind in general is said to have descended from Manu, the son of Vivasvat, that is, the "sun-god" (cf. Chanda 1976 : 17). In one of the earliest of *Upanishads*, man and woman are described as "sacrificial fire", while in the *Mahabharata* Draupadi and her brother are said to be "fire-born" (Hume 1949 : 162, VI : II : 12 & Lal 1980 : 98-99). But, above all, the content of the Gayatri Mantra, the most sacred verse of the Vedas, defines, once for all, the central thrust of the Indo-Aryan religious doctrine. This Mantra recognizes and celebrates the perennial supremacy of the sun-god over all other stellar deities: "We meditate on that excellent light of the divine sun; may he illuminate our minds" (cited in Lal 1980 : 380). In post-Vedic literature Vishnu and His Incarnations replace the sun-god. The transformation of the sun into Vishnu seems to be a natural consequence of the Puranic process of the replacement of stellar deities of the Vedas with personified gods. Traditionally, the lineage of Rama, the matchless imperial incarnation of Vishnu is directly linked with the sun-God by projecting Him as the most prominent king of the solar dynasty while Krishna, the unique philosophical incarnation of Vishnu, is represented despite his lunar lineage as one who "scorches the universe with his radiance" and whose effulgence is incomparable. A Verse in the *Gita* says : "If the effulgence of a thousand suns were to appear in the skies simultaneously it might compare somewhat with the splendour of that great form" (XI : 12 cf. XI : 19). The entire corpus of Indo-Aryan literature projects the sun or his personification as the supreme Deity probably because it combines light and fire with the creation and preservation of life. Is the sun supremely adorable because, above all, it symbolizes, as it shines and radiates, the effulgent superiority of white/fair-skin, always and everywhere?

Spencer's account of the pre-Vedic Aryans projects them as a very sophisticated and powerful people, no doubt, but their arrival in India seems to have brought about a great improvement in their understanding of life's philosophy. As soon as they entered India, they seem to have undergone a spiritual enrichment they had perhaps never experienced before. It seems reasonable to conjecture that at the very first sight of the dreamland, the incoming Aryans found themselves spell-bound by the unique simultaneity of the eloquent magnificence of the snowcapped Himalayas, the lustrous majesty of the daily sun, the tinkling music of the down-flowing rivers, the lush greenery of the beautiful meadows and the inviting looks of the vast and fertile tracts of land. The enchanting scenery of this magic world transformed traditional hunters and food gatherers into blissful bands of singers and poets. The ravishing panorama of the eternal Indian variety show flooded them with the countless wonders of Nature. The hymns of the *Rig-Veda,* the earliest in record the world knows of, were the first outpourings of a wonderstruck people (cf. Sengupta 1974 : 26). The transformation of traditional hunters and food gatherers into full-throated singers and poets took place so suddenly and spontaneously that before they could realize what was happening to them, they had uttered a whole saga of songs and hymns which celebrated, in an organized verbal form and for the first time in human history, the unprecedented alliance between man and nature. No previous panorama had ever flooded the Aryans with such abundant creativity as the Himalayan panorama did.

Once they abandoned their original habitat, Aryans became a nomadic people which they remained until they were able to settle down wherever chance took them. Their status as settlers in different parts of the world did have a definite impact on their psychology and on their attitude to the indigeneous people. The Aryans knew that the onset of the Ice-Age had played havoc with their life-style and they had to abandon their homes to become vagabonds. Their departure from home had been filled with uncertainties, risks and challenges of all sorts but they had persistently refused to succumb to those uncertainties, risks and challenges. They had decided instead to survive and go ahead. Such determination and fortitude had converted their odyssey into wonderful voyages of discovery. During their long and hazardous passage from country to country, they had been exposed to all types of peoples, places, climates and strategies. These encounters had never dampened their spirit. They had rather made them an army of invincible combatants. By the time they streamed into India, they had come to realize on the basis of their long racial experience that the only way to survive for them was to overcome difficulties by confronting and overcoming whatever came their way. If the natives in India did not want to live at peace with them, they were ready to fight and fight they did for long periods to have their way.

What did the early Indo-Aryans do to establish themselves in India? They invaded and conquered, one by one, in all walks of life and in all dimensions of civilization. Their greatest success however lay in imposing their own view of life on the people they had subdued. They institutionalized everything: language, culture, religion, politics, literature, philosophy, science, morality, wifehood, motherhood, social customs, relationships and behaviour-patterns. They ushered in an era of regimentation in every way and on every level. Their multi-dimensional, multi-level regimentation they carried out with caution and ruthlessness. They knew full well that their regimentation would command unswerving obedience to their inviolable and sacrosanct authority. They prescribed laws and patterns of behaviour (social, political and religious) which were intended to turn their institutions into centres of supremacy. The Indo-Aryan institutions and laws devoured the indigenous norms of excellence and centres of power.

Aryanism is a set of beliefs and values which postulates a rigidly defined hierarchial social structure in which the high and the low are clearly and permanently separated from each other on the basis of their gender and colour of skin. Aryanism creates a hiatus between the Aryan male on the one hand and the Aryan female, the non-Aryan male and the non-Aryan female on the other. It idolizes the Aryan male and denounces the Aryan female and the Shudra. It glorifies the inviolable purity of the Aryan male but condemns the congenital impurities of the Aryan female and the Shudra. It insists on the perception of the Aryan female and the Shudra as different, low and despicable. It is no coincidence that caste-Hindus still believe in the purity of their caste, even though Yudhishtira admits that "no one can be sure of his own caste's purity" because men of all four castes have been breeding children "from women of all four castes" (Lal 1980 : 157). Today we come across dark-skinned Brahmanas and fair-skinned Shudras which shows how confused and unsure has been the Hindu caste system. And yet the modern Brahmana considers himself an Aryan and therefore superior to the Shudra. As far as Aryanism is concerned, traditional ideology prevails over contemporary physical reality. When a dark-skinned

Brahmana flaunts the purity or superiority of his lineage to a fair-complexioned Shudra or when a stupid and wretched husband inflicts his claims for family leadership on his enlightened and smart wife, we are obliged to define Aryanism as a system of values and beliefs rather than as a set of physical features and intellectual characteristics. Normally, social conditions should change faster than ideological constructs. But it is unfortunate that in India neither ideological constructs nor social conditions have changed much since the arrival of the early Indo-Aryans. An average Shudra still belongs to the landless/homeless crowd. Similarly, an average woman, even a Brahmana woman, still finds herself in a milieu which prevailed in the Puranic age or even earlier. The persistence of such dichotomies between man and woman, on the one hand, and between high caste and low caste on the other, does certainly bear witness to the chronic nature of the Aryan ideology, beliefs and values.

Aryanism expands and flourishes by glorifying its ideals and by obliging the "other" to conform to its beliefs and values. The Aryan is apparently benign and normally persuasive but he does not hesitate to use coercion or force, if no other choice is left open. He sincerely and literally believes that he is the child of God and as such he is born to rule as the other is born to wait and obey, to serve and follow. He feels sure that his division of people into the ruler and the ruled or the master and the slave, is authentic and ultimate. If humanity has to survive, the *status-quo*, he thinks, must be maintained in all respects and at all costs. All his history, all his religion, all his science, all his literature, all his politics and all his ethics are motivated by a wish to retain a world-order which respects his leadership of the "other". His vision of the glory of life is the only vision possible. The world must be as he thinks it is. The age-old principles of "non-interference" and "peaceful co-existence" must remain as the only slogans of mankind for all times to come.

As the largest bulk of recorded history is post-Aryan or post-Vedic, little is known about pre-Aryan or pre-Vedic India. A scholar working in this area is therefore obliged to build up his story on indirect sources and intelligent conjectures. It is likely that people in pre-Aryan India lived mostly by agriculture, that theirs was an egalitarian society and that they recognized the female principle as the Alpha and Omega of creativity, as the highest Deity, as God. The Indian cult of Shakti, that is, Cosmic Energy personified as a Female is obviously pre-Vedic because an independent and power-wielding female deity is nowhere found in Aryan literature from the Vedas to the Grihyasutras. Female deities, as a rule, play very minor parts in the Vedic pantheon which is dominated by the "Monotheistic conception of Prajapati" (Chanda 1976 : 122). Names like Rudrani and Bhavani are "simply derivatives and do not show a belief in the existence of an independent powerful goddess". Uma, too, is the wife of a god and does not "overshadow her male consort" (Bhandarkar 1965 : 142). Therefore the conception of Shiva as the consort of the Devi must be traceable to pre-Vedic times (cf. Goetz 1980). The conception of the Mother Goddess rather than the Father God as the supreme Deity must be seen as a pre-Aryan conception. Even Havell's polemical references to non-Aryan customs and beliefs show that the mother reigned supreme only in pre-Aryan India. The pre-Aryan social structure, writes Havell, was different from the Aryan "in being matriarchal instead of patriarchal. Their mothers and children formed the nucleus of a settled society. They could never realize the Fatherhood of God; the Earth Mother ... embodied all their ideals of the divine. India was their mother, not their father ..... Durga was worshipped as the Mother" (1972 : 11-12 & 13).

Unlike the aggressive, virile and nomadic Aryans, the pre-Aryans (perhaps Afro-Dravidians) were a peace-loving and settled agricultural people. As far as we can guess, such peoples lived, a distinguished Indian scholar tells us, near the Mediterranean, in Africa, the Americas, India, and the islands and coasts, "Where agriculture was possible. The religion of all such regions was understandably connected with the earth, fertility, the cycle of procreation, decay and renewal. From the Mediterranean to the Pacific, the Mother Goddess was the eternal symbol of life" (Baig 1976 : 4). Goddess Shakti and God Shiva were, therefore, the oldest known deities in pre-Aryan India. As nuclear to the processes of reproduction and preservation of the infant, woman was certainly far more important than man in a society like this. Woman, like the earth, gave life, sustenance and strength (cf. p. 5).

The following passage describing the socio-religious situation in pre-Aryan India deserves to be quoted in full: "Upto about 2000 B C, we can assume, a dark-skinned, possibly matriarchal, people lived here in pockets of agricultural land hemmed in by huge forests. They lived by the rhythm of the seasons, worshipping the sun and the earth alike, likening the Gods to their own existences, as the stars and the moon moved across the heavens, the sun rose and fell, the seeds planted in earth and in woman bore fruit. Fertility was the perennial miracle. Life came from food. Woman gave life. It is not astonishing that God was a woman. She was the earth, strong and sustaining; she was worshipped ..... all her gifts of care, nursing and begetting led logically enough to the concept of Shakti: the strength of man and his household. Matriarchal power was the result. ... It is significant that the two early civilizations, Egyptian and Indian, both had Gods of creative force who were half man, half woman. The Mother Goddess of the neolithic period was made of strong stuff" (pp. 7-8 & 9).

Another Indian scholar invokes archaeological evidence in support of the conjecture that the pre-Vedic civilization was woman-centred. The many figures of goddesses discovered in the archaeological finds of Harappa and Mohan-jo-daro suggest that the popular deities of the pantheon were predominantly feminine and that the society was matriarchal (cf. Thomas 1964 : 6). To quote his words: "The importance of mother worship in religion, the abundance of female figurines with rich ornaments, the comparatively lesser importance given to males, would all indicate that society in ancient Indus-Valley was more favourable to women than men: it was possibly a matriarchate of the type of ancient Greece" (p. 7).

The absence of powerful and independent goddesses in Vedic literature clearly suggests that traditions like Shaktism and Tantrism originated and prospered only in pre-Aryan India. These traditions differ from the orthodox Vedic traditions in three crucial ways: first, they give prominence to the body-soul relationship, secondly, they have no use for social hierarchy or caste divisions and thirdly, they accord the highest position to the female principle in their socio-religious philosophy. Their highest deity is a goddess variously called Anand-Bhairavi, Kumari, Kali, Kapali, Mahakali, Chandi, Chamundi, Katyani, Kamala, Vijaya, Uma, Parvati, Lalita, Tripura-sundari, etc., (cf. Roy & Gidwani 1986 : 168). According to the Shakta or Tantric doctrine, the act of creation is a process which involves both male and female elements but in which the male element is thoroughly subdued by the female element. The predominant creative agent is the mother, not the father. The ambition of every pious follower of the system is, therefore, to become identical with the mother and his main religious exercise is to habituate himself to think that he is a woman (cf. Bhandarkar 1965 : 146).

Names of goddesses do occur in Vedic and post-Vedic texts but everywhere they refer to minor divinities. The worship of a goddess as a principal or even as an important deity is not common to the Vedic people or their descendants. Names like Usha and Aditi in the *Rig-Veda* do not eulogize independent goddesses. Likewise, Devi in *Atharvaveda* and Uma in the *Kena Upanishad* are mere derivatives (cf. Roy & Gidwani 1984 : 38-39). The intriguing legend of the omission of Shiva from Daksha's sacrifice seems to point to the refusal of the orthodox followers of Vedism to acknowledge the right of Shiva as the Devi's consort, to say nothing of the Devi herself, to a share of the sacrificial food along with the Vedic gods. Ravana's orthodox devotion to Shiva could have been one of the strong reasons for his confrontation with the Aryan king of Ayodhya.

In its long march from strict Vedism to Puranic liberalism, the Aryan doctrine of spiritual perception and desirable forms of worship assimilated some of the non-Aryan deities into their own pantheon. But it is significant to note in this context that the orthodox Aryan theology could not regard non-Aryan gods and goddesses as equal to Vedic gods and goddesses. The Aryan conceptions of the destructive Shiva and the blood-thirsty Kali were postulated, most probably to accommodate the one-time supreme Deities as subsidiary centres of divine power in the predominantly Puranic fold. In the Puranic order Shiva, even at his best, was designated as the third member of the Hindu Trinity and the Devi was reduced to a mere derivative of her already clipped Lord. Within the Puranic pantheon we have a Shiva and a Shakti who are not even proper replicas of what they had been in the Shakta tradition. The Supreme Being, The primordial Energy or the Adya Shakti and her Consort thus became total strangers to the followers of their original forms.

Once the Aryans were in full control of the Indian situation, they transposed every significant facet of the pre-Aryan social scene. They established a rigidly layered social structure in which there came to be the high and the low, the rich and the poor, the fair and the dark, the nosy and the noseless, the male and the female and the adorable and the hateful. An egalitarian and integrated society was replaced by a hierarchic and fragmented society. The caste-system was introduced in order that the selected few could flourish at the expense of the helpless and hopeless many. The custodians of social order and moral values founded a religion which eulogized the spirit and yet feasted on all the available pleasures of the body. Above all, they ushered in an era in which the father instead of the mother became the head of the family and the sole reference point for desirable social and moral behaviour.

The mother suddenly became a mere woman confined alternately to the labour room and the kitchen sink and yet subjected to all sorts of exploitation and ridicule. Borrowing certain phrases from Maud Bodkin's well known book on poetry, we might remark that a relation of high companionship between man and woman that existed in pre-Aryan, mother-centred India was replaced, with the coming of patriarchal conditions, by "a sequestered and survile domesticity" imposed on woman by man (cf. 1963 : 161). The Indo-Aryans thus succeeded in founding a social system, a political philosophy and a religious order which were pro-man and anti-woman, not only pro-Aryan and anti-non-Aryan.

1.2 Identification of Woman with Shudra

> "Early law books assessed a woman's *wergeld* as equivalent to that of a Shudra, whatever her class."
>
> —*Basham (1967 : 179)*

Not many years ago, pundits at a national seminar near Bombay suggested that the Hindu caste system should be seen as a scientific classification of people inspired by the noble purpose of making optimal use of their varying talents and capabilities for the highest good of the largest number rather than as a deliberate plan to divide people along ethnic lines so that the few could prosper at the expense of the many (cf. *Ind Ex* May 2, 1988). These pundits referred to the doctrine of hereditary differences to argue that people were bound to remain different because they were born different. Their most important argument was : Different groups of people manifest different sets of characteristics, tendencies and capabilities (collectively known as 'phenotypes') because their genetic constitutions (or 'genotypes') are different. Since genotypes and phenotypes are fixed and unchanging, castes and professions have to be fixed and unchanging. A Brahmana was not superior to a Shudra nor was a Shudra an inferior Brahmana in any absolute sense. One of them could be superior or inferior to the other in a given dimension but, on the whole, they were only different individually with different potentialities. It was only with a view to maximizing the social usefulness of the various segments of society that the Brahmana was entrusted with the acquisition and dissemination of knowledge, the Kshatriya with politics and administration, the Vaishya with agriculture and trade, and the Shudra with manual labour and menial chores. The ancient Hindu division of people into four castes was thus, the scientific pundits concluded, a harmonious and co-operative mobilization of their varying innate talents and potentialities so that the society as a whole could steadily move towards increasing prosperity and self-sufficiency without jeopardizing the interests of any caste or group.

If we examine this *genetic* approach to the Hindu caste system a little critically, we can easily see it as a hermeneutic rationalization of a system which is, in fact, indefensible from the point of view of social equality or human dignity. The genetic argument cannot bluff intelligent people into accepting the absurd thesis that since human beings are not born equal, they cannot be made equal. Genetic differences do not necessarily entail social inequality. Genetic constitutions or innate predispositions perhaps do make one an Einstein and the other a Buddha but they do not and must not make some people beggars and other princes. A system which makes some people slaves and lowly, and others powerful and respectable on the basis of their supposed hereditary differences cannot, by any logic, be viewed as scientific or humanistic. We do not yet know how much of an individual's personality is genuinely innate. Besides, there is no evidence to prove that Vedic Aryans assigned individuals or groups to their respective castes and professions on the basis of genetic tests. The truth seems to be that as soon as the Indo-Aryans consolidated their position, they divided people into different castes and professions in order that a handful of people could prosper at the expense of the majority. Rajmohan Gandhi rightly contends that democracy is incompatible with any excessive emphasis on self-advancement (whether spiritual or material) to the exclusion of the community's welfare; and that it is incompatible with any system of graded castes (1989). The Indian society, he suggests, must accept that for an "embarrassingly long time it tolerated values that ruined some by feeding their arrogance and others by humiliating them". He clearly points out that birth and not worth or the psychology of high and low was the basis of the grading of castes among the ancient Hindus.

There seems to be no doubt that the Hindu caste system was originally conceived as a binary classification of people along ethnic lines. The Aryan conquerors distinguished themselves from the vanquished non-Aryans with reference to physical features and the colour of the skin. Sharp-featured and fair-skinned Aryans intensely hated the snub-nosed and dark-skinned Dasas (slaves) or Dasyus (barbarians) and it was mainly with a view to maintaining their distinction from the latter on a permanent basis that the early Aryans conceived of the theory of 'colour' (Varna) to classify the contemporary population into different castes (cf. Thomas 1984 : 9, Havell 1972 : 8 & 13, Sengupta 1974 : 26 & 59, Bose 1975 : 108 and Chanda 1976 : 33-34). It is interesting to learn that the *Rig Veda* in its earlier parts (II : XII : 4 & III : XXXIV : 9) mentions only two *Varnas* : the *Aryavarna* and the *Dasavarna* (cf. Roy & Gidwani 1983 : 300). *Varna* naturally came to be the Vedic term to denote caste or class distinctions between the ruler and the ruled. In post-Vedic socio-political vocabulary *jati* meant the same thing. The Vedic Aryans generally referred to the vanquished majority as 'Dasas' or 'Dasyus'; 'Shudra' (the servile class) which occurs only once in the *Rig-Veda,* increasingly replaced Dasa or Dasyu in post-Vedic works (cf. Roy & Gidwani 1984 : 18 & 25, 1986 : 129-130 & 251). The Vedic perception of the unbridgeable gap between Aryans and Shudras gave rise to the formulation of the caste system. The Aryan "fours" like 'four colours', 'four aims', and 'four stages' have therefore to be examined in the light of the binary opposition between the fair and the dark.

With the passage of time, the scale of caste division was made more elaborate and rigid, perhaps to arrest the growing number of mixed progeny resulting from indiscriminate unions between Aryan males and non-Aryan females. Four colours and four levels of intellectual-spiritual development had to be distinguished in order to place the growing number of non-caste mixed progeny in a class separate from the so-called Aryan classes. The vertical stratification of the later Rig-Vedic society gives us a picture of four grades of people and of their mutual functions and relationships. The binary classification of fair and dark groups was replaced by a three-level division of Aryan castes in order of decreasing fairness and social significance and the fourth category of dark/black Shudras. People's professions were determined in accordance with their placement on the vertical scale. Super-fair Brahmanas were philosophers and spiritualists, fair Kshatriyas were political leaders and militarists, semi-fair Vaishyas were farmers and traders and the dark-skinned, casteless Shudras were slaves and labourers (see diagram 1). A clear line of demarcation had to be drawn between the Aryan castes on the one hand and the non-caste Shudras on the other because all power and resources—whether intellectual, spiritual, political or material—had to be shared only by the twice-born (dvija), the three higher castes. Brahmanas, Kshatriyas and Vaishyas had to study the scripture, perform the religious ceremonies and wear the sacred thread because all of them were twice-born. But the people on the lowest rung, the Shudras, were not allowed to do any of these except "to serve meekly" the higher castes and to stay in "a segregated corner of the village or outside the village" because they were descended from "exterior castes, low castes, out-casts and non-castes" (cf. Goetz 1980 & Bose 1975 : 91-94). Differences of colour, physical features and lineage thus combined to fix a logical connection between caste and profession so that a Brahmana's son could always be a Brahmana while a Shudra's son had ever to remain a Shudra: It was explicitly ordained through the scripture that Brahmanas were to be the sole custodian of intellectual, moral and spiritual matters, Kshatriyas were to be responsible for the management and preservation of the society and the State, Vaishyas had to look after the first two castes by supplying food and other commodities and resources, while the Shudras were there to do whatever was needed to make the three higher castes prosperous and happy. As both caste and occupation were hereditary, everyone was supposed to live and act according to the dictates of the tradition. Even a secular writer like Vatsyayana enumerates four methods of earning livelihood for the four varnas respectively: Brahmana—acceptance of gifts (Pratigraha), Kshatriya—conquest (Jaya), Vaishya—trade (Kraya) and Shudra—wages (Nirvesha cf. Chakladar 1976 : 98).

Diagram—1 : The Aryan Colour Spectrum: The Chaturvarna

Race	*Colour*	*Caste*	*Profession*
A	Super-Fair	Brahmanas	Intellectuals/Leaders
R			
	Fair	Kshatriyas	Militarists/Managers
Y			
A	Semi-Fair	Vaishyas	Agriculturlsts/Traders
N			
Non-Aryan	Dark	Shudras	Menials/Slaves

An interesting aspect of the four-fold division of society into intellectuals, militarists, traders, and labourers was the implicit claim that it had a divine sanction. In the following verses of the "Purusha-hymn" of the *Rig-Veda* (X : XC : 11-12) is contained the earliest account of the caste-system:

"When they divided the Purusha, into how many parts did they divide him? what was his mouth? What were his arms? What were his thighs and feet called?

The Brahmana was his mouth; of his arms, the Rajanya was made; the Vaishyas were his thighs; the Shudra sprang from his feet" (cf. Chanda 1976 : 34).

This theory of divine origin of the caste system finds a more elaborate and explicit account in the "Taittiriya—Samhita" of the *Yajur-Veda* (VII : I : I 4-6):

"Prajapati, desirous of offspring [performed the Agnishtoma sacrifice] and created ... god Agni ... Brahmana among men and goats among brutes from his mouth. As they were created from the mouth, therefore they were superior to all others.

He created ... god Indra ... Rajanya among men and sheep among brutes from his chest and arms. Therefore they are strong because they have been created from strength (strong arms).

He created ... Vishvadevas among the gods, ... Vaishya among men and cows among brutes from the belly. As they have been created from the store-house of the food (belly), so they are the food (or intended to be enjoyed by others). Therefore they are more numerous than others (among men) because many gods were created.

He created Shudra among men and horse among brutes from his feet. Therefore, the Shudra and the horse are dependent on other (castes). As no god was created from his feet, so the Shudra is not competent to perform sacrifice. As the Shudra and the horse were created from the feet, so they live by exerting their feet" (cf. Chanda 1976 : 34-35).

The divine origin of graded castes is alluded to or explicitly supported in several other texts. Krishna declares: "The four castes were created by Me according to differences in attitudes and actions of men" (*Gita* : IV : 13). At the beginning of the *Ramayana*, Rama is introduced to sage Valmiki by Narada as the "defender of religion and caste-system" (Sen 1976 : 2). The dying Bhishma tells Yuddhishthira: "A Brahmana's chief duty is to cultivate self—restraint, a Kshatriya's to protect the people, a Vaishya's to make gifts and acquire wealth by honest means, and a Shudra to serve the first three castes, in return for which he is maintained by them and receives old umbrellas, turbans, beds, shoes and hand-fans. A Shudra has no wealth of his own: whatever he has belongs to his master " (Lal 1980: 307). According to the *Panchavimsha Brahmana* a Shudra, even if prosperous, could not be "other than a servant", his business was "the washing of the feet of his superiors" (cited in Chanda 1976 : 2). In his *Laws* Manu ordains:

"The Shudra whether bought or unbought, should be made to act as a slave (dasyam), for the Shudra was created by the Self-existent for the service of the Brahmanas. Even if freed by his master, the Shudra is not released from servitude; for this (servitude) is innate in him; who then can take it away from him?" (Muller 1964 : VIII : 413-414).

Explaining what he means by 'slaves', Manu says (Muller 1964 : VIII : 415):

"A war captive, one serving as a slave for food, one born (of a female servant) within the house, one bought, one received as a gift, one inherited from the father, one condemned to act as a slave as a punishment—these are the seven kinds of slaves". A verse in the *Aitreya Brahmana* lays down: "One like a Shudra shall be born in thy line, the servant of another, who may be expelled or slain at will" (cited in Chanda 1976 : 2).

It is highly probable that the Vedic and the Puranic Aryans visualized the four—fold division of society as a progressive degeneration and populousness downwards. Brahmanas were glorified because they were on the top and just a handful in number but the lower one went, the more degenerate and populous group was to be encountered. By the time one reached the bottom of the scale, one was surrounded by the most despicable and the largest crowd.

Hindu texts greatly extol the religious significance of the *four—stages* (Chaturashrama) viz., studentship (Brahmacharya), family life (Garhastha), retirement (Vanaprastha) and renunciation or asceticism (Sanyasa) and the *four aims* (Chaturvarga) viz., material pursuits (Artha), procreation (Kama), spiritual pursuits (Dharma) and liberation (Moksha) in the life of a man. But if we look at these texts a little closely, we discover that these "fours" are not meant for all Hindus. Only the Brahmana passes through all the four stages and achieves all the four aims of life. According to the *Laws of Manu*, no other *Varna* except Brahmanas could take to sanyasa (cf. Muller 1964 : VI : 38). We do not hear of non-Brahmanas becoming sanyasis in any period of Hindu history. How astonishing it is that the restriction that only a Brahmana could become a Sanyasi was removed for the first time when Swami Vivekananda was allowed to become a Sanyasi towards the end of the nineteenth century (cf. Roy & Gidwani 1986 : 46)! The Brahmana alone is capable of renunciation because in orthodox Hinduism the Brahmana alone is a *complete* human being. The Shudra, who is a householder from birth to death and whose only aim in life is to serve the three upper castes in general and the Brahmana in particular, is only marginally human while the Kshatriya and the Vaishya occupy intermediate positions on the vertical scale. The *Vaikhanasa Dharmaprashna* clearly lays down that only a Brahmana could pass through all the four stages and achieve all the four aims of life; the Kshatriya had only three stages and three aims of life while the Vaishya had only two of each; the Shudra, of course, had only one stage and only one aim in life (see diagram 2 & cf. Chakladar 1976 : 113). In the four-fold division of Hindu castes, the Shudra is separated from the other three not only by being placed at the bottom of the scale but also because he is defined as a non-Aryan outcast. The Shudra is in fact not a caste but a non-caste. The Shudra is not comparable to any of the three castes; his proximity to the Vaishya means actually nothing in that the Shudra is casteless while the Vaishya is a caste. The division of the three upper castes is a family affair for the Aryans. The four graded castes therefore should be seen as a two-fold division between the Aryans on the one hand and the Shudras on the other.

Brahmanas and Shudras, as a matter of fact, represent the opposite end-points of the social spectrum prepared and glorified by the Vedic Aryans and preserved and maintained by their worthy successors through the ages. Brahmanas stand for all that is godly, spiritual, pure and adorable while Shudras represent all that is godless, material, impure and despicable. One is or is not born a Brahmana or a Shudra. Since orthodox Hinduism does not allow conversion, either external or internal, the separation of the Shudra from the Brahmana is crucial, final and sacrosanct. How intriguing it is that the

Brahmana shares his etymological kinship with 'Brahma' (the Absolute). The Purusha is both God and man. So is the Deva (literally the shining one). All references to the Aryan God include the Aryan, particularly the Brahmana. The Aryan religion therefore is merely a glossary of Aryanism, Vedism, Hinduism and Brahmanism.

Diagram—2 : The Aryan Fours—Four Castes, Four Stages and Four Aims

Castes	*Stages*	*Aims*
	Studentship	Material Pursuits
Brahmana	Family Life	Procreation
	Retirement	Spiritual Pursuits
	Renunciation	Liberation
	Studentship	Material Pursuits
Kshatriya	Family Life	Procreation
	Retirement	Spiritual Pursuits
	Studentship	Material Pursuits
Vaishya	Family Life	Procreation
Shudra	Family Life	Service of the upper castes

The Shudra, commonly treated as the eternal dustbin of the Hindu society, has traditionally been subjected to all sorts of insults, exclusions and deprivations. He has been a slave or a servant throughout Indo-Aryan history. The *Dharmashastras* describe the Shudra as the servile class: "One occupation only the Lord prescribed to the Shudra: to serve meekly even these (other) three *Varnas*" (Muller 1964 : I : 91). The Shudra is prohibited from learning the holy writ or performing religious rites. The Gautam *Dharmashastra* clearly ordains: "If a shudra hears the Vedas, his ears shall be stopped with molten tin or lac; if he repeats the sacred text, his tongue shall be cut out; if he stores them in his memory, his body shall be struck into two" (XII : 4-6 cited in Roy and Gidwani 1986 : 130). In the *Abhijnanashakuntalam*, Dushyanta declares that Shakuntala is fit for him only because she cannot possibly be "a girl of low caste", while Shakuntala's friends consider Dushyanta an ideal husband for her because he appears to be "a man of high caste" (Lal 1964 : 17 & 32-33). The *Mahabharata* displays the same type of rigidity on the exclusiveness of the Shudra from higher castes. A proposed arrow-shooting contest is going to take place between Karna and Arjuna to win Draupadi's hand. But before the contest begins, Kripacharya, one of the tallest scholars of his time, asks Karna: "Who are your father and mother? This Arjuna must know before he engages you, for sons of kings fight only with adversaries of equal status". Karna's face pales because he knows that his father and mother are of the low caste. Duryodhana therefore immediately makes him "the king of Anga" so that he can face Arjuna as an equal. At this Bhima sarcastically remarks: "A charioteer's son! ... You deserve a kingdom as much as a dog deserves the holy ghee of Yajna". Duryodhana then poses the rhetorical question: "which Kshatriya hero's lineage is clean?" Incidentally, we must remember in this connection that none of the Pandava princes, including Bhima, is the son of his father. And yet, as Karna rises to his string the bow and hit the target in order to marry Draupadi, she shrieks: "I will not marry a man of low caste" (cf. Lal 1980 : 91-92 & 99-100). Karna is ultimately excluded from the contest.

Orthodox Hinduism has always used caste to determine one's profession and profession to find out one's caste. Episode after episode and text after text seek to confirm and reinforce the rigidity of the Hindu caste system. It is interesting to note that there is a consistent attempt to eulogize the Brahmana and to denigrate the Shudra. The *Manusmriti* for example, contains numerous verses to highlight the age-old Brahmana-Shudra dichotomy. Let us look at the following verses which extol the innate supremacy of the Brahmana:

"By virtue of his birth alone, the Brahmana is the highest of all upon this earth.

Whatever is in the world belongs to the Brahmana.

Stupid or learned, the Brahmana is a great god.

Even though a Brahmana does evil deed, he is adorable in all respects; he is a great god.

By virtue of his birth alone, the Brahmana is the god of gods" (cited in Ratnesh 1987, my translation).

The following verses relate to the Shudra:

"To serve the Brahmana is the only religious duty of the Shudra.

If a Shudra speaks rudely to a Brahmana, the king must have the Shudra's tongue chopped off because he is born in a low caste.

If a Shudra addresses an evil word, ten burning rods should be inserted into his mouth.

If a Shudra vainly addresses a Brahmana, the king must have boiling oil poured into the Shudra's mouth" (*ibid.*, my translation).

As regards the Brahmana's attitude to the Shudra, Manu decrees:

"A Brahmana may give his servant or slave, the Shudra, leftovers of his food, tattered clothes, scattered grains and broken or condemned utensils" (*ibid.*, my translation).

Again:

"A Brahmana may take possession of the goods of a Shudra without any hesitation, for nothing that belongs to him is his own, he (Shudra) is one whose property may be taken away by his master" (quoted in Chanda 1976 : 2).

A verse in the *Vyasasmriti* prescribes: "The carpenter, the barber, the milkman, the potter, the grocer, the kirat, the Kayastha, the scavenger, the Kolas, the Chandala—all these are exterior castes. If one happens to see them, one has to purify oneself by looking at the sun, but if one talks to them, one has to purify oneself by having a ceremonial bath" (cited in Ratnesh 1987, my translation).

The *Ramacharitamanas* of Tulasidas, like the *Manusmriti*, is a notorious example of an otherwise great book which goes to the extreme to endorse casteist orthodoxy. Tulasidas, like Manu, maintains that the Brahmana is genetically superior to all other castes in all respects. Rama, the incarnation of Vishnu, Tulasidas says, has taken the human form for the sake of Brahmanas, cows, gods and saints and holds them dear to His heart (cf. Hill 1952 : 3, 60, 61, 86, 89, etc). Describing Rama's person, the poet says : "On His breast lay a jewelled necklace and the sparks of diamonds; there, too, was the mark of the Brahmana's foot, a sight to charm the soul" (*ibid.*, p. 92). Rama himself tells Kabandha : "I declare to you that I am not pleased with those who injure Brahmanas. He who in thought and word and deed does sincere service to those gods on earth may command myself and Brahma and Shiva and all other deities" (*ibid.*, p. 317). Rama again confides to Vibhishana: "Those who love the feet of the Brahmanas are dear to me as my own life" (p. 360). Just before he engages Ravana, Rama bows "his head before the Brahmanas' lotus feet" (p. 410). On his triumphant return to Ayodhya, Rama is anointed king. As king he addresses a general assembly of his subjects to announce: "There is one deed of merit in the world, no other, in thought and word and deed to worship the feet of Brahmanas; he who with unfeigned devotion serves the feet of Brahmanas finds favour with gods and sages" (p. 454). Shiva instructs a Shudra in these terms: "Now listen, brother, to my sure pronouncement, the only vow that pleases Hari is the vow to do service to Brahmanas. Never treat a Brahmana with disrespect but hold him to be the equal of god Himself. Even one who perishes not at the stroke of Indra's thunderbolt or my massive trident or Fate's decree or Hari's awful discus, is burned to ashes in the fire of the Brahmana's vengeance. Store up this wise counsel in your heart and there will be nothing in the world beyond your reach" (p. 484).

Tulasidas' view of the Shudra, embodied in the Kakabhushundi—Garuda episode of his grand epic, is a poetic apology for caste conservatism. How astonishing it is that a devotional poet should choose the concluding part of his *magnum opus* to describe the horrors of the *Shudra age* (Kaliyuga) which is incidentally the shortest and the last part of the Hindu cycle of "four ages' (*Chaturyugas*), commonly known as the "Iron age" (cf. Roy & Gidwani 1984 : 258). Recounting his painful experiences of a formal iron age in Ayodhya, Kakabhushundi laments that in that age Shudras had, against all spiritual injunctions, gone ahead of Brahmanas and upset all social and moral values. To quote part of that story: "Shudras gave Brahmanas lessons in wisdom, and putting on the sacred thread, accepted iniquitous gifts. Every one was lustful, avaricious and passionate, and flouted the gods, the Brahmanas, the scriptures and the saints.... Shudras argued with Brahmanas, 'Are we inferior to you? The true Brahmana is the one who knows the Brahma'. Such were impudent taunts..... men of the lowest caste—oilmen, potters, chandalas, kiratas, kolas, distillers—claimed reverence from Brahmanas, wantonly ruining their hopes of fortune in this world and the next .... Shudras indulged in all sorts of penances and vows and seated themselves on the dais to recite the Puranas. Everybody did just what he liked, it was an age of utterly unspeakable wickedness" (p. 477).

Since orthodox Hinduism did not provide for any variability between caste and profession, the Brahmana and the Shudra always stood, respectively, for the highest and the lowest in society. One may find evidence of the caste-profession rigidity in any work that deals with socio-religious life in ancient or medieval India but here I would like to refer to one of the greatest Hindu classics to illustrate the Brahmana—Shudra polarity so acutely represented in the Samvuka-episode of the *Ramayana*. The xenophobia of the orthodox Brahmana for the hapless Shudra is seldom better articulated. It is a vision of the horror of Aryan perception of the "other". Once during Rama's reign, a Brahmana's son died. He came to king Rama, charged him with impiety and questioned his authority to rule. Baffled by the Brahmana's accusations and grieved about his son's death, Rama summoned an urgent assembly of venerable sages like Vashishtha, Markandeya, Madgaulya, Vamadeva, Kashyapa, Katyayana, Javali, Gautama and Narada and sought their advice on what he could do to satisfy the enraged Brahmana. Narada, on behalf of the holy assembly, told the king: "It is highly sinful for a Shudra to be devoted to penance and meditation ... a Shudra is practising penance under your rule. Hence the Brahmana boy died so untimely".

Rama took the hint and immediately set out on the mission to track the culprit down. Ultimately he came to an ascetic who was practising penance. Suspecting him to be the culprit, king Rama asked him: "Tell me whether you are a Brahmana, a Kshatriya or a Shudra?" The ascetic replied: "O king! I am born of Shudra caste. I want to attain divinity by such penance. I am Shudra by caste and my name is Samvuka".

As soon as the ascetic uttered those words, Rama drew forth his sword and severed his head. The gods uttered praise of Rama, flowers were rained from above and the Brahmana boy revived. All were pleased" (cf. Sen 1976, Vol. III : 446-449).

The Aryan world is a world divided between the high and the low, the master and the slave, the Brahmana and the Shudra. This view of the Aryan world is further intensified by the meticulous nature of its definition of the split, half-ostracized Aryan female. Like the Brahmana and the Shudra, the He-Aryan and the Aryan female represent the opposite ends of the Aryan social spectrum. The Aryan female stands divided between two worlds: the world of the He-Aryan and the world of the Shudra. Her physical proximity with the He-Aryan is no compensation for the deprivations she is subjected to on account of her ideological dumping with the Shudra. The fact that she has to play both Aryan and Shudra at a time drives her into a very obnoxious kind of psychic ambivalence. She is not a Shudra nor is she an Aryan; she is half Aryan, half Shudra. In a sense, she is in a predicament worse than that of a Shudra. The Shudra has the consolation of having been born in the hopeless part of the society and he can at least curse his stars. His placement has, in his eyes, sufficient definitional clarity; he knows he suffers because he was unfortunately born in this rather than in that part of the world. The Aryan female lacks both the consolation of the hopelessness of her birth and the definitional clarity of her belonging to the hopeless part of the society. She suffers more intensely than her half brother (the Shudra) because she is neither here nor there or, unfortunately enough, both here and there. The awareness that she is not a Shudra hurts her more deeply because of her gnawing perception that she is not an Aryan either and yet an Aryan. That the Aryan female cannot situate herself positionally is her real tragedy. She is an archetype of corruptibility, vulnerability and ignorance while the He-Aryan is a symbol of purity, security and knowledge. Her identification with the Shudra at the hands of the He-Aryan confuses her, hurts her and swindles her throughout her destined and protracted physicality with the latter.

The Aryan female, in spite of her caste anomaly, is traditionally dumped with the Shudra. Like the Shudra's, her caste determines her profession and her profession determines her caste. She is considered inferior because she is assigned roles and functions which are inferior. In respect of her roles and functions she is one with the Shudra: neither of them can own property or be independent, neither of them can wear the sacred thread, study the scripture or perform religious rites; and neither of them can resist the tyranny of the master. Both of them have to serve others; both of them have to be maintained by others and both of them are fit only to be ordered about. Like children, the Shudra and the Aryan female, are to be treated as 'minor' in the eyes of law. This is decreed by the law books (cf. Altekar 1956 : 317, Bader 1964 : 12-13, Sengupta 1074 : 95 & Baig 1976 : 95-96). In his famous book on Indian history, Basham remarks: "A woman according to most authorities, was always a minor at law. As a girl, she was under the tutelage of her father, as an adult, of her husband, and as a widow, of her sons. Even under the liberal rules of Buddhism, a nun, however advanced in the faith, was always subordinated to the youngest novice among the brethren" (1967 : 179).

Diagram—3 : The Aryan Socio-Political Hierarchy

The Aryan Male ⋮ The Aryan Female	BORN TO RULE
⋮ The Shudra Male ⋮ The Shudra Female	BORN TO OBEY

When we discuss the woman-Shudra equation in Hindu society, we may incidentally take note of the parallels of such equations in other societies. Athenian laws of ancient Greece, for example, treated the wife as a veritable child, having the legal status of a minor. That the husband should rule over his wife and children was considered *natural* by no less a philosopher than Aristotle (cf. Pomeroy 1975 : 74), while women on their part always find an old connection between their position and that of the blacks: like the black man, the white woman in the west is forbidden "a thousand adventures, a thousand joys" (Beauvoir 1953 : 35, cf. Janewey 1981). Both of them are denied equality of opportunity with white men. There has been institutional sexism against women as there has been institutional racism against blacks in "all spheres of life" (Amundsen 1971 : 18). Many people believe, and very rightly, that the suppression of white women is even more severe and systematic than that of black people, even though it may be a great deal more subtle than the latter. In an opinion poll held in America in 1969 to ascertain whether a white woman or a black man should become the next president, 67 per cent of the electorate indicated their preference for a black man to a white woman (cf. *ibid.*, pp. 45 & 67). Not many years ago, a delegation of white women professionals called on a US official and requested him to stop discrimination against them. Reacting to this demand, the official blurted out : "You can't make that demand. We haven't even conceded it to blacks yet" (*ibid.*, p. 45).

As regards the Hindu identification of Aryan women with Shudras, we do not yet know if Shudra men would be preferable to Aryan women in any sphere of life. Aryan women and Shudras, ideologically speaking, belong to the same caste, no doubt, and yet we can place Aryan women, Shudra men and Shudra women on the vertical scale from the point of view of their respective deprivations and sufferings. Aryan women suffer because of their gender: Shudra men suffer because of their birth, while Shudra women suffer both because of their gender and their birth. Diagram 3 attempts to show the verticality of this horrific situation. To be a Shudra is bad, to be a woman is worse but to be a Shudra woman is definitely the worst that can happen to a human being in a human society.

1.3 Masculinization of Sex and Marriage

> "There are two marriages ... in every marital union, his and hers. And his is better than hers."
>
> —*Jessie Bernard cited in Mcphee (1979 : 80)*

Three factors determine the sex relations of human males and females: the male is much more muscular, libidinous and criminal than the female, the male can force sex on the female without her consent and against her will whenever he is in a position to do that, and the male does not have to bear the brunt of the sex act nor does he carry any evidence on his person of the sex act committed by him. The woman just happens to be on the wrong side of the table. She cannot revenge herself on the male in any of these three respects. She cannot overpower him, she cannot rape him, and she cannot lie about the consequences of the sex act if it has taken shape inside her. Both the male and the female know that these roles cannot be exchanged or wished away. This knowledge gives rise to male hypocrisy and female helplessness and resentment. We must face this fact squarely. Males and females are not yet equal, at least, in so far as their sex relation is concerned. Marriage and sex do not mean the same thing for man and woman. Man and woman respond to marriage (or sex) in very different ways. As Susan B. Anthony puts it, "Marriage has ever been a one-sided matter, resting most unequally upon the sexes. By it, man gains all—woman loses all; tyrant law and lust reign supreme with him—meek submission and ready obedience alone befit her. Woman has never been consulted; her wish has never been taken into consideration as regards the terms of the marriage compact" (cited in Mcphee 1979 : 75). A woman's response to marriage differs from that of a man in almost all respects: physiological, psychological, social, economic, moral, spiritual and so on. Marriage is much more of a commitment to a woman than it is to a man. Once a woman becomes a wife, she has to give up her personal freedom, ambition and comforts. A wife has no economic or sexual independence. She has no social status except as someone's wife. Once a wife becomes a mother, her commitment to the child adds a new dimension to the continuing erosion of her personal identity. For a woman, "Marriage is giving, marriage is sacrifice, marriage means abandoning one's inner identity, any self-imperative which conflicts with the demands that husband and children make.... [No] male genius avoids matrimony because he feels unable to give enough of himself. On the contrary, a man tends to think marriage essential to provide the right environment—*regular sex and hot meals*—so that he can work undisturbed" (Figes 1971). Marriage creates a split in woman's life, it separates her future from her past and renders her present cramped. The sky changes as soon as the beloved becomes a wife. As a fiancee, she was fresh and warm for years but as a wife she is stale and cold in less than a week. An ancient woman poet of India named Bhavakadevi, recounts her experience of conjugal love—making in the following lines: "So then this body of ours first became one and undivided, thereafter thou wert the beloved while I, bereft of all hope, was no longer thy darling. And now, thou art the lord, and I am only thy wife" (De 1969 : 47). These lines spontaneously call to mind Shakespeare's description of the sex act (in his sonnet 129) as something that is "enjoyed no sooner but despised straight". Christine Billson shares Bhavakadevi's experience of conjugal love-making: "Without me he would suffer; with him I am alone. I am as solitary as eternity and sometimes as stupid as clotted cream" (cited in Greer 1973 : 274). Greer draws attention to the wife's loneliness in marriage in these words: "Loneliness is never more cruel than when it is felt in close propinquity with someone who has ceased to communicate. Many a housewife staring at the back of her husband reading newspaper or listening to his breathing in bed is lonelier than any spinster in a rented room" (*ibid.*, p. 274).

Marriage, for most people, is not a union of souls; it is a union of two bodies in which one does and the other is done to. Marriage is the name given by society to the sex adventure of man which he carries out on the woman with absolute impunity. Marriage is a licence the society confers upon man to do whatever he likes with his woman to satisfy his sexuality. The wife is more helpless than the woman. The woman can refuse, run away or make a noise to resist sexual advances by a man. The wife cannot do any of these. There is no court of appeal for her. She cannot resist the sexual atrocities committed on her by her husband. She cannot get any support from her parents, from the husband's family, from the public, from the law-enforcing agencies or from voluntary social organizations. Willy-nilly, she has to put up with her husband. She knows her husband has all the authority: social, political and religious, to use her the way he likes to. One of the holiest of books states with patriarchal finality: "Men are protectors over women ... your wife is a tilth for you, then come to your tilth as you please" (Baig 1976 : 55). The wife knows that she is only a field her husband can plough and sow whenever he likes to. She knows only too well that even in America, the so-called `land of freedom', as late as 1769, the wife was not a legal person, but only a part of her husband; the wife did not own even the clothes she wore; she was liable to be sued for theft if she ran away from the heartless brute, called her husband, with clothes on (*ibid.*, pp. 32-34).

Ideally, and from the woman's point of view, sex is a sort of communication between two individuals, not "something unique and holy and awesome, but an activity which can on occasion be profound and moving, funny and gay ... friendly or romantic" (Kitzinger 1971). It is "the mutual search for a *shared identity*, for the mutual verification through an experience of finding oneself, as one loses oneself in another" (Erikson 1961). It is a sharing, a participation, a co-operation, a reciprocity and a union between two sensitive and authentic humans who respect each other. But, as it stands today, sex is generally a masculine adventure, a masculine pastime, a masculine monopoly and, therefore, it does not mean the same thing for man and woman.

There are two reasons why the masculine version of sex cannot be a shared activity between man and woman. First, male sex feeling, centred in his sex organ, rises like an arrow, reaches the height and dies abruptly in ejaculation. Female sex feeling, on the other hand, radiates throughout her whole body; it rises rhythmically and takes time to die out. The woman wants to prolong the act until the spell is completely dissipated. The famous biological taxonomist, Alfred Kinsey, through his massive statistical works: *Sexual Behaviour in the Human Male* (1948) and *Sexual Behaviour in the Human Female* (1953), shows that most males complete the sex act in less than two minutes while a very large proportion of females take ten to fifteen minutes of the most careful stimulation to reach orgasm (cf. Hunt 1961). How many males can continue the carnal contact beyond ejaculation? As soon as ejaculation takes place, the man disowns the flesh and turns away from the woman. The woman feels let down and cheated. It is for such frustrations that the woman is more liable to depression and masochism. The Margaret Sanger Research Bureau has found that twenty-five per cent of married women "feel at best apathy, and at worst, outright revulsion, about the sex act" (Hunt 1961). According to Beauvoir, nine out of ten "erotomaniacs are women and these are almost all forty to fifty years old" (1953 : 282). She points out that a woman reaches her full erotic development, overcoming all inhibitions, usually by the age of thirty-five. In support of her argument she quotes the case of an old woman: when asked at what age a woman ceases to feel the torments of the flesh, Princess Metternich replied: "I do not know. I am only sixty-five" (p. 284). Most women feel resentful towards their husbands or lovers for not co-operating with them till the end of the sex act and this leads them towards masochism, depression or erotomania, particularly, after thirty-five or forty when they are likely to be rejected as cold and stale by their husbands/lovers.

The second reason for the sexual incompatibility between man and woman is that orgasm is not the be-all and end-all of the sex act for most women as ejaculation is for all men. According to the *Hite Report*, an overwhelming number of women like the sex act only out of love and affection for the man, not for reaching orgasm (cf. Durden-Smith and De Simone 1983 : 202). Many women do not experience orgasm at all; even those who do, do so intermittently. As a woman puts it: "I do believe women can change channels in mid-stream or even switch-off; many women could go through life happily without having sex whereas it is an essential part of contented living for man .... a married woman, when and if she meets her handsome idol, does not automatically think in erotic terms, whereas the man, should he meet his blonde heroine, would directly fall into a fantasy of stripping her naked and leaping into bed with her" (Trench 1971). `Anatomic destiny' is so profoundly different in man and woman that for man sex is a necessity whereas for woman it is only a luxury in which many would not like to indulge at all.

The sex act has different effects on man and woman. In coition, the hypocritical male combines his service to the species with his pleasure. He carries out the sex act without disrupting the integrity of his person. But the female does not find much pleasure in the sex act forced on her. Her service to the species is "begun abruptly, fulfilled slowly and painfully in pregnancy, childbirth and lactation" with sufficient damage to the integrity of her body (Beauvoir 1953 : 100-101). Physiologically, the sex experience is not the same for woman as for man : "The man relieves himself of something. The woman receives something .... The something received may have momentous consequences for the woman" (Stocks 1971). The sex act involves "pollution of one person by another, confers a certain degree of pride on the polluter and some humiliation on the polluted, even when she consents" (Benda cited in Beauvoir 1953 : 107). From the male point of view, conception and abortion are the sole responsibility of the female because pregnancy and childbirth are specifically feminine liabilities. It is no wonder that in 1969 in a small country like the UK, 22,000 teenagers gave birth to fatherless babies while 10,000 teenagers had abortions (cf. Stocks 1971).

In a vast majority of civilized societies, the sex act is a peculiarly male prerogative. It is the male who decides the *position*, the *duration* and the *frequency* of the sex act. As the most libidinous of creatures in the universe, the human male takes his pleasure with the female, *he gives* pleasure to her. Woman *gives* herself, man *takes* her. The very words imply lack of reciprocity. For the male the sex is 'conquest', 'victory', 'assault', 'siege', 'attack', while for the female, it is 'loss', 'defeat', 'surrender', 'humiliation', 'pains and sufferings'. Even the most civilized, deferential and polite of men speak of the sex act in terms of assault and conquest. However understanding and sympathetic the husband may be, the first penetration for the wife is a violation. The defloration, strange and painful as it is, whether caused by husband or lover, creates a hiatus between the yesterday and the tomorrow of the virgin. She can no longer be what she has so far been (cf. Beauvoir 1953 : 102-111). The sex act is a one-way traffic: "man dives upon his prey like the eagle and the hawk; woman lies in wait like the carnivorous plant, the bog, in which children and insects are swallowed up" (*ibid.*, p. 112). Reminiscing about her own experience of defloration, the famous opera dancer, Isadora Duncan writes in *My Life*: "I confess that my first impressions were a horrible fright and an atrocious pain, as if someone had torn out several of my teeth at once ... I felt as if I were being mangled" (cited in Beauvoir 1953 : 110). We men seldom try to look within and see how ruthless, vicious and brutish we are and yet we never tire of glorifying our ideals of social and moral behaviour. We have no qualms of conscience when we put the blame for our delinquency on women. We never consider it necessary to ascertain if the other (and better) half of humanity looks at sex and marriage the same way as we do. We talk of our own morality and, at the same time, we exploit the physiology of others for our sensual gratification.

Generally speaking, a society controlled by men is both patriarchal and patrilocal. Name and property are decreed to pass from father to son and a man's wife and children are required to live at his home, on his land. The necessary association of the male child with name, property and home renders the child more significant and powerful than the female child. The continuation of the family line, in other words, is taken to mean a transmission from one male to another. "Bring forth and look after male children only" automatically becomes everyone's invocation to the would-be, child-bearing female. The male child is consistently groomed to become in course of time the head of the family, while the female child has to remain under some sort of tutelage throughout her life. In all relations, action is taken on behalf of the female by her `guardian' (Greek *Kurios* or Sanskrit *bharta*) because she is considered both physically weak and intellectually immature while the male is looked upon as a pillar of strength and maturity from the beginning. In such societies the family is regarded as the crucial socio-religious unit within which one has to find or lose one's identity. The family or clan (Greek *Oikos* or Sanskrit *Kula/gotra*) comes to be a source of limitless growth and the main reservoir of tradition. As the necessary and sole vehicle of transmission from the present to the future, that is, from the father to the son, the child-bearing female is held responsible for the preservation of the family line. She is therefore kept under strict surveillance so that she does not violate the family line or pollute the genealogy. She is kept under such surveillance by her male guardian or guardians because she is believed to be by nature vulnerable and fickle.

An interesting feature of a society like this is that it is perpetually torn between two contrary male pursuits. These male pursuits are: sex and morality. Both are indispensable to civilized life. The quality of civilized life depends upon the quality of their interaction. But they do not easily interact or integrate due to their opposite pulls and pressures. Sex is chaotic, rambunctious and unscrupulous. It knows no limits. It loves to repeat itself as frequently, and in as many forms as it can. Highly volatile, extremely amorphous and intensely personal, sex does not respect social relationships and moral laws. Its only aim is to obtain optimal self-fulfilment (open or clandestine), at times even at the cost of its possessor. Morality, on the other hand, is quiet and rational, pious and deferential, sincere and benevolent. It is the upholder of a stable rapport between the individual and the society. It belongs to the individual only to the extent that the individual belongs to the society. It requires the individual to be nice and honest to others as well as to himself. Morality has no room for equivocation and cunning. It says what it thinks. It does what it says. It is open and lawful. It is loud and clear.

When sex and morality are truly integrated into a single sociocultural construct, we have an institution called marriage. But marriage under patriarchal conditions becomes an extremely difficult proposition because the male is separately moral and sexual. The male wants marriage to be an arrangement which should combine his private pleasures with public morality by restricting the sexual conduct of his female to himself and yet allow him to keep his sexual options open to as many females as he can lay his hands upon. He wants his female to strictly abide by the social rules of sexual conduct and yet himself to remain above the rules. The married male is not contented with one female, his so-called life-partner. In spite of and outside of the bonds of matrimony, he wants many females, chases many females and seeks to overpower as many females as he can, by force or fraud, to have sex with. Marriage for the male is a smokescreen which he habitually uses to project his good image and to cheat his wife. A masculine marriage therefore turns out to be a moral flop also because even within its accepted limits the male refuses to treat the female as a true partner. A married male is an autocrat while a married female is only a sexual slave of her permanent male manipulator.

We do not have to distort history or to put words into the mouths of ancient law makers to show that controlled marriages in masculine societies are characterized by unlimited and shameless duplicity. Whether we refer to the Indo-Aryans or to the Graeco-Romans, we find sufficient evidence to conclude that marriage has always been used by the males of the society concerned to have the best of both worlds. Sex and marriage have seldom meant the same thing for males and females. Institutions like polygyny, concubinage and prostitution, customs like child-marriage, adultery, wife-sharing, widow-burning and seclusion of woman, practices like sex with helpless women, widows and minor girls and occurrences like extra-marital maternities do only expose the inherent contradictions of the masculinization of sex and marriage. The notorious deposition of Demosthenes, the fourth century (BC) Athenian philosopher, against Naera sums up for us the central tenet of patriarchal perspectives of marriage: "Courtesans we keep for pleasure, concubines for daily [sexual] attendance upon our persons, and wives to bear us legitimate children and be our housekeepers" (cited in Hunt 1961).

There are no virgins among Indian, Greek or Roman gods. Sexual promiscuity and rape are no causes for censure among the married ones. Both mortal and immortal husbands have free access to other females while both mortal and immortal wives are obliged to be faithful to their husbands. Besides, both mortal and immortal females are required to have sex only with males of equal or higher ranks while both types of males are free to have sex with females even of lower status. Adultery on the part of men and gods in these societies is common, even fashionable and yet Tacitus, a distinguished Roman scholar of the fourth century, has the cheek to eulogize the anti-adultery laws of contemporary Germany in these terms: "Adultery is very rare. ... Punishment is the prerogative of the husband: in the presence of the relatives, the husband expels the wife from the house, nude with hair cut, and drives her through the whole village with a whip. There is no pardon for prostituted chastity" (cited in Pomeroy 1975 : 212). In these societies chastity is a virtue peculiar to females. Even males who value chastity are obliged to worship this quality in a female deity. It is no accident that Hippolytus worships Artemis to attain chastity. Bridegrooms are nowhere required to produce evidence of their virginity. But it is astonishing that even today they demand positive proof of their brides' virginity. "There are parts of France", writes Beauvoir, "where the bridegroom's friends wait behind the door of the nuptial chamber, laughing and singing, until the husband comes out in triumph to show them the blood-stained sheet or the parents may display it next morning to the neighbours" (1953 : 160).

More hypocritical than any other patriarchal community, Hindus have always maintained contrary norms of sexual morality for men and women with absolute religiosity. What is freely available to men is strictly forbidden to women. Hindu women are ordained to combine their sexual behaviour to the males of their own rank and yet be ready to co-operate with the amorous dalliance of the males of the higher rank. They have to look straight or upward, never downward. Hindu males, on the other hand, are free to consort with women of lower ranks. Erotic adventures of the Hindu male operate on two levels. On the horizontal level, he has his wife (or wives), concubines, married women, unmarried women, and widows of his own caste, while on the vertical level, he has access to maid servants, slave girls, public women and other women of the lower caste or castes. By devising a hierarchy of sexual behaviour in terms of such horizontal and vertical levels or planes, the Hindu male, particularly the Brahmana male, assures himself that while he is free to avail of all possible sources of sensual satisfaction, his wife is not polluted by the casteless non-Aryan, the Shudra. Even the secular Vatsyayana lays down: "the practice of kama with women of higher caste is prohibited" (I : IV : p. 119). The Vedic Brahmana knows quite well that it was only through graded sexuality that he could ensure the chastity of Brahmana women despite his freedom to enjoy women of lower castes. He also knew that women of his caste were safe even from immortal visitors for the simple reason that such visitors did not exist in reality.

Like Aryans elsewhere, Indo-Aryans considered chastity a specifically feminine virtue. The obligation of virginity before marriage and chastity after marriage was laid on women alone. The curious Vedic ritual of *Varunapragahasa* applied only to women who had to declare at their wedding if they had had any lover or lovers before marriage. No such declaration was required of bridegrooms (cf. De 1969 : 4-5). Valmiki's society did not allow pre-marital or extra-marital sexual aberrations on the part of women but king Dasaratha had a harem of three hundred and fifty women in addition to his three principal wives. The *Ramayana* also mentions the presence of concubines and prostitutes in the kingdom (cf. Sharma 1971 : 6-8). The heroes of the *Mahabharata*, themselves born of mixed parentage, married women of lower orders. King Shantanu married Matsya-gandhi (or Satyavati), the fisherman's daughter, the sage Jagatkaru married a tribal princess, Bhima married Hidimba, the Rakshasi, Arjuna married the non-Aryan Ulupi, Krishna's grandson, Aniruddha married an Asura princess and king Yayati married Sharmishtha, a non-Aryan princess. But the epic does not refer to any Aryan woman, not to speak of an Aryan princess, who loved or married an Asura, a Rakshasa or a Shudra. Epic Aryans, like the Aryans of other ages, seem to have held the view that an Aryan woman marrying below her caste or status would demean herself, her family and her community, although no such stigma attached to an Aryan male who loved or married below his caste or status (cf. Thomas 1964 : 12-13). Diagram 4 represents the duplicity of Indo-Aryan sex morality.

Diagram-4 : The Aryan Sex Morality

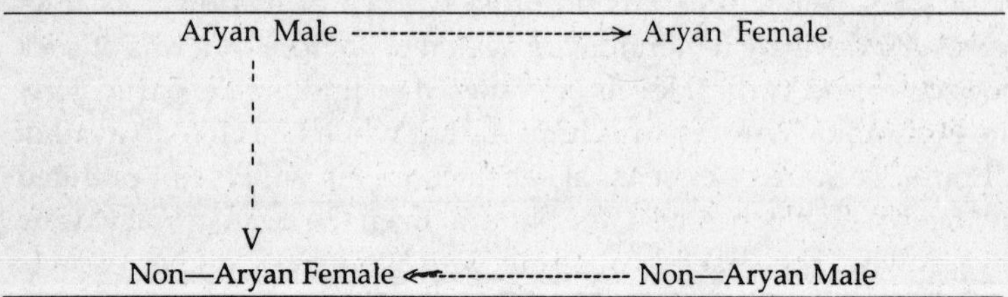

The Upanishads (written about 600 BC) are variously known as 'the Himalayas of the soul', 'the basic springs of Indian philosophy', 'the summits of early Indian thought', 'the first recorded attempts of the Hindus at systematic philosophy', and 'the earliest written presentation of their efforts to construe the world of experience as a rational whole' (cf. Hume 1949 : 2 & Mahadevan 1954). Paul Deussen writes: "To every Indian Brahmin the Upanishads are what the New Testament is to the Christians" (*ibid.*). In one of such wonderful texts, the *Chhandogya Upanishad*, a story is narrated which is highly instructive for the point I am trying to make here. The story goes as follows :

Satyakama, the son of Jabala, addressed his mother: "Venerable lady, I desire to lead the life of a religious student [Bramhachari]. To what Gotra do I belong?

She said to him: "O son, I do not know this, to what Gotra you belong. In my youth when I was moving about much and when I was a maid servant, I obtained you. I am Jabala by name and you are Satyakama by name. Therefore, you say you are Satyakama, son of Jabala".

Then Satyakama went to sage Gautama and asked him if he could admit him even if he had no Gotra. At this Gautama said:

"One who is not a Brahmin is not able to speak out like this. O beloved one, bring sacrificial fire. I shall initiate you" (IV : IV : 1-5, Mahadevan 1975 : 129-130).

This is fine enough. No one should be necessarily known by his Gotra or by his father's identity but the question is this: Do these great lovers of truth envisage a situation in which a Brahmana woman is involved in erotic or marital relation with a Shudra and yet remain socially acceptable? No Hindu text, one can easily generalize, endorses or accepts an Aryan female falling in love with or marrying a non-Aryan male and therefore Hindu literature cannot be regarded as a literature that respects or supports male-female equality. The Jabala story should not be considered an example of Hindu generosity or openness in matters of sex and morality. Despite its openness, this story must be taken as a concrete example of Hindu orthodoxy in the area of sex and marriage because Jabala is just one out of millions of non-Aryan females who had to suffer non-marital maternity at the hands of Aryan males.

1.4 Perception of Male—Female Polarity

> "It is certain that the man who avoids women and the woman who seeks men are abnormal."
>
> —*Krafft-Ebbing (quoted in Greer 1973 : 97).*

Nature creates polarity. Culture visualizes opposition. Nature creates difference. Culture visualizes gradation. Nature creates innocence. Culture visualizes guilt. It is this dichotomy between nature and culture that accounts for the traditional perception of men and women as sharers of mutual suspicion and exclusiveness rather than as partakers of a reciprocity based on co-operation and complementarity. From the point of view of nature, men and women are complementary to each other and, as such, equals. But from the point of view of culture, they are seen as polar opposites and, as such, placed on a scale of inequality. It is easy, not only possible and reasonable, to see woman as equal to man but it is easier to see her as inferior to him. We have plenty of evidence for both points of view.

Most educated people instinctively feel that there are wide statistical differences between human males and females and that these differences are independent of culture and climate. But few educated people realize that we now require a new lens to see such differences and a new semantic set to describe such differences truly. To be authentic, a description has to reflect real facts. No set of arbitrary criteria can prove that difference means inferiority. No male has the right to see himself as primary and to view a female as "an inferior version of himself" (Gohlke 1980). The male cannot treat himself as the point of reference to identify and project male-female differences to the disadvantage of the female. Freud's perception of the human female as a "castrated male" is a glaring example of the level to which a man of genius can stoop to convert difference into inferiority. Every conscientious analyst of male-female differences has therefore to take note of what Henry Adams once wrote: "The study of history is useful to the historian by teaching him his ignorance of woman. The woman who is known only through a man is known wrong" (cited in Janeway 1981). It is astonishing that women, until very recently, have been known wrong because they have been known only through men. As far as women are concerned, all recorded history is vulnerable and suspect. To say or believe that women are inferior to men is not only not based on truth; it is an act of cruelty and shame (cf. Huxley 1961).

We have now reached a stage in our intellectual history where we are called upon to examine, very critically, whatever men have so far written about women. We cannot and must not accept anything on faith. From the time of the *Rig-Veda* to our own, we have had very highly educated people who have been piling up tonnes and tonnes of nonsense about what women are and what they should be. Not many years ago, a respectable scholar could write: "physically and physiologically, it has been found that woman is inferior to man: her brain weighs less; her heart is smaller" (Kidwai 1976 : 89-90). That this statement is absurd should be clear to anybody. It is as absurd as Aristotle's remark that a woman had less teeth than a man. If Aristotle would have asked Mrs. Aristotle to keep her mouth open while he counted, he could not have said something so stupid as he did. If our contemporary scholar would have cared to ask a physiologist to educate him on the relationship between body-weight and brain-weight or between body-mass and the size of the heart he would not have made such an absurd statement. An average female's brain and heart are lighter and smaller than those of an average male for the simple reason that in terms of body mass and body weight an average female is smaller and lighter than an average male. The weight of the brain and the size of the heart of a female only indicate that a female is different from a male. Males and females are different but complementary. They complement each other only because they are different but equal. We can neither "ignore the differences nor the independence and equality between them ..... Neither is better, neither is worse" (Durden—Smith & De Simone 1983 : 232). The vicissitudes and crises of male-female relationships in actual life only reflect "the deepest polarities" of their different physiques and psyches (cf. Wurm 1976 : 561). If human life has to remain meaningful and enjoyable, the two must unite with full mutual respect for mutual differences. If masculinists argue that men are "more muscular" than women, they might as well be informed that women are "more resilient" than men (Trench 1971). Similarly, if they claim that men are more adventurous than women, one could show them the statistics of Church attendances to suggest that "women are more religious than men" or one could put before them police records of crimes to indicate that women are much less criminal and 'wicked' than men (Stocks 1971).

Traditional literature on male-female differences has consistently sought to put woman at the receiving end. It has filled her with guilt and diffidence to such an extent that even intelligent girls and educated women often see themselves as inferior to men. In his well known masterpiece, Havelock Ellis cites the case of Florie who accepts the 'superiority' of boys only from her observation of the way they urinate. The urinary function of the boy is so simple, convenient and unembarrassing, he does it standing, while the girl has to "sit or crouch, uncover herself and therefore hide" (Beauvoir

1953 : 9-15). The young girl fails to understand why "menstruating, gestating, giving birth and suckling are exclusively female experiences" (Stott 1971). Unlike a boy, a girl has to *bleed* and to *add flesh* on her bosom to grow. Unlike a boy, she finds her physiology and anatomy embarrassing. The adolescent girl is bewildered that on the street "men follow her with their eyes and comments on her anatomy. She would like to be invisible; it frightens her to become flesh and to show her flesh" (Beauvoir 1953 : 36137 & 43). She cannot make out why women do not follow young men on the street, why young men are not ashamed of their beard, moustache and muscles, and why things like periods and pregnancy do not happen to them. The young girl is baffled and shocked by the social context in which she has to become an individual. Her experiences of blood and flesh confuse and depress her. Frequent expressions like 'child of the same blood', 'pure blood' and 'mixed blood' coupled with her personal experiences of the 'monthly show of blood' lead the adolescent girl to the conclusion that man-woman partnership is perhaps nothing more than a solemn rite of blood transfusion in which the man is a gainer and the woman a loser (cf. *ibid.*, pp. 36-37). Such 'bloody' and 'fleshy' visions of life shake up the adolescent girl who begins to ask herself: does her difference from the boy make her 'inferior' to the boy? The girl grows into a woman but the question continues to nag her. It is therefore important that educated people, both men and women, take up the question of male-female differences and honestly seek to set the records straight so that every growing girl or mature woman may situate herself rightly and comfortably in society.

Two young scientists, Jo Durden-Smith and Diane de Simone brought out in 1983 *Sex and the Brain*, an excellent book on what is known as 'Brain Science'. In this book they present, among other things, a fascinating account of genetic differences between human males and females. It may be quite in order to have a quick look at some of the important points of this differential account which explains why men and women do what they do and why they are what they are. Men, for example, are physically much stronger than women because they have more muscle than fat (40% muscle and 15% fat), while women are more resilient and better at endurance-running than men because they have larger reserves of fat than muscle (25% fat and 23% muscle). Women cannot compete with men in high-speed running because their pelvis is too wide and too low. They cannot be as good hunters as men because their visual-spatial skills are not as developed as those of men. Women should be younger than men in marriage because they mature earlier and age faster than men. Married men are far healthier and happier than unmarried ones but the same thing cannot be said about women. Unmarried women are often healthier and happier than married women. (According to data presented at the Indian Society of Criminology held in Trivandrum in March 1988, more men than women commit suicide in almost every part of the world and that more unmarried than married people commit suicide—Ind. Exp. March 9, 1988). Statistically speaking, marriage is a greater necessity for men than for women. Working women are found to be healthier than housewives. Men can overpower women because they have more muscle, longer arms, wider shoulders and stronger upper body than women have. Women outnumber men because more male foetuses are aborted spontaneously and more male babies die in the first few months of life. More male babies are born deaf, blind and ambiguously sexed. Men are better than women in maths, mazes, goal-directedness and manipulation of the environment because the right hemisphere of their brain is more developed. Women are better than men in communication, co-ordination and language acquisition and they are more sensitive to context, odour, touch, sound and facial expression because the left hemisphere of their brain is more dominant. Women have a greater capacity for co-ordination and intuition because the two halves of their brain are better organized; male brain is more lateralized. The corpus callosum of the female brain is much wider and larger which accounts for their greater capacity for acceptance, flexibility and poise. Male sex hormones (androgens) have a greater tendency towards aggressiveness and diverse sexuality like rape, exhibitionism, homosexuality, incest, sexual sadism and paedophilia and towards criminality of various types, while female sex hormones (oestrogens) have much weaker tendencies towards these aberrations. It is because of the different natures of their sex hormones that women are much less aggressive, sexed and criminal than men. Men have a greater taste for variety of sexual partners, while women are more choosy and hesitant and therefore faithful. It is also due to the different sets of sex hormones that women are usually less arousable than men. Pornographic male magazines are full of nude females, while female magazines do not display nude males. Women can undergo servicing by male masseurs in a massage parlour abstractedly and without excitement, while male clients find it impossible to be perceived by female masseurs without sexual arousal. A man eats up a woman with his eyes, undressing her in his mind, constantly drawn to her mouth and lips and the rift-valley between her breasts. It is very likely that a female's attraction towards a male is not a physical one.

Differences between males and females, as noted above, only illustrate the basic complementarity and therefore equality between the two sexes. Their psychologies are different. It is a decree of nature that the two sexes are different. The difference between them cannot be a matter of pride or shame of the one to the disadvantage of the other. The authors of *Sex and the Brain* sound a note of caution for the unwary reader who should know first, that these differences are "statistical differences; averages. .... They are by no means cut and dried in every male and female. And second, the average sex differences that we do observe should never be allowed to have any effect on social policy" regarding males and females in a community (Durden-Smith & De Simone 1983 : 51). But the history of the perceptions of sex differences has not been benign and generous; the male has almost invariably used his superior muscular power and cunning to use and abuse the female for a variety of dehumanizing strategies. He has not only forced sex on her; he has also rejected and condemned her for it. He has often used pregnancy as a form of control on the female. Pregnancy, as we all know, means for woman, dependence on others. Reminiscing about her experiences during pregnancy, an enlightened woman has this to say: "I could not behave with dignity because I was totally dependent; I could only put up with the situation, like it or lump it, and we both [she and her husband] knew it" (Figes 1971). Men have abused and denounced women for those gifts of nature for which they should have been adored. Even if women had not done anything other than giving birth, they should have been elevated to the highest pedestal of glory.

Faster and more aggressive than female sex chromosomes, male sex chromosomes cause as many as 140 male conceptions for every 100 female conceptions. But as a number of male foetuses are miscarried, only 106 males are born for every 100 females. Even for those who begin their life on earth in good shape and health, it is not easy to survive for long. 30 per cent more males than females die during the first few months of life. Male babies are 5 per cent heavier at birth than female babies though they are 4 to 6 weeks behind female babies in physical maturity. Most male babies are born prematurely. They are genetically more prone to infantile diseases (except whooping cough) than female babies. Only castrated males and eunuchs have their immune systems that approach the physiological efficiency of females. Boys are more factious and irritable than girls. Girls sit up, crawl, walk and talk earlier than boys. More boys than girls suffer from genetic ambiguity or defect. Male babies are much less protected against viruses and bacteria than female babies. On account of disabilities like these, male babies lose their number much faster than female babies do so much so that by the time of puberty, they are just equal to female babies in number and then, if things go well for girls after puberty, they easily outnumber boys by the time of adulthood (cf. Durden-Smith & De Simone 1983 : 136-153).

If nature is allowed to prevail in respect of human survival, women should constitute at least 55 per cent of the total population in every community and they should be healthier, happier and longer-living. But it has not been so. Men have often interfered with nature and deliberately reduced the life span and the number of women as they have contaminated their health and happiness. Girl children have been subjected to infanticide by suffocation, strangulation, negligence, maltreatment, overdoses of exposure, and slow-killing drugs. For a long time in history, girls were sacrificed to gods and goddesses, buried alive, or exposed to nature in countries like Greece, Rome, the Arab World, China, Japan and India (cf. Kidwai 1976 : 9). Agamemnon's sacrifice of his daughter Iphigenia on the eve of the Trojan war is explicitly mentioned in Aeschylus' famous tragedy, *Agamemnon*.

The social status and the declining number of the womenfolk in India call for speculation and investigation. Available data clearly suggest that women are increasingly losing both in number and in work-participation in our country. The National Institute of Public Co-operation and Child Development organized a workshop on girls in collaboration with UNICEF in New Delhi in December 1987. It was pointed out by several participants that women are outnumbered by men in every field and that there are still deep prejudices against the social status of women in most parts of India (Ind. Exp. Dec., 29, 1987). Within the home the mother is handicapped by the birth of a girl and when the girl grows up, she is handicapped by the attitude of the mother and the family, thus creating a vicious circle around girls. Speakers at the workshop ruled out any correlation between economic backwardness and bias against girls. They emphasized that the centuries-old patriarchal bias against girls was responsible for their neglect and declining number. Isn't it shocking that in spite of government funding of girl education, there is a lower enrolment of girls in schools? The lower enrolment is further compounded by higher drop-out rates of girl students. Unless attitudinal changes in parents, particularly in mothers, with respect to girl babies are brought about urgently, we may not be able to improve the situation. If we are earnest about improving the social situation in India with respect to women, we must let nature have its way and we must redefine our culture. Unless we increase women population in our country at least comparable to the women population of developed countries, we must not talk about our humanistic philosophy. As of today, it does not simply lie in our mouth to brag about our glorious heritage and our belief in the so-called doctrine of non-injury to living beings. Our age-old hypocrisy in respect of women is systematically being exposed on two counts: girl infanticide and increasing number of women deaths. More and more women—unmarried, married, separated, divorced and widowed—are killed or forced to die through systematic neglect and torture. More and more women are openly killed. More and more women are pushed to death through a network of atrocities like rape, public humiliation, social boycott and repeated threats and assaults. Girl babies are done to death in a number of ways. As a scholar rightly puts it: "In a country where there have been such rigid doctrines of the sanctity of life, infanticide is extremely difficult to explain. ... It is significant that female deaths invariably increase between one week of age and twelve months" (Baig 1976 : 88-89). In a country which has had so many prophets of non-violence between Buddha and Gandhi, it is really mind-boggling to account for the increasing incidence of girl infanticide. A study conducted by a women's organization on the implications of sex-determination tests (Amniocentesis) revealed in January 1988 that out of 8,000 cases of abortion that were carried out in Bombay in the previous year, 7,999 involved female foetuses (Ind. Exp. January 4, 1988).

In countries like Japan and America, women now live on an average, for more that 80 years and they constitute nearly 54 per cent of the country's population whereas the average life expectancy of women in India is less than 55 years and they constitute less than 49 per cent of the country's population. Women in India can claim a mere 21 per cent of the country's work-force. Only 9 out of 412 districts in the country possess a satisfactory level of women education, even though Indian girls account for 77.3 per cent of non-school-going children in the age-group of 6-14 (cf. Amundsen 1971 : 12, Baig 1976 : 28 & Sahai 1985 : XVII-XX).

An analysis of the 1981 Census report reveals astounding facts about the position of women in our country. Some of the facts are: (i) Everywhere in the world there are more women than men whereas in India there are more men than women. (ii) Average life expectancy of women in India is one of the lowest in the world. (iii) Women population, like woman work-participation, has been consistently on the decline since the first Indian Census in 1901. (iv) The official forecast for the next five decades, that is, up to at least 2031 shows a downward trend both in population and work-participation for women in India. (v) Indian women are subjected to the cruelties of institutional sexism on a scale much larger than in many countries (*The Statesman* : Nov., 14 & 15, 1986). Statistics like these oblige us to look inward to take stock of the situation and to try to bring about a change for the better without any further loss of time.

1.5 Deification of the Aryan Hero

"... if God is male, then the male is God."

—*Mary Daly (cited in Mcphee 1979 : 130)*

Male-domination in Aryan society was not a historical or regional development; it was the fundamental principle on which Vedic Aryans based their social philosophy. The problems of today are conditioned by a male sex-domination which has existed" since the first man pleaded mitigation of guilt by blaming his delinquency on the first woman. It was a bad beginning, and the sons of Adam have done it ever since" (Stocks 1971). People often think that women mostly suffer from legal injustices or from defects in the law. But they seldom realize that parliamentarians and lawyers until very recently have all been men (cf Summerskill 1971). Women are treated in all sorts of ways in literature and their sufferings are often attributed to their own faults or vices but it is seldom noted that their sufferings and vices are all created by men. Patriarchal values pervade the whole canon of literature because, aside from a few texts here and there, all extant literary texts have been written by men (cf Lenz *et al* 1980). It is often argued that women must/mustn't do such and such things because they are/aren't sanctioned by religious authorities but no one cares to ascertain as to why religious texts/

authorities prescribe what they do in relation to women. If we take note of the simple fact that since almost all religious establishments, texts, rituals and values are sponsored, managed and preserved by men, it becomes easier to understand why religious authorities/texts maintain what they do. According to the *Bhagavata Purana*, the Supreme Being is a Man. He creates the Creator who is a Man and the Creator creates the first human being who is a Man, a Man who is a Patriarch (cf Bader 1964 : 76). How intriguing it is that in almost every established religion God is a He-Man, a Patriarch, having extraordinary virile attributes!

The advancement of science and technology is generally considered a hall-mark of modern civilization. Revolutionary thinkers like Darwin, Marx and Freud are often credited with having reduced religious orthodoxy to an extent that modern culture is sharply distinguished from ancient culture. We frequently claim to have developed an adequately scientific attitude to socio-religious conventions and practices. But, despite these claims, it comes as a miracle to the sensitive that primitive attitudes towards women and their roles in the socio-religious set-up have endured through the centuries. Mythologies are full of tales which show that self-sacrifice or martyrdom is the standard way for women, even for women like Sita and Desdemona and that self-assertion earns an evil reputation for women, even for women like Draupadi and Medea. Are these myths lies or concoctions designed to impose a symbolic order upon the universe created by men ? Mythological goddesses seem to be archetypal images of human females, as envisioned by human males (cf Pomeroy 1975 : 1 & 8). The divine kingdom is ruled by Indra with his Vajra or by Zeus with his thunderbolt (the synonymity between Vajra and thunderbolt is intriguing), the unfailing weapon. Indra seduces Ahalya and Zeus abducts Persephone, although both of them are already married to ravishingly beautiful goddesses. All the gods drink nectar and ambrosia which keep them externally youthful and vivacious so that they can molest, rape or destroy pretty mortal women. Mortal women cannot and must not resist their advances or protest against their wilfulness. The *Manusmriti* lays down : " a wife ought to revere as god even that husband who has repeatedly transgressed his marriage vows" (VI : 154). Manu's decree applies to both mortal and immortal wives. Every woman is an Ismene who has been indoctrinated into beliefs of patriarchal society: men are born to rule and women to obey. In Sophocles' *Antigone*

Ismene says : "We were born women, showing that we were not meant to fight with men" (line 61-62).

Mythology is a people's vision of life here and hereafter. It deals with a world which is both real and imaginary, historical and mythical, earthy and ethereal. It is a link between "this world" and the "other world". The other world is an extension of this world. Mythology constructs a continuum between this world and the other world so that gods and men may change places, exchange roles and thus form a common fraternity. The two worlds share a unity of substance and a diversity of powers. An eminent critic of Greek tragedy and mythology writes : "The anthropomorphization of the Greek gods was total. No human attribute, physical or psychological, was excluded from them. With the exception of death, which was the absolute defining-point between man and god, and which was fatal to cross, the Greeks give all kinds of human form and feelings to their deities, often unconscious of any absurdities. ... The Greek gods have human bodies, they are male or female, have intercourse as we do, bear children as we do" (Vickers 1973 : 122-123). Like Greek men, Greek gods are loved, hated, cheated, tried, rewarded, punished or purified. Although of widely differing powers, Greek men and gods are identical in substance and form. Pindar celebrates the kinship between such men and gods in the opening lines of his *Sixth Nemean* :

"Single is the race

of men and gods

From a single mother we both draw breath.

But a difference of power in everything keeps us apart". (quoted in *ibid* p. 121).

The only dividing line between Greek men and gods is that the former are mortal while the latter are immortal. The "other world" is both logically sensible and emotionally satisfying to the denizens of "this world" and these twin attributes of the other world make it necessary and enjoyable to the innocent and the credulous.

To continue and flourish as a well-structured and firmly established hierarchic society, ancient Hindus, like ancient Greeks, thought it expedient to create a superstructure, the other world of religion and mythology. They stipulated a network of practices and behaviour patterns for the constituents of the superstructure that might support and sustain this world. It was for this purpose that they elected to humanize God and His Deputies as well as to deify man. The two worlds, the divine and the terrestrial, thus created, could come so close to each other that people living in either of them could step into the other at will. The divine kingdom was clearly and entirely anthropomorphic. The gods of the ancient Hindus were just like themselves. Their gods were as highly sexed, wily, cruel and mean as themselves. They were as scheming, unscrupulous, polygynous and heartless as their divine mentors. The early Aryans, quite naturally, developed a habit of thought that could easily identify one God with multiple forms and multiple forms with one God.

The logical connection between multiplicity and oneness gave rise to the doctrine of incarnation (Avatara) in Hindu philosophy. This doctrine is Vedic in origin. In one of the hymns of the *Rig-Veda* reference is made to Vishnu's capacity to assume multiple forms : "Do not assume this form, since thou didst assume another in battle" (VII : 100 : 6, cf Chanda 1976 : 111). Vedic Vishnu was a powerful deity, no doubt, but he was not yet the Supreme Being or the Absolute. He grew, in all respects, into the Supreme Being by the time of the epics. Vasudeva (*i.e.* the earliest name of the god of gods), Hari and Narayana became synonyms of Vishnu (cf Bhandarkar 1965 : 33-34). Once the doctrine of incarnation was firmly established in Hinduism, it became convenient to transform an Aryan hero into an Avatara of Vishnu. To recognize a hero as an Avatara of Vishnu was the highest honour that Aryans could bestow on their symbol of power and triumph. As time drew on, the Hindu pantheon came to be headed absolutely by Vishnu, the Supreme Deity. The system would not allow any god transferred from other systems to rival Vishnu.

The divine pantheon was rigidly graded so that other gods could be placed in the right order. The Hindu Trinity consisting of Vishnu, Brahma and Mahesh (Shiva) was created. As Hinduism became more and more Brahmanized, several incarnations of Vishnu were envisioned. The number of incarnations varies from six to twenty-three : the Narayaniya section of the *Mahabharata* mentions six incarnations, while the *Bhagavata-Purana* variously enumerates sixteen, twenty-two and twenty-three incarnations. But the *Varaha-Purana* mentions only ten incarnations of Vishnu. This number is traditionally accepted by the orthodox. These ten incarnations are : the Boar, the Man-lion, the Dwarf, Vasudeva-Krishna, Parashurama, Rama, the

Tortoise, the Fish, the Buddha and Kalkin (cf. Bhandarkar 1965 : 33-34, 41-42).

An interesting feature of the doctrine of Avatara is that the story of the apotheosization of a name starts later than the actual occurrence of the name. Vishnu, for example, was a powerful Vedic deity, capable of assuming forms at will but he became all-powerful centuries after the Vedas. Similarly, Vasudeva-Krishna lived long before the writing of the *Gita*. It was only by the time of the composition of the *Gita* and the *Mahabharata* (the former being a part of the latter), that is, about the third century BC that Vasudeva-Krishna emerged as the all-powerful deity, the Supreme Being, the Ishvara and was identified with Vedic Vishnu. Krishna became the first Avatara of Vishnu, or Vishnu re-emerged as omnipotent Krishna only about the third century BC. The Mahabharata war seems to have preceded the composition of the epic (*Mahabharata*) by several centuries. By the time the Epic came to be composed, Krishna had become the most important legend in Hindu history. As Bhandarkar puts it : "Vasudeva could not have been living when the *Bhagavata-Gita* was composed as a discourse delivered by Him, any more than Buddha was living when his discoureses were reduced to the form of books" (1965 : 30 cf. Chanda 1976 : 99). The Ikshvaku hero Rama was probably recognized as an incarnation of Vishnu much later than his supposed time and in imitation of Vasudeva-Krishna (cf Bhandarkar 1965 : 46-48 & Chanda 1976 : 111). Rama's transformation into an Avatara of Vishnu appears to have taken shape even after the *Ramayana* of Valmiki. All references to Rama as an Avatara in Books I & VII of the Epic are generally considered interpolations by scholars (cf Bhandarkar 1965 : 47 & Chanda 1976: 116 & Nath 1979). One could similarly separate the historicity of a personage from his tranformation into an Avatara because the whole theory of Avatara is a construct of the Puranic Aryans.

The personalization of God and the apotheosization of man constitute the doctrine of incarnation. In course of time incarnations build a system and a long line of heroes are idealised and deified by the Aryans to maintain their hold on the future. No question is ever supposed to be asked about the alchemy of the man-God or God-man transformation. A fundamental question is raised by the sceptical wife of Shiva in the *Ramacharitamanasa* : "Can the Absolute, which is all-pervading, passionless, unborn, indivisible, desireless, without parts—and that which even the Vedas do not know — take a bodily form as a man ?" (Hill 1952 : 30). By dismissing this question as an unnecessary question by the unbelieving or uninitiated, Hindu orthodoxy seeks to use its philosophy of the religious suprestructure to take every one for a ride. The fear of God and the reward of heaven are natural to man. The Hindu doctrine of incarnation uses the fear of God and the reward of heaven to silence opposition and to abort scepticism. But the one-to-one correspondence between the Hindu this world and the Hindu that world is there for anyone to see and judge. The literalness of the that world is repeatedly displayed by the texts themselves. In a Greek myth, Hera, the queen of the Olympian kingdom and wife of Zeus, curses Echo : "your punishment will be to stay invisible for ever and only able to repeat other people's words" (cf. Graves 1960 : 153). Similarly, here is an incantation for ritual coition to be chanted by the husband to his wife in the *Brihadaranyaka-Upanishad* :

"I am the Saman, thou the Rig!

I am the heaven, thou the earth!

Come, let us together clasp!

Together let us semen mix!

A male, a son to produce" (VI : 4 : 2, Hume 1949 : 171).

The Rig in this text and the Echo in Hera's, it hardly needs to be pointed out, are first cousins who suffer physically in this world due to the spiritualizing requirements of the other world. Rig and Echo are forced into compliance and silence by and for the males of the other world. How significant it is that Ismene uses the verb *phyo* in *Antigone* to imply that it is by "nature' (physis) rather than by man-made conventon that women "do not attempt to rival men" (cf. Pomeroy 1975 : 99)!

Full of great beauty, wisdom and poetry, the *Mahabharata* and the *Ramayana* are, by all standards, the greatest of Hindu classics, outside the Vedas and the Upanishadas. They form the central part of Hindu mythology. They are wonderful masterpieces of literature and religion. They represent the life history of the ancient Hindus. They articulate the collective unconscious of the Indo-Aryans. They glorify male values. But they differ from each other in certain respects. The *Mahabharata* is four times the size of the *Ramayana*. The *Mahabharata* represents intra-racial conflicts while the *Ramayana* is a classic record of the inter-racial confrontation as well as of the decisive triumph of the Aryan over the non-Aryan. The *Mahabharata*, the longest poem in the world, containing a hundred thousand verses, delineates a society in transition, a society which is full of diverse elements, practices and customs, a society which maintains institutions like polygyny, polyandry, pre-marital maternity, extra-marital sexuality, inter-racial marriages, matrilocal marriages, sacramental marriages, contract marriages, marriages by purchase, wife-sharing, widowhood and widow-burning. In view of all these conflicting institutions, practices and customs, the *Mahabharata* may be said to have been composed earlier than the other Epic. One of the fifteen greatest books of the world, (cf Chatterjee 1978 : 5), the *Ramayana* is longer than the *Iliad* and the *Odyssey* put together. It depicts a later, better organized and more developed society than the *Mahabharata* does.

The *Mahabharata* and the *Ramayana* represent different societies, different world-views and different ends. Unlike the *Ramayana*, the *Mahabharata* displays the naked and embarrassing realities of life. It is less idealistic, more frank and therefore, more embarrassing than the *Ramayana*. As an eminent scholar puts it : "The *Ramayana* rouses compassion; the *Mahabharata* an almost cosmic awe ... Valmiki rules the Hindu heart, Vyasa goes into his very guts ... Valmiki delineates the Hindu, the Indian dream of perfection, Vyasa pricks the Hindu, the Indian, conscience. Valmiki's epic is a vision; Vyasa's epic is a mirror in which the Indian sees himself undeceived ... Vyasa is ubiquitous and inescapable; he will not let us be; he is like an eczema itch, a chronic toothache, a betrayed love" (Lal 1980). To summarize the difference between these two epics in one sentence, we can say that the *Ramayana* is more Brahmanized and Brahmanizing than the *Mahabharata* and this is the secret of its undiminishing and universal appeal to the Hindus.

The *Ramayana* deals with an age in which "Brahmanic ideals of religion and sexual morality were fully developed and non-Aryan practices were hailed in extreme contempt" and it appears to articulate a social philosophy which believed in "a progressive racial degeneration southwards from Ayodhya" (Thomas 1964 : 13). "Rama's exile is sometimes seen as years of preparation with non-Aryan allies for a massive compaign to drive out the formidable Rakshasas from the mainland as well as to pursue them right into their teritory and to rout their power once for all" (cf Spencer 1965 : 249 & Sen 1976). One can never be sure about the definitive interpretation of a classic like the *Ramayana* but it is possible to read it as an account of "colonial penetration by the Aryans of Ayodhya led by Rama who, with the help of a faithful mercenary army of forest folk or tree-men called Vanaras, routed the Asura, the anti-God of Lanka, Ravana" (cf Lal 1980). The matchless popularity of the Rama legend with the millions of Hindu masses may be taken as the support for a political interpretation of the war epic.

As a war epic, the *Ramayana* bears a striking resemblance to the first epic and the earliest extant work of Western literature, the *Iliad*, composed by the blind bard, Homer in the eighth century BC. The *Iliad*, as is so well known, relates the events of the first and the most disasterous war in Western history, known as the Trojan War, which probably took place around 1184 BC. According to the *Iliad*, Helen was the cause of the Trojan War. It is alleged in the epic that Paris, the Prince of Troy, abducted Helen, the Queen of Sparta, to his kingdom and married her. The Spartans took it as their national humiliation and therefore decided to revenge themselves on the Trojans. As Sparta was one of the Greek states, the other Greeks joined the offended Spartan hero, Menelaus, in his campaign against Troy. As a combined force, the Greeks launched a massive attack on Troy, destroyed the kingdom and recovered Helen. This is the *Iliad* version of the Trojan War. But reputed classical Greek historians like Herodotus and Thucydides reject this claim. They suggest instead that the Greeks invaded and destroyed the Trojan kingdom only to extend their politico-economic domination over the eastern Mediterranean (cf Pomeroy 1975 : 16-17). Like the *Iliad*, the *Ramayana* could easily be read as an account of a political war, fought for political purposes and concluded with the political triumph of the powerful Aryans over the non-Aryans. Besides, as there was a gap between the time of the Trojan War and the composition of the *Iliad*, there was perhaps a long gap between the time of the Lankan War and the actual writing of the *Ramayana*. Valmiki does not seem to have been a contemporary of Rama. Perhaps he got the story of his epic from folk tales about the Rama-Ravana confrontation (cf Rajgopalachari 1951 a). The *Ramayana* was probably composed later than the *Mahabharata*, not only because it is less embarrassing a book than the *Mahabharata*, but also because it depicts a social set-up which is more consistent with regard to Hindu institutions, practices and customs. The *Ramayana* is much more conservative a book than the *Mahabharata*.

2

Politics of Discrimination

"The son is a boat of salvation, a light in the highest heaven but ... a daughter is a misery."

—*Aitareya Brahmana*

2.1 Exaltation of Male Values

All patri-centric societies, independent of culture or climate, age or system of faith, derive from and justify the universal assumption that the world is essentially a world of men—created by and for men. All the names of the absolute, Ishwara, are masculine; all sages, messiahs and prophets are men; all philosophies, revelations, sciences and literatures are formulated by men; all theories of evolution and progress are invented by men; all norms of social behaviour and religious thinking are controlled by men. It is no wonder that, in a world so prominently masculine, the female is reduced to a means, a scapegoat, an excuse for everything the male wants to do. It is no wonder that the Athenian in Plato's *Laws* declares with absolute finality and without any qualms of conscience that "the origin of society was patriarchal" (p. 680). It is no wonder that Puranic Vishnu acquires more than a thousand names, accumulated in the form of a book of names (*Vishnusahasranaam*).

In the Jewish account of creation, God not only makes Adam first; He makes Eve as "an help meet for him" because he feels that it is "not good that the man should be alone" (Genesis 2 : 18). In the *Brihadaranyaka Upnishada* (VI : IV : 2), after creating man, Prajapati, the lord of creation, bethinks himself "Come, let me provide him a firm basis !" So he creates woman. The Rig-Vedic hymn visualizes the "origin of creation" as a He (X : 129 : 7). *The Avesta* describes the Omniscient Lord, Ahura Mazda, and the first Prophet, Holy Zarathushtra, as He's. The founders of Buddhism, Jainism and Sikhism were men. The Prophet of Islam was a man. One of the most ancient systems of Indian Philosophy, the Samkhya, traces the evolution of the universe to the inter-play (samyoga) of two ultimate principles, viz., spirit and primal matter, Purusha and Prakriti (cf. Chatterjee & Datta 1960 : 25-88). If we look at the Samkhya account of creation a bit critically, we will find that the scale is very shrewdly tilted in favour of the male principle, the spirit, the Purusha which (outside the Samkhya, though) is incidentally a term that refers both to Vishnu and his Aryan male. Radiating with pure consciousness, the Purusha remains unmoved and unchanged even though it is the *enjoyer* (bhokta) of Prakriti. The Purusha is lame and inactive (the lion never goes a hunting but claims the largest share in the lioness' catch) but its mere presence (sannidhi) is sufficient to move Prakriti to act. Prakriti is active and ever-changing but blind and unintelligent (Jada-a typical male perception of femininity!). Purusha needs Prakriti to attain self-knowledge and liberation, while Prakriti requires Purusha to achieve self-fulfilment. The summum bonum of Prakriti is manifestation (darsḥanartham) whereas the highest end of the Purushạ is final liberation (kaivalyartham). By the analogy of the lame and the blind, the Samkhya places Purusha, beyond doubt, above Prakriti. To interact with Purusha, Prakriti has to carry him on her shoulders but, more importantly, to submit herself to be led by him. The Samkhya cosmology is, quite clearly, a metaphoric pronouncement of the primordial supremacy of the male over the female.

Hindu gods, like their Olympian cousins, both outnumber and overpower goddesses. It is they who manage and control the heavenly kingdom. Goddesses are there only to keep them company and to do their bidding. The gods make laws but they are above the laws. They transgress their laws with absolute impunity. The greatest law of a patriarchal system is an ordinance which keeps its men free to do what they like but enjoins upon its women to act according to the dictates of their men. Under the orthodox Muslim Law, one Muslim male is equivalent to two Muslim females in all respects, including rights to property. A Muslim male has the right to unilateral divorce without any reason; the wife has no such right; a Muslim male can marry four women at a time, a Muslim female cannot do that; a Muslim male is allowed to marry outside his religion but a Muslim female is not (cf. Pickthall 1924 : IV : 11 & Islam 1986). King Dasharatha has 350 concubines, besides three wives and Lord Krishna has 16008 wives, including 8 regularly married wives but no mortal or immortal female (Draupadi's case may be enigmatic) is wedded to more than one male at a time. Until a few decades ago, a Hindu male could marry any number of women at a time but Manu decrees that a woman cannot think of another man even after the death of her husband (cf. *Manusmriti* : V : 157). A Hindu woman acquired right to property for the first time in Hindu history in 1956. The heroes of the *Mahabharata* marry outside their caste but no Aryan woman in that great book is mentioned as having done so.

The ancient Athenians do not seem to have had any regard for the maternal contribution to the foetus. Apollo in Aeschylus' *Eumenides* (458 BC) denies the mother's contribution to conception. The mother is only the receptacle for the father's seed: "She who is called the mother is not her off-spring's parent, but nurse to the newly sown embryo. The male who mounts begets" (cf. Pomeroy 1975 : 65). When the modern Hindu refers to his son or daughter as `my child', he only echoes Apollo in his daily chit-chat. Patriarchal bias is rampant even today in many parts of Greece. If a Greek peasant with three sons and two daughters is asked today how many children he has, his first answer is `three' (*ibid.*, p. 70). The situation is not very different with modern Hindus. In orthodox Hindu families, parents without sons do often say that they are `childless'. The universal practice of tagging the man's surname to his wife and children is tantamount to denying the mother's share in genetic continuity.

It is not a case of linguistic accident that in a morphologically related pair of nouns, the feminine form is generally derived from the masculine root (cf. Quirk *et. al.*, 1972 : 188). The English 'she' is graphologically longer than 'he' like any number of feminine nouns. The masculine base forms (or roots) like 'prince', 'duke', 'god', etc., can exist by themselves but feminine derivatives like 'princess', 'duchess' and 'goddess' cannot. Sanskrit synonyms of 'women', 'girl', 'wife', and 'sister' are some of the numerous examples in which the feminine derivatives owe their existence in the language to their masculine base forms. Besides, in the semantic analysis of lexical items, pairs of words are seen as *unmarked* and *marked* on the ground that the latter is more *specific* than the former. Unmarked forms (or words) have a larger semantic area or greater *value* (in the Saussurean sense) than marked forms. One can, for example, speak of male or female 'dog' but one cannot speak of male or female 'bitch' because 'dog' refers to either gender whereas 'bitch' is confined only to the feminine gender. Male forms are unmarked and female forms are marked. 'Woman', for example, is marked for gender but 'man' is not because it is neither idiomatic nor acceptable in the structure of English to make a sentence like "Woman is a social animal" (cf. Crystal 1980: 219-21).

What really intrigues one in a context like this is the choice of the term *marked* to refer to feminine nouns. It is possible that linguists use this term without any conscious implication of alleged female sexuality. It is possible that they have no bias against women. It is possible that they do not conspire to restrict women. Possibilities like these, however, do not rule out the possibility for the choice of this term. It is likely that by coining and popularizing *Markedness* in respect of feminine nouns, the linguist is unconsciously trying to set women as a class apart. The denigration of women throughout history owes its existence to their gender. They have always suffered on account of their gender because they have always been *marked* for their gender. The sage Vatsyayana recommends the *physical marking* of women as a means to make them sexy (cf. *Kamasutra* : II : IV & V).

Most educated people need to be educated about the conditions in which women still live in millions of Hindu families. They are still literally, physically marked. According to an FIR lodged with the Bhubaneshwar Police (case no. 1322/1987), a nineteen-year-old Brahmana girl was spotted, while begging for food in the streets of Cuttack, on June 26, 1987 and taken to the home for the homeless by the volunteers of a social organization. The eldest of six daughters and five sons of a responsible in-service officer of the Orissa government, Ms Sanghamitra Mishra, was branded with a redhot iron rod when she was born. As her parents hated female children, she was subjected to all sorts of torture during her childhood. Her parents would often whip her. They would break hard coconuts on her head. They would pour boiling oil on her head. In the final phase of her torture, when she was in her teens, she was compelled to survive on raw onion and pickings from the drain until she escaped from her home in Bhubaneshwar and went to Cuttack begging for food. And it was here that she revealed to the world the horror story of her growth from childhood to adolescence (cf. Ind. Exp., July 21, 1987 p. 6).

The tradition of glorifying the birth of a male child in India and Greece is as old as the Vedas and the Homeric Epics. The early Indo-Aryans often repeat in their hymns the earnest prayer "May we possess a family of males" (Bader 1964 : 3). Indrani exclaims in a verse in the *Rig-Veda*: "The mother of a son deserves honour" (*ibid.*, pp. 51-52). One of the benedictions of elderly guests present at the wedding says to the bride: "Be amenable; be glorious; be the mother of males" (*Rig-Veda* cited in Shastri 1969 : 15). The birth of a daughter is emphatically deprecated in the *Atharva-Veda*. Prayers and ceremonies to prevent the birth of female children are frequently invoked. A characteristic incantation in the *Atharva-Veda* runs as follows:

> "The birth of a girl, O Prajapati, grant elsewhere!
>
> Here grant a boy" (Baig 1976 : 83).

The *Aitareya Brahmana* mentions the dialogue between king Harish Chandra and the sage Narada on the value of a son. Harish Chandra has a hundred wives and no son. He asks the sage, "What is the fruit to be attained by having a son?" The sage tells him: "The father gains immortality when he sees the face of a son born to him. The son is a boat of salvation" (cited in Shastri 1969 : 75). Manu lays down that the house-holder can get out of the debt to his ancestors (Pitririna) only by: "begetting sons". (VI : 36). In the *Ramayana* parents perform sacrifices or practise penance for the sake of a son (cf. Sharma 1971 : 67). Perhaps no Hindu text prescribes or recommends prayers and ceremonials for the birth of a daughter. The birth of a daughter even today deceives the parents' expectations. Not too many years ago, one octogenarian Punjabi woman was asked what it was like in her youth when she gave birth to her first daughter. Pat came the terse reply : "It was a funeral" (Baig 1976 : 83).

The *Brihadaranyaka Upanishada* offers an etymological justification for glorifying the arrival of a male child in the family: "Because a son 'delivers' (*trayate*) his father from `hell' (*put*), he is called `deliverer from hell' *i.e., putra* (I : I : 17). It prescribes elaborate rituals for the couple to procure sons (already quoted in the previous chapter cf. VI : IV : 20). As soon as the son is born, the father must repeat the following incantations:

"In this son may I be increased, And have a thousand in my house.

He reaches the highest pinnacle of splendour and glory, and sacred knowledge, who is born as the son of a Brahmana" (VI : IV : 24 & 28). In Kalidasa's *Abhijnanashakuntalam*, Kanva blesses the departing Shakuntala with these words: "May you bear him a son as brave as Puru" (Lal 1964 : 42).

As in India, so in Greece, the value of the son in the eyes of parents, a primary symbolic feature of a patri-centric society, is emphasized in both the *Iliad* and the *Odyssey*. In ancient Athenian marriages, before the groom joined her on the wedding day, the bride had to eat a fruit with many seeds, symbolizing fertility. The birth of a son was generally considered a fulfilment of the goals of such marriages (cf. Pomeroy 1975 : 28 & 62). The Indian custom of wives eating specially prepared food to ensure the birth of a son is related in the *Ramayana*. The three wives of Dasharatha eat the celestial "porridge" (payas) to beget sons (cf. I : XV : p. 35). Such fruit-eating or porridge-eating ceremonies were never performed for the birth of a daughter. For all practical purposes, fertility meant both in India and Greece, the woman's capacity to produce male children. The ancient Greeks were so much obsessed with the value of male children that even philosophers and scientists had to propound the doctrine that to give birth to a son was the noblest act of a wife. In his epoch-making medical *Aphorism* Hippocrates, the renowned medical scientist of classical Athens, observes in Aphorism No. 42: "A pregnant woman has a good complexion if the child is male; a poor complexion if the child is female" (Pomeroy 1975 : 84). Aristotle opposed child-bearing by child-wives on the ground that the babies born of very young wives were likely to be female (cf. *ibid.*, p. 85).

The doctrine of male superiority was so thoroughly preached and so religiously practised that even women came to view themselves as essentially inferior to men. In Euripides' famous tragedy, *Iphigenia in Tauris*, the heroine offers to sacrifice herself for her brother, Orestes, simply because he is a male and she is a female. Iphigenia articulates what most men and women of her age and society believe in:

"My life is little. I would gladly die to earn your safety and your reaching home. If a man die, a house, a name is lost. But if a woman die, what does it matter". (cf. Vickers 1973 : 116).

Sad it is that things have not changed over the centuries. If modern parents in Greece (or in India for that matter) were asked today to sacrifice either their sons or daughters, they would willingly sacrifice all their daughters to retain their sons. Whenever possible, Iphigenias continue to die for their brothers even now but seldom does an Orestes care for his self-sacrificing sister.

A society so overtly masculine cannot be expected to be fair to girls in a family where there are boys as well as girls. One can easily find girls being discriminated against in almost all dimensions. Boys go out to play games or to idle away their time, while girls are required to help in the kitchen. Boys can be naughty and mischievous, while girls have to be polite and well-behaved. Higher education is a necessity for boys whereas for girls it is a luxury. Boys grow up to inherit the father's property and authority whereas girls have to be married and packed off. A boy marries to decorate the house whereas the house is decorated for a girl to be married off. In a milieu like this, it is only natural that the male baby becomes a household pet and the female baby a chronic curse in a Hindu family (cf. Wiser and Wiser 1963 : 75). If a small boy does not get what he desires, he "lies on the ground and kicks and cries and refuses to move until he gets it ... Little sisters seldom resort to this" (*ibid.*, p. 77). Their training in self-restraint begins at a time when the girls can hardly realize why it should be so. They do not understand why their parents treat them differently from their brothers. A woman writer rightly protests: "As a girl, I inwardly raged at having to help with the washing up whilst my brother went off to play football" (Figes 1971). Indira Gandhi, just twenty years ago, loudly declared that the notion of the superiority of "one race or sex" was out of date (1974). It is unfortunate that there are not even a dozen Indira Gandhis in India to change the centuries-old philosophy of male chauvinism into a string of nonsense words.

2.2 Subordination of Woman

> "I have a very clear, keen memory of myself the day after I was married. I was sweeping a floor."
>
> —*Adrienne Rich (Mcphee 1979 : 87)*

A vast majority of educated males need to be reminded that it is socially damaging and morally indefensible to concoct and perpetuate the axiom that women are an inferior variety of men. It is no complement to a woman to be 'masculine' as it is no complement to a man to be 'feminine'. Mythological females cannot be allowed to float as archetypal images of modern women. We cannot divide women into intellectual/asexual/career women, frivolous sex objects and respectable symbols of domesticity. Women cannot be forced to choose between an Athena or a Gargi, an Aphrodite or an Ambapali, and a Hera or a Savitri. Women cannot be judged with reference to men as the norms of human excellence. Women are as much human as men and they have the same rights to the equality of opportunity and development as men have. Men have no right to fix and inflict standards of female behaviour on women. They have no business to poke their nose in the affairs of women in the same sense in which they would not like women to decide for them and to impose upon them the norms of male behaviour.

It is, however, baffling to note that throughout history men have inflicted their false notions of womanhood on women. The very word 'woman' recounts a tedious history of subordination and harassment. Few people would ever try to find out what true femininity actually means. We seldom care to realize that the characteristics popularly held to be *typical* of women are quite simply and viciously determined by those who want to perpetuate male superiority over females. Men have converted the history of human civilization into a series of subtle and systematic attempts to acquire absolute control on women. It is a history of indoctrination which seeks to convert women into slaves so much so that now even the majority of women do not know that the roles and functions they aspire for are in fact the tools of their subordination and dependence. It is, by and large, "the socialization process that is responsible for the mental sets, the emotional dispositions and the prevalent behaviour of women" (Amundsen : 18). Those who talk about the ideal or typical behaviour of women do not care to note that behaviour need not be biologically determined for women any more that it is for men. Biology cannot and must not be the destiny for women any more than it is for men. Willy-nilly, we are at a stage of human development where one is not born, but rather made a woman. "No biological, psychological or economic fate determines the figure that the human female presents in society; it is civilization as a whole that produces this creature, intermediate between male and eunuch which is described as feminine" (Beauvoir 1953 : 8).

To say and believe that woman is less responsible, virtuous and intelligent and more emotional and dependent than man is to propagate an atrocious lie. Great books and great men are often full of monstrous untruths about women. The wicked Athenian in Plato's *Laws*, for example, has no basis, whatsoever, for his pronouncement that the female sex is "by nature inferior to man in the capacity for virtue" (p. 781). Timaeus is just a wicked lier when he propounds that men are created asexually while women and animals are "created through biological procreation involving both sexes" and that "cowardly and unrighteous men are born as women in their next life" (*Timaeus* pp. 18-19). It does not behove Socrates to hold the view that women "should be assimilated and brought into harmony with men" (*ibid.*, p. 18). It is sheer mischief on the part of Demetrius, a Greek thinker of the fourth century BC, to float the doctrine that the "deliberative part" of women's soul is "impotent"and hence needs supervision (Pomeroy 1975 : 13). Equally mischievous is the old Russian proverb: "there is only one soul among ten women" (Kidwai 1976 : 8). Theophrates, a disciple of Aristotle, has no logical support for his theory that more education would turn women into "lazy, talkative, busibodies" (Pomeroy 1975 : 131) as Jung has no sociological justification for his condemnation of universities as "animus incubators" because they make women "competitive, argumentative and full of ideas" (Storr 1973 : 54). In his testimony before a House subcommittee considering legislation to stop discrimination against American women in 1970, Shirley Chisholm revealed: "To keep them in their place, the same characteristics are imputed to women as to blacks—that they are more childish, emotional and irresponsible than men, that they are of lower intelligence than men, that they are happiest in routine, undemanding jobs, and that they lack ambition and executive ability" (Amundsen 1971 : 43-44). It is these notions of femininity that make silence and submissiveness in girls admirable qualities while in adolescent boys they are thought to be unbecoming. It is these notions of ideal womanhood that deny access to, and opportunities for, socio-economic benefits and political power to women even in the great democracies of the world.

Betti Friedman, very rightly, dismisses the prevalent image of the happy, fulfilled, and secure housewife as "pure bunk" in *The Feminine Mystique* (cf. Amundsen 1971 : 6). As a matter of fact, the modern woman is still "cajoled, manipulated, and brainwashed into accepting the role of wife and mother as the only possible and proper outlet for her talents and energies. Stifled, bored and frustrated, she eventually takes refuge in day-dreaming, drinking and neurotic activity of various kinds, unconscious that these may be genuine alternatives to spending one's days by the kitchen sink and stove" (*ibid.*, p. 6). Because she has played the game by the rule, the modern woman discovers to her cost that the dice were loaded against her right from the beginning. The more she has conformed to the socially accepted image of womanhood, the more she has invested in the traditional concepts of marriage, motherhood and domesticity, "the more bankrupt, economically and psychologically, she will now find herself" (Figes 1971).

The expectations of the society about the female role preclude the development of intellectual independence and the drive to compete in girls. They are, instead, encouraged to be polite, popular, charming, marriageable and able and willing to bear children. The ideals of manhood are diametrically opposed to those of womanhood : "For a woman to be expressive means .... for her to be kind, obedient, cheerful, affectionate and sensitive .... For a man to be expressive means to be tenacious, curious, ambitious, responsible, original and competitive, all qualities required of a governing class" (Amundsen 1971 : 110). W.A. Mischel agrees that from early childhood on, dependent behaviour is less rewarded for males and physically aggressive behaviour less rewarded for females in all patriarchal cultures (cf. *ibid.*, p. 115). "Nature", says Freud, "has determined a woman's destiny through beauty, charm and sweetness" (cf. Sharma 1986). Everything invites the little girl to surrender herself to the demands of the society and to enjoy or suffer life as others dictate. The adolescent girl has to wait till she is in a man's arms to be transported into a heaven of glory. As Beauvoir puts it : "She learns that to be happy she must be loved, to be loved she must await love's coming. Woman is the sleeping Beauty, Cindrella, Snow White, she who receives and submits. In song and story the young man is seen departing adventurously in search of woman, he slays the dragon, he battles giants, she is locked in a tower, a palace, a garden, a cave, she is chained to a rock, a captive, sound asleep, she waits" (1953 : 29). Joseph Campbell in *The Hero with A Thousand Faces* describes the most persistent theme (in oral tradition and recorded literature) of the myth of the hero. In his study of world hero myths, he discovers that they are all basically the same story—retold endlessly in infinite variation. The hero myth is the monomyth in which the hero is called to adventure, forms alliances, goes on the trying journey, enters the inmost cave, kills the dragon or the beast, frees the sleeping or suffering beauty, and returns home with the beauty in one hand and elixir in the other (cf. Vogler 1988). Unlike the girl, the boy is not expected to cry or to please. Friends envy and admire the girl who gets most masculine attention. Everything in the circumambient universe instructs the growing girl that it is in her own interest to be womanlike in order that she may deserve and draw the attention of prospective bridegrooms. It is not for nothing that in colleges and universities now the social standing of a girl is measured by the number of 'dates' she has with boyfriends.

Patri-centric cultures use fashions to curtail the independence of women. Dress for women is considered decoration and decoration means display. Traditional women's fashions are designed to hamper movement as traditional female roles hamper mobility. Any attempt by women to ignore or outstrip the boundaries of fashion and role is resented by men. Men automatically protest against women putting on trousers or cropping their hair. Trousers facilitate movement and short hair reduces vulnerability. Women with long hair and flowing sarees or gowns can easily be outrun, caught, overpowered and dragged. Draupadi is a classic example of dragging by the hair. A girl in a short skirt is a prey to male desires: "The skirt is less convenient than trousers, high heeled shoes impede walking, the least practical of gowns and dress shoes, the most fragile of hats and stockings, are most elegant, the costume may disguise the body, deform it or follow its curves, in any case, it puts it on display" (Beauvoir 1953 : 237).

There is no valid, cultural, climatic or hygienic reason for only women to use tonnes and tonnes of body cover, cosmetics, ornaments and fixtures. Women are subjected to covering the body in public only to be stripped in private. Sparkling ornaments and gaudy dresses make them objects of display; they also render them incapable of their natural speed or movement. Vatsyayana recommends that the parents of a girl of marriageable age should have their daughter arrayed in smart dress and beautiful ornaments and taken to parties whenever there is a chance, because a girl at this age must be displayed as an "article of trade" (cf. Chakladar 1976 : 123). An adage in the *Grihyasutra* of Apastamba declares: "he will be a happy husband who marries the woman on whom his heart and his eyes are set" (*ibid.*, p. 123). Smart appearance for a woman is considered a letter of recommendation. There seems to be no justification for the dictates of fashion and taste to be more tempting to women than to men, except as a string to bind women with.

A patrilocal marriage is a stereotyped mechanism to subordinate the bride to the groom for life. The bride after marriage is immediately consigned to a family dominated by the father and his cronies. A bride is given in marriage by a man to a man. A marriage like this requires the bride to leave her history and home and to abandon herself to her captors and masters. The married woman takes her man's name, her man's religion and her man's philosophy of life. She is appended to his family and is made his half. She follows him like a shadow everywhere and in everything. She breaks with her past and looks to a future she knows nothing of. She gives him her person, her virginity and her identity only to be required to prove her fidelity at every step and on a life-long basis.

If girls are found to be gullible, docile, narcissistic and all-accepting, one should note that characteristics such as these are attributable to centuries of social conditioning rather than to their genetic structure. Women accept the leadership of the male and the vision of his world not through sound or critical judgement but by an act of faith, and faith is "blind, impassioned, obstinate, stupid; what it declares, it declares unconditionally, against all denial" (Beauvoir 1953 : 300). Recent studies have demonstrated that women are no less intelligent and talented than men and that they display attitudes and dispositions which have been conditioned rather than consciously acquired (cf. Amundsen 1971 : 127-129). Margaret Mead, the distinguished American Anthropologist, effectively shattered the popular notions of universal and eternal roles and characteristics of women through her classic study *Sex and Temperament in Three Primitive Societies* as early as in 1935. Mead shows that women display different attitudes and mental sets in different societies : in one society, both men and women tend to be ruthless, aggressive, severe and unresponsive; in another, both men and women are submissive, responsive and co-operative and in the third, women are found to be dominant, impersonal and managing while men are meek, dependent and childish (cf. Amundsen 1971 : 120).

One of the most disastrous effects of patrilocal marriages for women has manifested itself in making marriageability a peculiarly feminine liability. It is the onus of the girl to prove that she is marriageable. Hindu texts hardly ever refer to the qualifications of the would-be bridegroom. He may be stupid, old, deaf, dumb, blind, diseased, crooked, lecherous, married, criminal, heartless and impotent and yet he is not disqualified for marriage with a young and pretty woman. It is shocking that the same texts are so insistent about the qualifications of the would-be bride. Some of the essential requirements of desirable bridehood are: youth, virginity, amiability, beauty, fertility, submissiveness and authentic guarantee for life-long fidelity to the husband. The texts ordain that only three values relate to girls. They (girls) are for 'gift' (dana), 'sale' (vikraya) or 'abandonment' (atisarga cf. Baig 1976 : 89). Perhaps no patriarchal people are as discriminatory against women as Hindu Law-makers are. They seem to have no qualms of conscience when they prescribe contrary codes of conduct for men and women. If a woman loves a man, she should not, warns Vatsyayana, make the first overtures, for a woman who does so loses her dignity and is liable to be scorned and rejected. But if a man is inclined to enjoy her, she should be co-operative and should receive all his manifestations of love as cherishable blessings (cf. III : IV pp. 187-188). The sole qualification of the husband (howsoever deformed, ugly or obnoxious) is his maleness but demands are made upon the wife which are impossible to fulfill even for the exceptionally gifted. An ancient Sanskrit proverb, for example, characterizes a worthy wife as one who is "In work a slave, in business a diplomat; in form a goddess; in sex a courtesan; in virtue as firm as the earth and in looking after the husband as good as the mother" (Baig 1976 : 81). References to scriptural mandate for the complete devotion of the wife to the husband, even if he is a moral wreck, deserve to be viewed as a mockery of the Hindu philosophy of gender distinction.

A girl's eligibility for marriage, according to Hindu texts depends, among other things, upon the loveliness of her form and her willingness to submit to a man's desire. No reference is made to her intellectual and spiritual accomplishments as necessary conditions for marriageability. A girl, says Manu, "should be free from bodily defects, should have an agreeable name, should be of graceful gait like a swan or elephant, should have a moderate quantity of hair on the body, and on the head, small teeth and soft limbs" (cf. Thomas 1964 : 221). Vatsyayana prescribes that marriageable girls should master the sixty-four skills and the sixty-four erotic postures. In the opening paragraph of the chapter on marriage, Vatsyayana observes: "When the girl of the same caste, and a virgin, is married in accordance with the precepts of the Holy Writ, the results of such a union are the acquisition of Dharma and Artha, offspring, affinity, increase of friends, and untarnished love. For this reason a man should fix his affections upon a girl who is of good family, whose parents are alive, and who is three years or more younger than himself. She should be born of a highly respectable family, possessed of wealth, well connected and with many relations and friends. She should also be beautiful, of a good disposition, with lucky marks on her body, and with good hair, nails, teeth, ears, eyes and breasts, neither more nor less than they ought to be, and no one of them entirely wanting, and not troubled with a sickly body" (III : I p. 178). Vatsyayana also forbids marriage with a girl who has already been polluted by others, who has been kept in concealment, who is found sleeping, crying or absconding when sought in marriage, who has an ill-sounding name, a depressed nose, turned-up nostrils, crooked thighs, glandular enlargements in any part of the body, a masculine appearance, a hunch back, a bald head, a projecting forehead, perspiring soles and palms and who has not fully arrived at puberty (cf. *ibid.*, p. 174). He says in an earlier chapter that a man should not have any erotic relation with a woman who is a lunatic, a leper, an outcast, one incapable of keeping secrets, making overtures for sexual enjoyment, a bad-smelling woman, an ascetic, wife of a friend, king or a learned Brahmana (cf. I : IV pp. 119-122).

With such stringent demands on the eligibility of the bride, we can take a quick look at some representative lovers and husbands who stalk through the Puranas and the Epics. The *Ramayana* represents Dashratha as a doddering old man with lustful attachment to his youngest queen. The *Mahabharata* contains a long line of despicable husbands and sex-doers. Shantanu is an octogenerian when he falls in love with the fisherman's daughter. It does not prick his conscience to have his marriage negotiations with Satyavati finalized by his own son, who has to undertake a vow of celibacy for life in order that his stepmother's eldest son may become king. Bhishma, the venerable old man of the epic, feels no embarrassment when he advises his step-mother to persuade her widowed daughters-in-law to procure sons through the monstrous-looking Vyasa, who incidentally happens to be Satyavati's son from her pre-marital union with a holy man known as Parashara (orthodox tradition does not allow a Hindu male to have sex with the wife or widow of his younger brother or half-brother). When Vyasa enters the bed room of Ambika, she is filled with horror to see his frightening face, coppery hair, livid eyes, black beard and repugnant smell and yet with closed eyes she allows him to have sex with her. Similarly, the other widow, Ambalika, pales with fear to see him and yet offers him her body. From such frightful unions are born Dhritarashtra, the blind one (from Ambika) and Pandu, the pale one (from Ambalika). Apart from these widows, there are other victims of evil husbands or sex-doers. Pradveshi's blind husband curses her for not being sufficiently faithful to him. Gandhari keeps a bandage of a multi-folded peace of cloth on her eyes for life in deference to her blind husband and yet bears him a hundred sons. Kunti and Madri have to put up with a jaundiced and impotent husband who compells them to procure five sons (three and two respectively) through intercourse with various gods. One of the most revered Upanishadic sages, Yajnavalkya has two wives. According to a legend in one of the Puranas, there is an old leper who is in love with a prostitute. He cannot stay with or marry the prostitute (according to law) nor can he walk the distance from his house to that of his beloved. He therefore commands his faithful wife to carry him daily on her back to and from the prostitute's house so that he may have sex with her. The leper's wife is not reported to have ever complained against the tyranny of her lecherous husband. According to another famous legend, Savitri marries Satyavana in spite of the knowledge that he cannot live for more than a hundred days. When Satyavana dies, Savitri follows him to the world of the dead, entreating Yama to revive and return her husband. For a long time the god of death does not relent but finally grants him life. Savitri retrieves her husband from the world of death and becomes a famous wife.

Hindu texts eulogize Amba, Ambalika, Kunti, Madri, Gandhari, Savitri and others as models of wifely devotion and commitment.

But questions like the following erupt in a context like this: Can one locate a single husband in the annals of Hindu history who would carry his leperous wife to a sex-doer even once, if not for years, as a matter of daily routine? Can one locate in any Hindu text a single youthful husband who blinds himself in deference to his blind wife? Is there a frigid or barren wife who commands her husband to procure children from other women and publicly acknowledge them as her children? Scriptural eulogies for wayward, sick, or devilish husbands or sex-doers do not glorify the history of Hindu marriages nor do they bear witness to the Hindu claim on gender equality.

2.3 Seclusion of Woman

> "The institution of marriage makes a parasite of woman, ... incapacitates her for life's struggle, annihilates her social consciousness."
>
> —*Emma Goldman (Mcphee 1979 : 77)*

Civilization and confinement share a common history. Civilization for man began as confinement for woman. Confinement was respectable while mobility was a synonym of corruptibility. In the onward march of civilization women were classified as 'private' and 'public'. Private women were to be respectable women. Public women could freely move about in civilized areas because they were corrupt and corruptible women, even though 'public' men were both mobile and respectable.

With the onset of civilization systematic confinement of respectable women began to be practised in *civilized* parts of the world which included India and Greece, among others. In classical Athens the separation of the sexes was spatially emphasized. 'Free' or 'citizen' women were secluded from free or citizen men and male slaves so that they could not be seen by men who were not members of the family. While public women and female slaves could spend their day in areas such as the market place and the gymnasium, mostly frequented by men, free, private or respectable women had to remain at home within the four walls of the building. Besides, in contrast to the admired public buildings and clean public areas, the residential quarters meant for private women in classical Athens were "dark, squalid and unsanitary" (Pomeroy 1975 : 79).

The Arab version of the seclusion of women is evident from the etymology of the woman-specific term 'harem'. Derived from the Arabic *maharain*, 'harem' means "private or forbidden". It originally referred to those rooms in a Turkish home which were exclusively meant for women (cf. Kidwai 1976 : 137). The Arabs achieved a unique distinction by combining confinement with the veil. A woman was normally confined to the harem and if or when she moved out for reasons unavoidable she had to be veiled so that she could not be seen by anyone. As regards the seclusion of women in India, early Hindus went far ahead of the Greeks and the Arabs. They created a society in which the private or respectable women could not be seen even by the sun. Seclusion came to be another term for invisibility in Hindu sociological vocabulary. A respectable, free and private Aryan woman had to be 'invisible to the sun' (*asuryampashya*), even though the *Rig-Veda i.e.*, the earliest text of the Indo-Aryans, has references to different classes of 'public' women.

It is possible to argue that the sociology of seclusion was originally determined by a biological disparity between human and non-human females. Unlike non-human females, human females have to be provided for during periods like late pregnancy, child-birth, and the first few weeks or months after child-birth. Human females may find it very difficult, if not impossible, to look after themselves during such periods. It is probable that confinement or seclusion of Aryan females began in the Polar phase of Aryan history. Given the topography and terrain of the Polar region, it was inconvenient as well as unsafe for women and children to accompany men on their expeditions for collecting food and fire-wood, often in inclement weather. Women and children were therefore obliged to stay at home and to do household chores (cf. Baig 1976 : 6). But it was unfortunate for women and wicked of men that the latter turned, in course of time, the locational custom (of confinement) of the Polar woman into the eternal destiny of the Indo-Aryan female even when they migrated to safer regions. The *Ramayana* describes a society in which women perform rigidly defined duties like domestic chores, bearing and rearing of children and attending to the menfolk (cf. Sharma 1971 : 114). Manu lays down, once for all, that woman is "responsible for the bearing of children, for the nurture of those born and for the daily life of men."

Factors like those of biology and location may have led to the practice of the confinement of women. But the most important factor responsible for the philosophy of confining women appears to have been that of the male psychology of paternity and sexuality. Among animals, it does not matter who has sex with whom or whose babies are whose. Assurance of paternity is not part of their sexual package because the females can look after themselves during late pregnancy and childbirth and their infants after childbirth. In case of human beings, males arrogate to themselves the responsibility for providing shelter, protection, food and care to the child-bearing female and the offspring over long periods. This may be a significant element in the "sexual trade off" that governs the sexual and reproductive behaviour of human males. Maybe because of this attitude, male parenting in our species acquires a ridiculous significance. In exchange for what he chooses to do for the child-bearing female and the offspring, the male demands a guarantee of reliable sex with the female and reliable parenting of the offspring (cf. Durden-Smith & De Simone 1983 : 174, 178 & 179). Besides, the human male, unlike his animal cousin, can have sex with the female at will and even outside the period of her ovulation. It is mainly because of the availability of recreational sex that the male seeks to ensure his monopoly over the female by confining her within the house. Still another reason for the seclusion of women may be the peculiar nature of newly born babies. Human babies, unlike non-human babies, are born foetal and completely helpless. They need lots of care to survive and grow for quite some time. Mothers are obliged to remain with their babies not only because fathers are indifferent and often not available but also because they have to suckle their babies.

When we examine the practice of the seclusion of women from a historical point of view, we come to the heart of the matter. The primitive Aryans may have been obliged to keep women at home because they had to be protected from wild beasts and from the hazards of the climate. The constant terror of the surroundings and the scarcity of food and firewood could have genuinely necessitated a neat division between indoor and outdoor duties and women may have preferred to stay indoors with their babies. But there was no reason for the practice to continue once the Aryans moved out to safer and better surroundings. In surroundings which had plenty of food and firewood and few threats from wild beasts, men and women could have easily chosen to work, play or rest together. As regards the assurance of parenting, there was never a reason to suspect women of infidelity, unless there were coercive sex-doers among men. If every man strictly adhered to the one-man-one-woman formula for sexual behaviour, the question of suspecting women could never arise. The problem of child-rearing could have been taken care of by male or female baby-sitters. There was thus no reason for the seclusion of women to have ever been practised in India.

Seclusion of women was imported into India by the incoming Aryans and it came to stay as a principle of social organization for all time to come. Women continued to be secluded or confined even when there was no reason to do so in the Indian context. Apart from this, seclusion of women gradually came to be looked upon as necessary and respectable in the eyes of Hindu males. Even a secular writer like Vatsyayana was all praise for this obnoxious custom. Describing his society, Vatsyayana says with pride that the king kept the royal women in his harem, guarded by officers of proven honesty and integrity. No man except servants, members of the family and close relatives was even allowed to enter the royal harem. Vatsyayana's description of the inner apartments (antah-pura) of respectable citizens show that women were systematically confined within the house so that they could not meet other men or even doubtful women. He agrees with Manu that, as women cannot guard themselves against temptations, they must be kept in confinement (cf. Chakaladar 1976 : 33 & 178-179).

Vatsyayana's description, however, presents the daily life of the male as "a round of pleasures" and but that of his wife as "a round of duties" (*ibid.*, p. 172). Times changed but the disparity between male and female modes of life did not change. A very large part of the Hindu society maintains the age-old separation between the masculine round of pleasures and the feminine round of duties even today. Commenting on the life style of average housewives in an Uttar Pradesh village in the early sixties, the authors of a book about that village remark: "Round and round the same circle they move—babies, husbands, food, ailments, all interwoven with their simple faith in spiritdom" (Wiser & Wiser 1963 : 74). There are still millions and millions of women who have to put up with the drudgery of daily domestic chores without being able to move out of their prison-like houses. Confined within squalid houses, millions and millions of women daily "conglomerate behind millions of sinks where they wash millions of nappies, a million times over" (cf. Trench 1971).

2.4 Ambivalence Towards Woman

".... the heaven that leads men to ... hell."

—*Shakespeare*

Women in general are caught in the 'damned if you do and damned if you don't' sort of dilemma in their relation to men. If they are vital and assertive, they are rejected as "aggressive bitches out to castrate men" and if they are quiet and submissive, they are rejected as useless creatures, "unlikely to amount to much" (cf. Amundsen 1971 : 4). Men hanker after women out of love for their flesh and despise them for reminding them (men) that they are creatures of the flesh. This basic contradiction in man's attitude to woman is photographically displayed in the following poem by Shakespeare:

Th' expense of spirit in a waste of shame
Is lust in action; and till action, lust
Is perjur'd, murd'rous, bloody, full of blame,
Savage, extreme, rude, cruel, not to trust;
Enjoy'd no sooner but despised straight;
Past reason hunted, and, no sooner had,
Past reason hated, as a swallowed bait,
On purpose laid to make the taker mad—
Mad in pursuit, and in possession so;
Had, having, and in quest to have, extreme;
A bliss in proof, and prov'd, a very woe;
Before, a joy proposed; behind, a dream.
All this the world knows; yet none knows well
To shun the heaven that leads men to this hell.

(Sonnet 129).

Reading Shakespeare from a woman's point of view may reveal a persistent theme throughout the canon of his plays—men's inability to reconcile tender affection with sexual desire and their consequent vascillation between idealization and degradation of women. There is a dual ideal of sexuality and chastity held up before women. A typical Shakespeare heroine might as well repeat the words of Vivian Gormick to place herself in relation to her man : "I am not real to him. I am not real to my civilization. I am not real to the culture that has spawned me and made use of me. I am only a collection of myths. I am an existential stand-in. The idea of me is real—the temptress, the goddess, the child, the mother—but I am not real. The mythic proportions of woman are recognizable and real; it is only the human dimensions that are patently false and will be denied to the death, our death" (cited in Mcphee 1979 : 45). One may contend that the central element in Shakespeare's treatment of women is always their sex, not as a focus for cultural observation or social criticism but primarily as a mythic power, and archetypal symbol that arouses both love and loathing in the male. "The curse of the tragic world", writes Berggren, "is to be barren; the salvation of the comic is fecundity" (1980). Men condemn women for the same thing as they are mostly looking for, always without reason. There is no justification for Lear's angry outburst : "Down from the waist. They are centaurs" (IV : IV : 126). To be born of woman, laments Macbeth, is to be mortal (cf. Gohlke 1980). Antony perceives himself as having been feminized by love. Romeo bemoans : "O sweet Juliet Thy love hath made me effeminate" (III : I : 115-16). Cleopatra is, in many ways the epitome of what is hated, loved, and feared in a woman by Shakespeare's tragic heroes. She can betray as well as dominate; she has the power to give but the authority to demand; she can submit to man but she can also reject him. One may see some reason in Antony's chronic vascillation between love and duty, Cleopatra and Rome but there is no reason why other heroes in Shakespeare should vascillate in relation to the women they love. In *Othello* Roderigo articulates the pernicious combination of romanticism and cynicism and the dissociation of love and sex which most heroes in Shakespeare seems to share (cf. Neely 1980). Othello's attitude towards Desdemona is full of contradictions:

> "O, ay; as summer flies are in the shambles,
> That quicken even with blowing. O thou weed
> Who art so lovely fair and smell'st so sweet
> That the sense aches at thee !
> Would thou, had'st never been born!" (IV : II : 66-70).

Othello's love-hate attitude to Desdemona is so typically echoed in Adam's complaint about Eve:

> "O why did God
> Creator wise, that peopled highest heaven

With spirits masculine, create at last
This novelty on earth, this fair
Defect of Nature". (*Paradise Lost* X : 888-892).

The paradox of marriage lies in the fact that it has at once an erotic and a social function. The husband is the custodian of moral values, the sponsor of truth and the ethical vindicator of the coupling. These roles notwithstanding, he is also a male with whom the wife must daily share and experience that which is shameful, grotesque and often upsetting. He leads her towards Religion and God and yet he bullies her into bestial sexuality. The following incident reported in a French novel will amply illustrate the chronic paradox of marital sharing:

"One evening in Paris, Bernard made a conspicuous exit from a music Hall where the show had shocked him. `Just think of foreigners seeing that! It's a shame, and we will be judged on that sort of thing'. Therise was amazed that this model soul was no other than the man to whose prolonged nocturnal ingenuities she would be subjected in less than an hour" (cf. Beauvoir 1953 : 179)!

It is common knowledge that the husband/lover privately urges his wife/beloved to sex, abortion, betrayal, wrong-doing and lies, while he condemns these in public. He makes an impossible dual demand on the woman; he wants her to be fully exciting and fresh and yet entirely his own; he wants her to conform exactly to his dreams and yet to be different from anything he can imagine, a response to his expectations and yet a complete surprise (cf. *ibid.*, p. 357). The woman is torn by this contradiction and doomed to frustration. If she emphasizes her sex appeal, she shows bad taste in the eyes of her husband—the husband who likes only sexy women. The husband condemns her to drudgery and then complains that she is no longer exciting. Woman is shut-up in a kitchen and then rejected as one whose horizon is limited. Her wings are clipped and then it is deplored that she cannot fly. At least Montaigne has the honesty to acknowledge that men make contradictory demands upon women: "we want them healthy, vigorous, plump and chaste, all at once—that is to say both hot and cold" (cited *ibid.*, p. 158).

Hindus have quite a large share in the universal patriarchal ambivalence towards woman. In Vedic literature woman is called *devi ie* 'the shining one' (derived from the root *diva ie* 'to shine') but she is also called *bharya* or *bhagini ie* 'the one who is protected'. The Vedic word for husband is *bharta* and for brother is *bhrata* both of which mean the 'one who protects'. In a protector/protected opposition, the protector is definitely above the protected. The very terms (bharya, bhagini, devi, etc.), are patronizing (cf. Bader 1964 : 9 & Sharma 1971 : 85). So are *patni* (wife), *srimati* (Mrs, wife) and a host of others.

The Vedic ambivalence towards woman becomes a habitual thought structure of the Hindus by the time of Puranas, the Epics and the Smritis. Manu's code, for instance, manifests throughout "a singular mixture of love and fear, of respect and scorn. Raising the woman upon a magnificent pedestal, Manu appears to present her as the source of all good, worthy of the adoration of man; then suddenly brutally throwing her down and seeing in her the genius of evil, he casts her down at the feet of man as a stinking beggar" (Bader 1964 : 55). The following verses from the *Manusmriti* illustrate this generalization:

"Women must be honoured and adorned by their fathers, brothers, husbands and brothers-in-law who desire (their own) welfare. Where women are honoured, there the gods are pleased; but where they are not honoured, no sacred rite yields results (III : 55-56).

And then: "A prudent man should not marry (a maiden) who has no brother, nor one whose father is not known" (III : 11).

And again: "When creating them, Manu allotted to women, a love of their bed, of their seat and of ornaments, impure desires, wrath, dishonesty, malice, and bad conduct" (IX : 13).

Like Manu, Bhartrihari, a philosopher-poet who vascillates as many as seven times between love and renunciation before he finally begins a life of renunciation, expresses his contradictions in the following lines: "I am telling the truth without any bias that in the seven worlds this is a fact that there is nothing more delightful than a young woman and nothing which is a greater source of sorrow to man" (quoted in De 1969 : 34). Likewise, Ashvaghosh, the earliest known writer in the Kavya-style of Sanskrit poetry, remarks: "Passionate women cause intoxication; women without passion cause fear" (quoted *ibid.*, p. 13). Whether he knows it or not, Ashvaghosh reveals a truth which most men share in their experience of women:

"Hence doth one drink from those lips/ And strike at that heart with the fist" (*ibid.*, p. 13). In view of remarks and observations like these, we can fully agree with Basham's conclusion that the ancient Hindu attitude to woman "was, in fact, ambivalent. She was at once a goddess and a slave, a saint and a strumpet" (1967: 183). Unfortunately such ambivalence still characterizes the perception of woman for a vast majority of Hindu males.

An ideological contradiction still exists in the mores and attitudes towards sex. The sexual desire is considered "evil in the infant, naughty in the adolescent and desirable in the adult" (Hunt 1961). The mere ceremony of marriage cannot suddenly overcome this sense of contradictions; tensions, inhibitions, fears and suspicions affect the sex life of millions of couples in contemporary Hindu society. Hindus do generally, at least publicly, label the sex act as 'animal' or 'bestial', on the one hand, but display on the sly or in private a life-long obsession with sexuality, on the other. The double standard of the Hindu sex philosophy shapes the Hindu ambivalence towards women (cf. Cormack 1961 : 117). A Hindu wife still continues to find contradictions in her husband's attitude towards her : "Husbands have an ambivalent attitude towards their wives; they like their wives to be uninhibited, modern, smart, and even westernized but at the same time they would not like their wives to mix with men" (Kapoor 1974 : 34-35). The main reason for such contradiction or ambivalence emanates from the paradoxial nature of male sexuality itself. Man is by nature polygamous. He loves variety but anything that is readily available turns him sour. We have in this context the testimony of no less a philosopher than Schopenhauer : "Most men fall in love with a pretty face but find themselves bound for life to a hateful stranger, alternating between a workshop and a witch's kitchen" (cited in Greer 1973 : 270).

3

Ritualization of Marriage

3.1 Marriage and Divorce

> "The gods have given thee to me that I may be the master of a household."
>
> —*Rig-Veda*

As a wonderful bridge between nature and civilization, biology and culture, sex and righteousness, private rivalry and public order, pristine innocence and sophisticated artistry, the institution of marriage marks a unique development in the evolutionary history of humanity. It brings two adults of opposite sexes together to combine mutual fulfilment with positive service to the species. It inaugurates the family with full commitment to the community. Based on a free and fair selection between two individuals, marriage is ideally a secular and amoral contract. A union of souls, marriage is an honest recognition of the native equality between man and woman. As an agreement to share between themselves the joys and the responsibilities of the joint adventure, marriage is an equal necessity for both partners. It does not set up the one above the other. Neither is better, neither is worse. Both seek to co-operate in every sphere of their shared existence and it is this co-operation that makes marriage a unique institution. Other institutions of human civilization require either less or more than two individuals of either the same sex or of opposite sexes. Marriage is perhaps the only enterprise that, of necessity, requires two individuals of opposite sexes to share a series of experiences which are, of necessity, partly private and partly public. It is the only joint experience of two individuals which preserves the species with full social sanction. There is no other option for the species to continue in an ordered and socially acceptable way. Neither 'cloning' nor 'crowding' is likely to become an alternative way of preserving the species in the foreseeable future.

Marriage, however, is not the only means of reproduction. From the beginning of human history non-marital reproduction has been a fact of life. Reproduction is included in matrimony but it is not the other way about. Marriage is much more than reproduction and it is this additional benefit of marriage that accounts for its uniqueness as a necessary and desirable institution but it must be a matter of choice rather than a part of destiny for either man or woman. An individual man or woman must be absolutely free to choose his or her marriage partner, to marry for a mutually agreed period of time, to dissolve the marriage at any time or not to marry at all.

Marriage has two forms: (i) an alliance forged between the male members of two families, and (ii) an alliance forged between two individuals. According to the first, the bride is gifted by the male head of her family to the groom with full authority. It is a transfer of authority from the bride's family to the family of her husband. Such transfer of authority has a socio-religious sanction which effectively subordinates the bride to her husband and his family. The husband, like her father before her marriage, becomes after her marriage her mentor, protector, patron, master, lord and God. The bride suddenly becomes a slave, a vassal, a servant and a thing. This form of marriage is a compulsion or mandate that every bride must accept as her only and final destiny. It is an indissoluble bond, a sacrament which can never be violated or broken. It has no provision for divorce or if it has a provision for divorce, the divorce is an exception rather than a rule. Until a woman gets rid of her wifehood, she has to play the game by the rules of the game. Patriarchal societies accept such marriages as the only form of marriage. Whether we think of Vedic India, of Homeric Greece or of Modern Arab, we find the same structure of marriage throughout.

'Piety', 'progeny' and 'pleasure' (dharma, artha and kama) are the three goals of patriarchal marriages. Marriage and motherhood are logically connected in such unions. The situation of the wife in a patriarchal marriage does not normally change across age or nationality (cf. Basham 1967 : 167). Because marriage has traditionally defined 'femininity', it continues to be the reference point for women. Women have been married. Women have to plan to be married. Or women have to suffer from being married. The unmarried or unmarrying woman has to be explained or defined with reference to marriage because marriage is 'emancipation' or 'fulfilment'. It is a logical consequence of this patriarchal philosophy that 'spinster' and 'old maid' still continue to be the ugliest words in the language, "implying rejection, the faulty product which nobody wants to buy, the flawed pot doomed to gather dust, left on the shelf" (Figes 1971 cf. Beauvoir 1953 : 148 & Summerskill 1971). The very structure of such marriages condemns the woman in the home to the same roles and functions, whatever her capacity. The organized conspiracy of husbands, religious authorities and the propaganda media bind her so fast that she loses all visions of freedom. Her flutterings and murmurs are drowned by the bustle of the vicious majority of males and she is subjected to "a barrage of advertising which seeks to persuade her that she is wrong" (Summerskill 1971).

The other form of marriage is a secular contract, an amoral partnership or a neutral reciprocity between two equal and free individuals. In a marriage like this, two individuals, who have felt drawn to each other over a span of time, voluntarily choose to share their body and mind for an unspecified period of time for mutual benefit and fulfilment. As a true fellowship of body and spirit, a marriage like this develops in course of time as the most intimate, valuable and blissful of all human partnerships. No other human relationship is as intensely bilateral and mutually enjoyable as such partnership between a man and a woman. Relationships like those between father and son, mother and daughter, father and daughter, mother and son, brother and sister, brother and brother, and so on, even at their best, retain a duality between the individuals involved. It is only in this form of marriage that two wonderful human beings find themselves spontaneously dissolving their separate identities and merging with each other to become one and whole.

For want of a better set of terms, we can classify marriages into 'patricentric' marriages and 'matricentric' marriages to define the two types or forms of marriage noted above. It does not really matter for this distinction whether the bride goes to stay with the groom or the groom goes to stay with the bride. The point which is crucial for this distinction, however, is whether a particular marriage alliance is forged by external agencies or by the individuals themselves. If a marriage alliance is forged by the individuals themselves, it will certainly have a thrust which is totally different from the one accompanying a marriage alliance forged by others on behalf of the individuals concerned. A patricentric marriage is motivated by a network of masculinist manipulations which treat woman as innately inferior to man. The agents of such marriages do therefore invoke God and bring in religion to execute a bond between man and woman to the utter disadvantage of the latter. From the woman's point of view, a marital bond like this turns out to be something like imprisonment for life. A patricentric marriage is a sacrament and has no provision for meaningful divorce. A matricentric marriage, on the other hand, is a secular contract by which two independent, equal and valuable human beings choose to live together and share all that life offers them. The moment there is a threat to the contract on account of either of the partners getting jealous, suspicious or bitter, the partners agree to have a parting of ways without any sense of rancour or ill will. In a marriage like this, the right to disagree is reciprocally recognized by both partners. Divorce is therefore a necessary, though not an inevitable, component of a matricentric marriage. The reason for designating such marriages as matricentric marriages accrues from the belief that a society governed by women is both secular and egalitarian because women do not divide human beings into high and low, white and black, rich and poor, 'we' and 'they' or male and female. Since it does not recognize a third party, whether man, god, or religion, a matricentric marriage is by definition both contractual and non-sacramental. Available forms of marriage may therefore be classified as patricentric and matricentric marriages. Men have dithered, cheated and sinned too long. It's time they were stopped dithering, cheating and sinning any longer about something so valuable as a heterosexual union by marriage. This classification need not recognize a homosexual union as a form of marriage for the simple reason that a homosexual union is not based on the motive of preserving and expanding the community or the species. If humanity has to continue as a self- conscious and developing species, it has to make a decisive choice between patricentric and matricentric marriages, once for all.

There have been some notable conventions of matricentric marriages in our country. Among ancient Tamils marriage was considered a 'private' (*Kalavu*) arrangement between a young man and a young woman. The 'public' (*karapu*) ritualization of marriage, allegedly introduced much later and under Aryan influence, was generally considered an undesirable innovation. Similarly, among ancient Nayars who denied Aryan descent, marriage was called an auspicious connection (*sambandham*). Sambandham was a contract according to which the couple would stay together for three days and then would separate, the man returning to his home and the woman staying back with her mother. Once this ceremony was over, the husband became a visiting husband who would have no legal control over his wife. In both these types of marriage, the wife was an equal to her husband in every respect (cf. Thomas 1964 : 30-41).

Contract marriages appear, at times, to have taken place even among ancient Indo-Aryans. In a delightful poem, which incidentally happens to be the earliest extant love-poem in the world, the *Rig-Veda* (x : 95) celebrates the intense attachment between Urvashi and Pururvas. Urvashi agreed to marry Pururvas on the condition that he would never appear naked before her. They were thus obliged to conduct their sexual activities in the dark. Time passed on and she gave him a son. The prolonged absence of Urvashi from heaven, however, made the Gandharvas restive. They contrived to wake Pururvas at night in such a hurry that he could not put on clothes. He appeared naked before Urvashi who immediately decided to return to heaven. The Urvashi-Pururvas story is also recounted in the *Mahabhurata* (I : 75) and the *Vishnupurana* (IV : 6). Kalidasa wrote a full play, *Vikramorvashiyam*, on this theme with some modifications in the original story (cf. Ray & Gidwani 1985 Vol. III : 237-38). Another example of contract marriage is described in the first book of the *Mahabharata*. Enamoured of Ganga, King Shantanu begged her to be his wife. Ganga agreed to marry him on the condition that he would never speak a harsh word to her nor would he ever interfere with anything she wanted to do. Shantanu agreed. They were married. Months, seasons, and years passed. Then was born a son. Ganga threw him into the river. After this six sons were born and thrown into the Ganga one by one. Now the eighth son was born. As Ganga started going to the river with the baby in her arms, Shantanu stopped her. On this Ganga suddenly abandoned him and returned to heaven. The eight sons of Ganga are known as the eight Vasus. It was the eighth Vasu, the lone survivor of the sons of Ganga, that later became known as Bhishma, the grand old man of the *Mahabharata* (cf. Lal 1980 : 67-68).

References to contract marriages like these do not go well with the Aryan view of marriage. Why are they then mentioned in Aryan texts? This 'why' calls for reflection. One has to sit back and think about this anomaly. It should not be difficult for a thinking reader to account for such anomalous marriages in the Aryan canon. Both Urvashi and Ganga are superhuman damsels (Apsaras). According to the scale of Aryan sex morality, no male is allowed to look up to have sex relations with a female. As has already been pointed out, in his sexual behaviour the Aryan male has to look straight or below but never up. The Urvashi-Pururvas and Ganga-Shantanu alliances should be viewed as accidental (though lovable) deviations from the Aryan norm. The Aryan male would love to have a sexual trade-off with superhuman females, if and when they were available. Unfortunately they were not generally forthcoming. The Aryan male therefore had to define the structure of marriage with human females in mind. Since human females could not be placed on a par with males, marriage had to be a sacrament based on a proper grading between male and female. No woman married to an Aryan male could ever lay down conditions for her marriage with him. Indo-Aryan marriages had, of necessity, to be patricentric marriages.

To illustrate the striking difference between a patricentric marriage and a matricentric marriage, one can easily refer to the way the central female character is treated in the *Iliad* and the *Ramayana*, respectively. In each of these epics, the war is fought to recover a woman. But the picture of the woman that emerges from the *Iliad* is just the reverse of the picture that emerges from the *Ramayana*. The war of Troy is fought and concluded with catastrophic implications for the Trojans but nothing is done to the woman who causes the war. Helen elopes with Paris, the Prince of Troy. The Greeks declare a war on Troy. At the end of the war Helen is recovered and brought to Sparta with honour because Menelaus owes his kingship to his marriage with Helen. The loss of Helen would mean the loss of his kingship. With the return of Helen, Menelaus retains his kingship. Unlike Helen, Sita is abducted by Ravana and taken to Lanka by force. A war is declared on Lanka. The war concludes, unlike the Trojan war, with devastating consequences both for Ravana and Sita. Ravana is killed. His kith and kin and his army are routed. The kingship is handed over to an Aryan surrogate. Sita is recovered only to be continually insulted and harrassed till such time as she terminates her life. Rama does not own his kingship to his marriage with Sita. He fights the war and recovers her only to defend the honour and reputation of his great family. The abducted and recovered Sita is treated as a bleeding ulcer which must be eliminated to preserve the name and fame of the illustrious king and his line.

Hindu texts enumerate eight types of marriage, originally formulated by the law-giver Ashvalayana in his *Grihyasutra,* named after various gods and supernatural beings and widely accepted as authoritative by later scholars (cf. Thomas 1969 : 62, Basham 1967 : 169-70, Shastri 1969 : 129-30 & Baig 1976 : 118-19). These eight types are:

(1) *Brahma Vivaha*—The marriage of a duly dowered girl to a man of the same class solemnized by the singing of Vedic verses. At such public ceremonies the father of the bride formally gives her to the groom who promises that he would never behave falsely to her in respect of the three aims of marriage *i.e.,* piety, progeny and pleasure.

(2) *Daiva Vivaha*—The marriage of a girl to a sacrificial priest. The father of the bride gives her to the priest as part of his fee.

(3) *Arsa Vivaha*—The marriage of a girl in which the father gives dowry to the groom and also accepts a token bride-price of a cow and a bull.

(4) *Prajapatya Vivaha*—The marriage of a girl in which the father does not give dowry or demand bride price.

(5) *Gandharva Vivaha*—The marriage of a girl to a man who is supposed to have won her heart. To be acceptable to society, such clandestine marriages are often solemnized at religious ceremonies.

(6) *Asura Vivaha*—The marriage of a girl to a man who has paid pride price to her father. This is marriage by purchase.

(7) *Rakshasa Vivaha*—The marriage of a girl or woman to a man who has captured her in war or otherwise.

(8) *Paishacha Vivaha*—The marriage of a girl to a man who has seduced her through his tricks.

Of these eight forms of marriage, the first four are generally approved as religious marriages. The other four are looked on with varying degrees of disfavour by the orthodox, though there is evidence that Gandharva marriages and Svayamvara (self-choice) marriages are respected. Marriage by purchase as well as marriage with dowry existed even in Vedic times (cf. Basham 1967 : 169-170). It is difficult to believe that a marriage could ever take place without dowry or bride-price in the Aryan social set-up. A girl could not be given to a man in marriage unless the father gave dowry or sold her. The only forms of marriage without dowry or bride-price seem to have been the last two *i.e.*, Rakshasa and Paishacha marriages.

The orthodox classification of Hindu marriages into eight types deserves to be seen as a notorious example of the vicious priestcraft that was hellbent on rationalizing all forms of enslaving and exploiting women. Given the rigidly patriarchal biases of the orthodox Hindu society, it is impossible to believe that a woman could be married in those dark days without dowry or bride-price or that a woman was ever free to marry a man she loved or selected. Only three values were attached to Hindu girls. They were for gift, sale or abandonment. Now, a society which believed that a girl could only be gifted, sold or abandoned, could not have allowed any measure of freedom to girls or women. It is difficult to locate any genuine example of love marriage in Hindu society. The so-called svayamvara marriages were, in fact, marriages by lottery. Whosoever won the lot, automatically became the husband of the girl. The lot itself was fixed by the father or the guardian of the girl. There was no choice involved in such ceremonies. No girl could really choose to marry the man she liked. In most cases such 'selections' by the bride were already fixed by her father or guardian. If we ever think that a Hindu girl could select a man to marry at such ceremonies, we must treat the so-called Svayamvara as a hoax put up by the males of the family to project a good image of the family.

Similarly, the so-called Gandharva marriage was a hoax. Inspite of Kalidasa's great classic, Dushyanta's marriage with Shakuntala does not emerge as an example of love marriage. An elderly and polygynous King, Dushyanta, comes to a holiday resort, presumably hunting for young, pretty and innocent girls. His eyes fall and fix on a hauntingly beautiful maiden who is deceived into believing that he loves her. Illegitimately born, abandoned by parents and brought up by a poor mendicant, Shakuntala finds in Dushyanta an assurance of a lavish and stable family life. She agrees to marry him then and there without any fanfare or fuss. A few months of merry-making quickly pass. She is thick with child. Dushyanta has had enough of her. He decides to return to his capital, leaving her behind. She is asked to wait. Wait she does for quite a length of time. He does not come back. She goes to his palace and it is there that she finds herself swindled. Pregnant Shakuntala is of no use to a king who has been hunting, enjoying and rejecting women one after another just for the sake of variety.

For royal heroes like Agnimitra, Pururvas and Dushyanta, attachment to a woman—call it 'love' if you like—is a light-hearted pursuit, a momentary affair. As soon as the fever of the hero's passion for the woman cools down, she is discarded as a condemned object, a piece of junk, and just forgotten about. Every heroine in Kalidasa, whether Malvika or Shakuntala, is ultimately dumped in the secluded corner of an obnoxious harem (cf. Ghosal 1971 : XLVII). In the *Abhijnanashakuntalam*, the jester warns his king: "If you don't watch, you will be turning this ashrama into a harem" (Lal 1964 : 26). The jester describes his king as a 'hunter' of women: "This king will be my death! what a hunter—he does nothing but hunt!" (*ibid.*, p. 22). Much later, the king tells him that once he loved Shakuntala. The jester's rejoinder runs like the following: "But you said once it was just a little game you were playing and I believed you" (*ibid.*, p. 60). Anyone who looks into this account of a Gandharva marriage in Kalidasa's masterpiece—the greatest masterpiece in Sanskrit drama—should be able to make out what this type of marriage has in store for young and hopeful women.

The eight types of Hindu marriage can easily be reduced to just two types: the first six belonging to what may be called *dowered marriages* and the last two belonging to what might be called *marriages by capture*. As dowry or bride-price seems to have been a necessary condition for marriages except those by capture, it is theoretically important to draw a line of demarcation between marriages which were dowered and marriages which were not. Despite the law books, both types of marriages appear to have been acceptable to the general run of Hindus in ancient India.

Both dowered marriages and marriages by capture are variants of patricentric marriages. It is immaterial for the purpose of the present study whether a girl is bought or sold, gifted to a priest as his fee or married to a man with dowry. If a marriage alliance involves a transaction between the two parties as part of the negotiations, it should be considered a dowered marriage. Again, it is immaterial for the purposes of this study whether a girl is abducted openly or clandestinely, seduced or drugged, mentally fit or deranged. If a marriage alliance is forged without a ceremony and transaction, it should be considered a marriage by capture. Needless to add, a Hindu marriage, according to the sacred law, whether dowered or not, was a sacramental union which could never be dissolved (cf. Basham 1967 : 173, Mehta 1970 : 17 & Kapoor 1974 : 6-16). Besides, the Law established a necessary bond between marriage and the bride's destiny. Once married off (or abandoned or abducted), a girl/woman could not return to the father's/guardian's family. A girl, it was often said, was "like a spit on the ground (sic): once taken out, it could not be taken back into the owner's mouth" (Baig 1976 : 90). Even the holy Kanva blurts out in Kalidasa's *magnum opus*: "A daughter never really belongs to her father. I am glad she has gone to her husband. It is where she belongs" (Lal 1964 : 46).

Marriages by capture, purchase and dowry are freely discussed and generally approved in the Epics. "The forcible abduction of a woman", says the *Mahabharata*, "for the sake of marriage is commended for heroic Kshatriyas; those who are versed in the *dharma* say so" (Banerjee 1976 : 12 : 51). Fascinated by Shakuntala's spellbinding charms, Dushyanta bursts out: "I know she cannot be an easy prize" (Lal 1964 : 23). Abduction of women for marriage was quite lawful in the Epic times. The etymology of the Sanskrit word *Vivaha* itself points to the custom of "carrying away" of women for marriage. The hordes of elephants, horses and people with arms accompanying a matrimonial procession even in our own times is just a spill-over of that ancient custom (cf. Bader 1964 : 39, 44 & Baig 1976 : 90). Out of sixteen thousand and eight wives of Krishna, only eight were regularly married wives while the rest were collected as spoils of wars, rewards of adventures and prizes of abductions (cf. Thomas 1964 : 145). Even Rukmini had been abducted while she was on her way to the temple for her marriage with Shisupala, the king of Chedis (cf. Lal 1980 : 384-85). Krishna himself instigated Arjuna to abduct Subhadra before her marriage to Duryodhana (*ibid.*, p. 386). Minutes before carrying away Amba, Ambika and Ambalika, the three daughters of the king of Varanasi, from a Svayamvara gathering for their marriage with his half brother Vichitravirya, the great Bhishma proclaimed: "The wise have declared that a girl can be given finely dressed and with much dowry to a noble guest who is invited for that purpose. Others give girls in exchange for cows. Some give money, some girls are abducted. Some consult the girl, and secure the parents' approval. Some get girls as presents to help at rituals and sacrifices. The learned approve of the last; a king prefers to be chosen by the girl herself; but the wise applaud a girl taken by force from an assembly of kings. I take these three girls by force! Stop me, if you dare! I throw you an open challenge" (*ibid.*, p. 70). The following account is given of Bhishma's escape:

"He raced his chariot around the assembly. The kings rose slapping their arm-pits like wrestlers, and biting their lower lips. Ornaments were cast off, and armours put on, both flashing like bright meteors in the sky. Brows furrowed and eyes flaming in the anger, they lined up, shooting ten thousand arrows at Bhishma. But Bhishma raged a shower of his own arrows, as thick as the hair on his body. And as their arrow-cloud was about to fall on his mountain breast, Bhishma pierced it, pinning down each king with two shafts; after which he raced towards Hastinapura" (*ibid.*, p. 70-71).

A representative example of marriage by purchase is Pandu's marriage with Madri. When Bhishma asks for the hand of Madri on behalf of Pandu, Madri's brother Salya tells him that he must pay bride-price. Bhishma offers him vast treasures of pure gold and minted gold, thousands of precious stones, elephants, horses and chariots, robes and ornaments, pearls and corals and other gems. Happy with the offer, Salya hands over his sister to Bhishma (*ibid.*, p. 77).

The *Mahabharata*, equally explicitly, describes dowry for the bridegroom even in cases where the marriage is based on Svayamvara. At Draupadi's marriage with the five Pandava brothers, a lavish dowry is bestowed on them by king Drupada: each bridegroom is offered a hundred chariots with golden banners and golden-reined horses, a hundred elephants and a hundred young and attractive female servants (*ibid.*, p. 103). The *Ramayana* describes how king Janaka offers vast treasures of cash and kind to each of his four sons-in-law. He offers each of them thousands of cows, a number of fine blankets, heaps of silken cloth, well-adorned elephants, horses, guards, and profuse gold, silver, pearls, corals and hundreds of maids (I :

XXXVII : 95). The *Ramacharitamanasa* offers a more systematic account of the dowry-giving ceremony:

"The value of the dowry defies description; the pavilion was filled with gold and jewels; blankets and garments and silks of every kind, and priceless; elephants, chariots, horses, men-servants and maid-servants and cows adorned like the cow of plenty-everything in such profusion that none could reckon them; they must be seen to be believed! The guardians of the spheres were envious when they saw the dowry; the king of Awadh received it all with pleasure ... Various kinds of fruit and confections, and an indescribable amount of food materials, all laden on innumerable bullock-carts .... Janaka also sent a number of comfortable beds, a hundred thousand horses and twenty five thousand chariots, all adorned throughout; ten thousand proud elephants, too, richly caparisoned, at the site of which the elephants of the quarters were mortified, with wagons full of gold and raiment and jewels; buffaloes, too, and cows and all things needed. A limitless dowry, again, beyond all telling Videha gave, compared with which the wealth of the spheres was a mere nothing in the eyes of their lords" (Balakanda : verses 323-333).

Kautilya's *Arthashastra* says that divorce could be allowed by mutual consent on grounds of incompatibility and that even one party could obtain divorce without the consent of the other, if apprehensive of physical danger from the other party. These provisions, however, do not appear in Law books or in later texts. This means that except for a short period, divorce was not possible for women of the higher castes, even though the husband could abandon his wife on charges of infidelity or barrenness (cf. Basham 1967 : 174). Divorce is now part of the Hindu marriage laws but it is still a male privilege. Hindu wives, like wives in other systems, continue to be discriminated against—in spite of the availability of divorce as a way out of an unhappy marriage. The main reason for the woman's disadvantage, to a much greater extent for Hindus than for others, is that a divorced woman is considered an anathema by the vast majority of Hindu men. Traditions and customs die hard. The modern Hindu woman is torn between dowry and divorce. Dowry has now acquired murderous implications for Hindu women. Indiscriminate bride-burning incidents taking place in different segments of Hindu population bear sufficient testimony to the horrors of the age-old dowry system. As the word *Talaque* is to a Muslim wife, the word 'Dowry' is to a Hindu bride (cf. Sahai 1985 : XXV).

As a measure of social reform, divorce should have become for married woman a way of effective protest against exploitation by her husband and his family. Divorce has not yet become an alternative to harassment and torture within marriage because an average Hindu marriage is still a patricentric arrangement. Marriages are seldom based on freedom and love between man and woman. One does not require any statistics to prove that a majority of married women are still inhibited by marriage and afflicted by divorce. Men still think that the wife is a servant or a thing and that she has to obey and hero-worship her husband. Unless marriage laws are drastically liberalized in favour of women, divorce cannot become an effective remedy for the ills of an unhappy marriage.

3.2 Polygyny, Polyandry and Prostitution

> "Kings have many wives, Shakuntala. You must make allowance for that."
>
> —*Abhijnanashakuntalam*

'Marriage' in this study is used in the sense of a monogamous arrangement between a man and a woman on a long term basis. Unions like those between one man and another man, one woman and another woman, one man and several women and, one woman and several men are therefore excluded from its purview. Unless otherwise mentioned, marriage as used here is a monogamous marriage. Non-monogamous marriages are referred to by other names.

It is assumed in this study that no discussion of the institution of marriage can ever acquire academic viability unless it takes note of parallel developments like polygyny, prostitution and concubinage. One can reasonably surmise that developments or customs like these could not have existed in the pre-marital phase of human history. This would mean that developments like these must owe their existence to the structure of marriage itself. It is intriguing that polygyny, prostitution and concubinage are traditionally looked upon with varying degrees of disfavour and yet they have been coterminus with the institution of marriage. The fact that these customs have been the indispensable by-ways of marriage points to the probability that they did not come into existence as inevitable side-effects of marriage but were deliberately created as additional avenues for extra-marital gratification. It is highly probable that the proponents of one man-one woman formula did not want to be limited by marriage. Marriage could not succeed as a form of control over unlimited sexuality mainly because men never wanted it to be so. Based on the perception of woman as inferior and disposable, marriage appears to have been formulated by men as a camouflage for controlled male sexuality as well as a limiting bond for women, as for underpriviliged men. As a civilizing institution, marriage has largely been a flop because it was designed to be a privilege to the few and a disadvantage to the majority.

Structurally analysed, marriage seems to be a concrete illustration of the masculine philosophy of having a cake and eating it too. There is a woman always available at home and then there are others, whether married or not, for cohabitation and enjoyment. To call other women additional wives, concubines or prostitutes is a linguistic luxury in which only the powerful male can indulge, if and when he so desires. It is immaterial whether he shares a woman with several men or he obliges several women to share him. He is always at the centre and they are always around the centre. It is his privilege to use them, abuse them or dispose them of. He has access to an infinite variety of ways to amuse himself and to abuse them.

Polygyny need not be seen as a special Islamic institution. It was practised in Vedic India, Homeric Greece, Pagan Arab and in several other parts of the civilized world. King Priam of Troy had numerous wives and concubines, the foremost of whom was Hecuba. In ancient Jewish society it was practised even by the wisest of men on an enormous scale. In Pagan Arab the number of wives had no upper limit (cf. Pomeroy 1975 : 27 & Kidwai 1976 : 8, 30).

By nature polygynous, the Indo-Aryan male inaugurates the history of Hindu marriage by prescribing the desirability of having a plurality of wives. The *Atharva Veda* explicitly ordains: "For one husband has many wives" (quoted in Sengupta 1974 : 56). That polygyny was freely practised in the Vedic age is clearly illustrated by the numerous references to women uttering magic spells for the destruction of their rivals or co-wives. Women are frequently described as those `who run after men' (*punshachali*) in the *Atharva Veda* and the *Yajur Veda* (cf. De 1969 : 4-5). In his well known classic *The Wonder That was India*, A.L. Basham observes: "Even in the time of the *Rig-Veda* polygamy was not unknown. Kings and chiefs were almost invariably polygamous as were many Brahmanas and wealthier members of the lower orders. Polygamous marriages are so frequently mentioned that we may assume that they were fairly common among all sections of the community who could afford them" (1967 : 174-175 cf. Thomas 1964 : 52). The *Ramayana* tells us that king Dasharatha had three hundred and fifty wives over and above the three principal queens (cf. Sharma 1971 : 108). Legendary accounts of Lord Krishna idealize him as the sole master of more than sixteen thousand wives (cf. Thomas 1964 : 145 & Lal 1980 : 352). Almost all important personalities in the *Mahabharata* are polygynous: Shantanu marries Ganga and Satyavati, Vichitravirya Ambika and Ambalika, Dhristarshtra Gandhari and a Vaishya woman, and Bhima Hidimba and Draupadi. But of all Pandava heroes, Arjuna turns out to be his mentor's faithful protege. His variety of "erotic adventures suggests a restless twentieth-century hero relentlessly seeking self-fulfilment through sexual satisfaction. He marries the Princesses of Kalinga, Chedi, Madra, Magadha and Yavana, besides those of Haridwar [Ulupi] and Manipur" [Chitrangada] (Lal 1980). He is also the darling of Draupadi.

Vatsyayana's work presents an interesting portrait of the social life in ancient India. The *Kamasutra* recommends that a man can remarry in his wife's lifetime for the following reasons : the folly or ill-temper of the wife, her husband's dislike to her, the want of offspring, the continual birth of daughters and the incontinence of the husband (IV : II : 202). It goes on to suggest that when the second wife comes, the first wife "should give her a position superior to her own" and "should not mind all the husband's favour being given to her" (IV : II : 202). With pity for wives in the royal harem, Vatsyayana suggests that as these wives cannot meet other men due to strict vigilance and are therefore sexually starving, they can obtain sexual satisfaction in a variety of ways by using artificial means (V : VI : 236).

A Reuter report from Hong Kong disclosed a few years ago that a Chinese peasant Ye Xianfa (33) *rented* his wife in 1984 to a bachelor living nearby for 500 Yuans (US $ 140) for a period of six years. The wife started living with the bachelor and soon bore him a son. The bachelor and the woman were living happily. But suddenly something went wrong somewhere. The fact that a wife had been rented to someone was brought to the notice of the local authorities. The authorities declared this contract void in October 1986 and ordered the husband to take back his wife, leaving the son with the bachelor. Social workers then started a vigorous campaign against *wife-renting* among local Chinese peasants (The Statesman, 22 October, 1986). A modern educated Hindu may find this report amusing, even obnoxious, unless he is informed that *wife-lending* or *wife-sharing* was once upon a time a common practice in Sparta and India.

The custom of lending one's wife to another man to beget an heir to his estate was not considered evil in Sparta nor was it thought to be repugnant to requisition the services of another man to get a good 'breed' for one's family. By the end of the eighth century BC, Spartans came to believe that since the interests of the community prevailed over those of individual citizens, it did not matter whether a child was born of the mother's husband or not. Women were encouraged, often compelled, to have sex even with slaves, known as *helots*, so that the state could have plenty of male children. Children born of the wife-helot union were euphemistically called 'the children of unmarried mothers'. Curiously enough, the *Rig-Veda* contains references to 'sons of unwed mothers' (kumari-putra), 'wife-sharing' (niyoga) and 'levirate marriage' or *Vidhawa-Vivaha* (cf. De 1969 : 4-5, Pomeroy 1975 : 36-37 & Kidwai 1976 : 6).

The famous sons of unwed mothers in the *Mahabharata* are Vyasa and Karna: the former born of the union of Matsyagandhi with sage Parashara and the latter of that of Kunti with the Sun-God. Besides, Vichitravirya's widows Ambika and Ambalika are forced to have sex with Vyasa, the elder brother of their dead husband, to bear the blind Dhritarashtra and the jaundiced Pandu, respectively. Ambalika's maid also has to bear the brunt of Vyasa's sex spree and she gives birth to the learned Vidura. The five Pandava brothers are born by Kunti and Madri through their extra-marital unions with gods: Yudhishtira is born of Dharma (god of righteousness), Bhima of Vayu (Wind-god), Arjuna of Indra (the king of heaven), and the twins Nakula and Sahadeva of the Ashvins. It should be sufficiently embarrassing for a contemporary righteous Hindu to recollect by scratching his conscience that none of his beloved Pandava heroes was born of his father. When Kunti refuses to go in for unions outside marriage to beget sons, her impotent husband has the cheek to admonish her in words like the following: "The scriptures say there are six kinds of sons who become heirs: the son from a lawful wife, the son born to one's wife from a good man acting out of kindness, the son born to one's wife from a man paid for the purpose, the son born after a husband's death, the son born to a virgin, and the son of an unchaste wife. Manu says that husbands without offspring should obtain the services of others for their wives, because sons bring the highest merit .... I command you, Kunti, give sons from someone either equal or superior to me". Pandu goes on to add: "The moral sages speak of a time in the past when women were free, neither confined to their homes nor dependent on their husbands. Nor was fidelity valued in those days; yet the charge of immorality was never brought against them. One wife married to one husband is a recent custom" (Lal 1980 : 80-81).

The *Mahabharata* also refers to the custom of inviting guests to share the bed with one's wife. 'Adultery' was not known to the epic people. The Brahmana who had a nice time with Oghavati, the wife of the fellow Brahaman Sudarshana, was not embarrassed when he was caught red-handed by the latter. Sudarshana was rather pleased that his wife had at least been so good to a Brahmana guest. Likewise, king Shrinjaya's daughter Sukumari gave such nice time to the holiest of sages, Narada, that he fell in love with her and finally married her (cf. Thomas 1964 : 150-151).

The social ethos of the *Mahabharata*, particularly in relation to the sex life of the people, is full of contradictions. The Epic says, for example, that the custom of monogamous marriages is a recent one but its general tenor points in the opposite direction. There are a number of verses which declare, quite unequivocally, that polygyny is in conformity with the Dharmashastras but polyandry is not and that a woman who has sex relation with several men, Draupadi's example notwithstanding, is a prostitute. Let us look at the following:

"O offspring of Kuru, many queens of one are ordained. Many men (*i.e.*, husbands) of one woman are never prescribed.

O blessed one, polygamy is not contrary to religion for men. It is a great violation of Dharma for women to desert their first husband.

O fortunate one, to have many wives is not a fault on the part of men. But for a woman, it is a fault to have many husbands" (Banerjee 1976 : 12 : 17, 18, 36, 42).

Chitrangada, Arjuna's Manipuri wife, enlightens co-wife 'Ulupi': "Blame does not attach to a man if he marries more than one wife; blame attaches only to a woman if she marries more than one husband" (Lal 1980 : 333). This view is perfectly in line with the Atharva-Vedic injunction: "For one man has many wives, one wife has not many husbands at the same time" (cf. 178 Sengupta 1974 : 56). Kunti goes far ahead of such formulations when she tells her coercive husband: "A woman who has intercourse with four men is defiled; and one who has intercourse with five is a prostitute" (*ibid.*, p. 82). Even elsewhere in the text, it is held: "A woman who is under the control of many men is considered to be a harlot" (Banerji 1976 : 23 : 4).

It is evident from such formulations that the general opinion in the *Mahabharata* does not look upon polyandry as an acceptable form of marital relationship. That a Hindu woman could have more than one husband at a time does not find favour with the scripture nor is it found acceptable even within the *Mahabharata*. Draupadi's so-called marriage with five men therefore cannot be taken as an example of *polyandry*, if by this term is meant a woman's legal competence to have several husbands at a time (as by *polygyny* is meant a man's legal competence to have several wives at a time). 'Polyandry' is not an antonym of 'polygyny', that is, these terms do not have the same *value* in the Saussurian sense. A man acquires women to be his wives or concubines as a matter of right; a woman is acquired by several men at a time to be their common wife, concubine or prostitute. The Hindu system does not recognize woman as a full citizen with legal rights. There is therefore no question of a woman having the freedom to choose a husband or husbands, be the woman a Draupadi, or any other. Draupadi is tied down to the Pandava brothers rather than *married* to them, in spite of her father and brother. Draupadi's bond with a company of husbands should be seen as an instance of wife-sharing at best or prostitution at worst. A close reading of the text should support this contention.

It is true that, in spite of distortions, Draupadi remains the heart of the Epic. A *Mahabharata* without Draupadi would be a body without the soul. Draupadi must be there to give the epic life and intensity. It is also true that Draupadi's association with the Pandava brothers was an essential part of the legend and the author of the epic could not have glossed over it or wished it away. Draupadi and the joint-stock company of her husbands have to be there as ingredients essential to the structure of the epic. The author of the *Mahabharata* was therefore obliged to come up with a rationalization of this embarrassing episode without offending the orthodox but finally he turned up with a formulation of the episode which could only be clumsy and ridiculous.

Arjuna wins at the arrow-shooting competition which is held to decide who is going to marry Draupadi. He becomes eligible to marry her. But when news is brought to Yudhishthira, the epic "embodiment of righteousness" (Dharamaraja), he immediatlely decrees: "She will be our common wife". One day king Drupada goes to Yudhishthira to say that he should allow Arjuna to marry Draupadi. "But I must marry too", says Yudhishthira. "You are welcome to marry her if you like", says Drupada. "Or marry her to any of the brothers, if that is your wish". But Yudhishthira insists that Draupadi must marry all the five brothers at a time. The king is baffled. He tells Yudhishthira, "I have heard of the practice of polygamy but this is the first time I hear of one wife having many husbands. You know this is wrong, Yudhishthira, and the Vedas forbid it". Yudhishthira does not listen to him. He points out to the king that he always speaks the truth and avoids doing wrong but on this question his conscience is with him and Draupadi must marry all the brothers. The discussion goes on. Vyasa suddenly drops in and Drupada asks him, "How is it possible, O holy one, for one woman to have many husbands without defiling Dharma". Vyasa agrees that the Vedas do not sanction such marriages. At this moment there comes Dhristadyumna, Draupadi's brother, to say, "I cannot with a good conscience allow my sister to become the wife of five men". Yudhishthira, to justify his stand, digs up the Puranic story of Jatila who is alleged to have married seven sages. He also refers to an ascetic's daughter, without naming her, who is believed to have married ten brothers. Yudhishthira's strongest argument is based on his mother's reported decree that all the five brothers must share (they do not share everything, though) everything that anyone of them acquires. And so the king must allow his daughter to be married to all the brothers. Kunti then joins them to support her eldest son. And then comes the final judgement from Vyasa: "This is not the time for a lecture. But I can say this much—Yudhishthira is within the Dharma in saying what he does. This is an old and honoured practice which I will explain to you in private" (Lal 1980 : 101-103 cf. Chandra 1970 : 387-89). Draupadi is ultimately tied down to all the five brothers, without her consent and against her will.

Human sex relations may be divided into single and multiple physical unions. It is single when it is limited to a man and a woman at a time; it is multiple when it involves one man and several women or one woman and several men at a time. Marriage (derived from the Greek *gamos*) is ideally one man—one woman relationship at a time and over a period of time. Marriage (derived from the Latin maritos *i.e.*, 'husband' or ultimately from *mas maris i.e.*, 'male') is also a male coinage and monopoly. In other words, marriage is a construct strictly etymologically speaking, devised by a male for a male to be a husband. Marriage, therefore, is a male-centred, husband-oriented institution that formalizes and justifies a masculine view of human sex relations but, as it is masculine, it has to have alternative devices to satisfy and justify informal male pursuits. Informal male sexuality acquires the form of multiple male sexuality which is polygyny or polygamy which is another name for prostitution. If marriage is limited to monogamy or single sexuality, as is done in this study, then prostitution becomes a necessary alternative to it and as such another term for multiple sexuality. Since a patriarchal society does not allow a woman to ever become the single source or centre of sexuality, polyandry does not exist and prostitution is never a one woman-many men kind of sexual trade-off. Both monogamy and prostitution are male-centred institutions and should be defined as one man—one woman and many men-one woman sex relations, respectively. Annie Besant very aptly describes 'prostitution' as "polygamy without responsibility" and remarks that "the righteous sex-relation" between one man and one woman is preached in many parts of the world but is practised in none (cf. Kidwai 1976 : 29). The philosopher Schopenhauer sees prostitutes as "human sacrifices offered upon the altar of monogamy" (*ibid.*, p. 30).

As an alternative to marriage, prostitution has followed patriarchal humanity from ancient to modern times like a dark shadow and it is there still. The dustbin of civilization, prostitution reflects the innate duplicity of male philosophy which sweeps the dirt under the carpet to keep the house clean. The prostitute is a scapegoat; she is both a necessity and a pariah. Man vents his turpitude upon her and rejects her and yet runs after her again. All prostitutes feel that all men are vicious and sadistic. Prostitution continues as a social phenomenon because it has been a social necessity. Prostitutes are both disgusted with and involved in their profession. They often feel intrigued because they know they are rejected but sought, hated but wanted and that is the secret of the game called prostitution. Prostitutes are integrated and integrative because society manifests a constant and universal "demand for their services" (Beauvoir 1953 : 268).

Prostitution is often divided into three categories: respectable prostitution, temple prostitution and common prostitution. Beginning with the last, we may note that common prostitution is a miserable occupation, a dreadful occupation. Exploited sexually and economically, subjected to the police and to the other custodians of the social order and doomed to infection, disease and endless misery, the prostitute is reduced "to the level of a thing" (*ibid.*, p. 269). This category of prostitution is practised in India on a larger scale. Minor girls are forced into this inhuman trade to cater to the perverted demands of their clients (cf. Barse 1985). Common prostitutes form the garbage dump of Indian society. Their daughters grow up to be prostitutes and their sons pimps or castrated eunuchs (euphemistically known as the `third' sex) while the `legitimate' children of their clients grow up to be happy and respectable citizens of our great republic. In keeping with our double standards, we condone the man "who sneaks off into a fleshpot to have sex without relationship with a stranger he has bought and whom he considers too gross, polluted and depraved a being to be allowed to participate in normal social activities. On the other hand, we ostracize, condemn and legally punish the woman who sells sex. Worst still, we treat her progeny as desecrated, and deny them any oppurtunity to break away from the rut into which they have been born" (*ibid.*).

Temple prostitution is one of the murkiest facets of human civilization. According to the *Bhavishya Purana*, the best way for a man to obtain heaven of the 'Sun-god' (Surya-Loka) is to dedicate a bevy of dancing girls to a temple of the sun. It is no wonder that the sun temples are profusely decorated with paintings and sculptures of nude couples engaged in sexual acts. The Prostitutes (*devadasees*, literally, 'slaves of the gods') have been a necessary part of temple life. Though not peculiar to Hindus, this type of prostitution seems to have been associated with Hinduism in a much more systematic way than with any other system. The holy priests successfully convinced the ancient masses that the easiest means of securing a blissful after-life was to dedicate as many girls as possible to a temple for the service of the gods inside. Gods in India, like those in Greece, needed girls, more than anything else, to look after them. There were masses of the pious ready to avail of such meritorious opportunities offered by the priesthood. The same Brahmanas who had imagined the absolute, all-powerful, all-knowing and omnipresent Brahma, who had propounded the Sacred Law and who had taken upon themselves the responsibilities of enlightening the masses, attached themselves to temples with hundreds of Prostitutes on their staff (cf. Thomas 1964 : 236-38, Basham 1967 : 187, Sengupta 1974 : 99 & Baig 1976 : 69). With the progress of Hinduism from age to age, prostitution in temples became increasingly popular, so much so that by the medieval times almost every temple was crowded by women. It is not surprising therefore that even today, the notorious practice of dedicating girls to temples continues unabated (cf. Sahai 1985 : XXV). We have official statistics available to support the contention that the devadasee system is still a social reality (cf. *Hindustan Times* April 2, 1987 & *Ind. Exp.*, April 24, 1988).

No ingredient of male behaviour exposes the gnawing gap between what men preach and what they practise as the contrary attitudes of civilized men towards the free courtesan and the confined wife, respectively. Both the Vedic Indian and the Archaic Greek admired and respected a certain class of women who, strange though it might seem, combined prostitution with self-respect and power. The Indian Ganika, like Greek Hetaira, possessed wealth, power, beauty, literary taste and cultural sophistication which the wife envied and missed. References to the courtesans (hetairas or ganikas) are found in the *Rig Veda* as well as in the earliest of Greek chronicles (cf. De 1969 : 4-5 & Pomeroy 1975 : 88). State-owned brothels were established and maintained both in Periclean Athens and Mauryan Magadh to make their cities attractive for tourists (Thomas 1964 : 69, Pomeroy 1975 : 88-89 & Baig 1976 : 68). These brothels contained women who were called 'common public women' (*sadharani*, to use the Rig-Vedic term vide De 1969 : 4-5), women who were generally sought after but not always admired. Such prostitutes were loved and hated by people who needed and enjoyed their company. A typical example of the popular view of such women is found in an ancient Sanskrit play called *Mrichchhakatika* or *The Toy Clay Cart* of Shudraka which deals with the love-life of Charudatta, a married man, and Vasantasena, a prostitute. The Vita (*i.e.*, the clown or parasite of the hero) tells Vasantasena that the prostitute is "like a creeper that grows by the roadside; her person is like an article for sale [incidentally derived from the Latin *prot statuere*, `Prostitute' means `one who offers herself for sale']; her love is a thing that money will buy; and her welcome is equally bestowed on the amiable and the disgusting. The sage and the idiot, the Brahmana and the outcast, all bathe in the same stream; and the crow and the peacock perch on the same branches of the same tree" (De 1969 : 80).

But unlike the ordinary public woman, the Ganika is always highly spoken of. She is honoured by the king and highly lauded by men qualified to appreciate merit, her favours and company are sought for and she is considered a pattern for desirable conduct. Being highly skilled, educated and refined, the Ganikas were, in Vatsyayana's age, "far more acceptable as companions than the generality of the married or unmarried women of the period" (Archer 1963 : 243). The *Kamasutra* tells us that the Ganika is "always respected by the king, and praised by learned men, and her favour being sought for by all, she becomes an object of universal regard" (*ibid.*, p. 111). About the Greek equivalent of the Ganika, Pomeroy writes : "Those at the top of this social scale were called *hetairas* or `companion to men', many of these, in addition to physical beauty, had had intellectual training and possessed artistic talents, attributes that made them more entertaining to Athenian men at parties than their legitimate wives. It is no accident that the most famous woman in fifth-century Athens was the foreign born Aspasia, who .... in the course of her life lived with Pericles, the political leader of Athens. ... Aristophanes claims that due to her influence Pericles started the Peloponnesian War. ... Plutarch says that even Socrates occasionally visited her, presumably for intellectual discussion" (1975 : 89). Later in her book, Pomeroy comments: "Like Aspasia, Hellenistic courtesans mingled with many of the leading men in the state. ... The famous courtesan Thais was rumoured to have captivated Alexander and then Plotemy I to whom she bore three children" (p. 141).

References to Aspasia's association with Socrates and Pericles at once reminds us of the association of the sixth-century courtesan of Vaishali with Buddha and Ajatshatru. The historical eminence of Ambapali bears witness to the Hindu attitude to courtesans and city women. Except Ajatshatru and Lord Buddha, no man or woman of that age is ever spoken of with a greater sense of awe than is Ambapali. As K.M. Pannikar puts it: " In India the courtesan enjoyed at all times a special position. In the time of the Buddha (sixth-century BC) we hear of the famous courtesan ... Ambapali who held a high position in the great city of Vaishali. It was in her mango grove that the Blessed One stayed during his visit to the city. ... In the Jataka tales there are many stories which indicate that learned and accomplished courtesans were held in high respect and esteem ... Kautilya's *Arthashastra* (Circa 300 BC) bears witness to the fact that courtesans held high positions near the person of the King. ... Indeed they were at one time considered models of deportment, courtly behaviour and politeness and young princes and nobles were sent to elderly courtesans to be instructed in manners" (1963). How astonishing it is that masses of the educated elite, despite such accounts, seek to glorify the ancient Hindu ideals of marriage and womanhood! Who can ever cure us of our chronic self-deception?

3.3 Maternity, Child-Marriage and Widowhood

> "Whatever a man really wishes to do, he will finally discover a means of doing."
>
> —*G.B. Shaw*

Contraceptions, conceptions and abortions annually humiliate, hurt or kill hundreds of thousands of women in our country, a vast majority of whom are Hindus. Immaterial it is whether such deeds or misdeeds are marital or extra-marital, legal or illegal. Do educated Hindu males realize that abortions and contraceptions by far outnumber live births? Do they realize that incidents like contraceptions, abortions and live births are anti-women, even though they are carried out by men and for women? Why do such incidents take place at all? Is there any reason to identify contraceptions and abortions with freedom for women? Does the question 'freedom for what?' ever prick the conscience of men who persuade or force women to avoid or to get rid of unwanted conceptions?

Conceptions outside marriage may be (or often are) horrifying experiences for the victims of male sexuality. Stories of children born out of wedlock are legion in Hindu history and yet the unwed mother remains an offence to public opinion. Children born out of non-marital unions live and grow to be baffling anomalies and shameful reminders to the custodians of marital sanctity, apart from turning the helpless mothers into a community of outcasts. Even within marriage a conception or a child birth acquires various implications for women. It may be for one a cherishable experience, an act of self-fulfilment; for another it may be an act of temporary inconvenience or even a symbol of pollution, while for the third it may be a permanent handicap.

As an experience, maternity is unique to woman and as such it is only proper that in matters like conception, contraception and abortion the woman has the last word. Men cannot and must not impose on women their notions of maternity or femininity. It is therefore obligatory for a society to ensure that there is no coercion of a woman into a sex act so that there is no coercion later on for contraception or abortion. Any sex act which is not based on the emotional involvement of the woman, whether wife or non-wife, must be declared an incidence of rape by law. Husbands, Hindu husbands in particular, should be compelled to realize that any sexual act without the consent of the wife is an act of rape and therefore punishable under the law.

Not many years ago, a Japanese district court sentenced a twenty-six-year old husband to two years' imprisonment on the charge of raping his wife (cf. *Hindu* 18 Dec., 1986). If Hindu husbands were to be brought to court on charges of marital rape, millions of them would find themselves behind the bars almost every day of the year. The sexual exploitation of the wife by the husband is so common in our society that one does not need to invoke statistics to prove that husbands are guilty of numerous rapes. Havelock Ellis rightly holds that many more rapes are committed within marriage than outside (cf. Beauvoir 1953 : 162). A Hindu writer says that husbands in general tend to use their wives just as sex objects with no regard to their mood or health (cf. Kapoor 1974 : 34-35). Unless men develop a healthier attitude to heterosexual relationships and recognize women's autonomy in matters like maternity, incidents like unwanted conceptions, contraceptions and abortions will continue to plague the generality of women.

The ancient Hindu institution of what is known as 'child marriage' points to the age-old masculinist philosophy of exploiting and limiting women on all levels. Most authorities on ancient India agree that the ideal age of marriage for girls in those days varied from seven to ten years (cf. Basham 1967 : 167, Shastri 1969 : 87-88 & Chakladar 1976 : 125-126). The general view in ancient times was that the ideal marriage was a marriage in which the bride was one-third of the age of the groom—so that a man of twenty-four could marry a girl of eight and a man of thirty could marry a girl of ten. A verse in the *Mahabharata* explicitly states: "A thirty year old man should marry a girl of ten years called *Nagnika*. Or, a twenty-one year old man should get a girl of seven years" (Banerji 1976 : 12 : 29). The

Vishnu Purana recommends: "One should marry a girl whose age is one-third of one's own" (cited in Chakladar 1976 : 124). Vatsyayana suggests that the bride should be three to seven years younger than the groom but he also insists that the bride must be a Nagnika (cf. *ibid.*, pp. 125-26). The law books warn that if a father does not give his daughter in marriage before her first menstruation, he incurs a sin worse than murder (cf. Basham 1967 : 167). Manu's code, for example, lays down that a father "who gives in marriage a girl of eight goes to heaven, the giver of a girl of nine to Vaikuntha; one who gives his daughter in marriage before she obtains the age of ten attains the heaven of Brahma. But the father of a girl married after puberty goes to hell" (cf. Thomas 1964 : 225). One of the most notorious statements in favour of child-marriage occurs in the *Bhagavata Purana*: "an unmarried girl who menstruates, living in her father's or mother's house, should be regarded as a degraded woman; a man commits no sin by carrying her away from the custody of her guardian" (cf. Baig 1976 : 118).

Shakuntala Rao Shastri is not correct in her assertion that child-wives are mentioned for the first time in the *Chhandogya Upanishada*. Perhaps with the single exception of widow-burning (sati), almost all Hindu customs, practices and views may be traced back to the Vedas. Of course, the Vedas do not insist on child marriage as the only form of marriage for girls; there are mentioned adult wives as well. It is probable that Vedic Aryans recommended child marriage for girls even though they tolerated adult marriage. Ghosha is described as an adult-wife while Romasha is spoken of as a child-wife in the *Rig Veda* itself (cf. Chakladar 1976 : 126). It is, however, interesting to note that child-husbands, even boy-husbands, are not mentioned in ancient Hindu texts. The hero of the *Ramayana* may be a solitary example of a boy-husband. Ravana meets Sita to abduct her but he engages her in a pleasant conversation by introducing himself as a mendicant and in the hope that he might as well win her over. It is during this conversation that Sita informs him that at the time of her marriage she was only six years of age while Rama was just thirteen (cf. III : IXX p. 390).

The rigidity of the scriptural demand that girls must be married at the earliest possible age, in any case before the first menstruation, should be viewed as a concrete example of what might be called *sadistic paedophilia*. We may bear in mind that while the marriage age prescribed for girls varies from seven to ten, that for men varies from twenty-one to thirty. Even the latest Marriage Act prescribes twenty-one as the age for men to marry. As regards men, the ancient Law makers were so generous and forward-looking! They were obnoxious only with regard to women, whether it was marriage or maternity.

The doctrinization of such disparity between Hindu males and females in respect of their desirable age for marriage finds its parallels also in Greece. The Athenian in Plato's *Laws* declares that the marriage age for girls "shall be sixteen to twenty years and for a man from thirty to thirty-five years" (p. 785). The main reason for prescribing an earlier age for women than for men to marry was the same as that among ancient Hindus. The necessity that the bride be "a virgin, coupled with the ancient belief that the young girls were lustful, made early marriage [in Greece] desirable" (Pomeroy 1975 : 64). As for the Hindus, Basham observes: "A woman was thought to be naturally libidinous; an unmarried girl attaining puberty would proceed to find a lover, however strictly her parents guarded her" (1967 : 168). Imaginary apprehensions like these motivated the custodians of communal morality to make laws that could catch girls young so that they could not defile the family or defame the community. Child marriage was therefore made compulsory for all girls. Such were the views of daughters and sisters held by their noble and enlightened guardians in the golden age of Hindu civilization!

Pointing to the inevitable consequences of child marriage, a scholar has this to say: "Condemned to domestic drudgery, ignorance and premature motherhood, developing in most cases, physical infirmities or deformities, the married woman in respectable households was not fit company for a normal healthy man, and this was in no small measure responsible for the extraordinary high position prostitutes gained in later India and for the hold they obtained even in temples and places of pilgrimages" (Thomas 1964 : 228). Also, as frequent pregnancies and child births rendered these young women sick, ugly and uncouth, men hated and tortured their wives to spit out the deep-rooted frustrations of their conjugal hopes. The modern Hindu starts gasping for breath when he finds such condemned, helpless and hopeless women glorified both in holy texts and literary masterpieces.

Centuries have come and gone but we are still stayput with our obsolete Law Books. As we Hindus have always steadfastly held on to our 'glorious' past, we have religiously refused to change with the times. The world goes ahead, but we refuse to move forward because, by heredity and nature, we are a backward-looking, crab-like people. Because we always look back to our illustrious ancestors to illumine our minds and direct our conduct about everything in life, we fail to criticize our heritage. We are probably the only community on earth who can fish out millions and millions from our depleted bank accounts and near-empty purses to watch on portable black-and-white TV sets the antique tales of men and monkeys as picturized. It is no wonder therefore that we still have hundreds of millions of child-wives and child-mothers in our midst. The Sharda Act of 1929 had decreed that girls before sixteen could not be married off without their parents risking the rigours of the law and yet a study conducted by Lucknow University in 1971 revealed that in Uttar Pradesh alone 52 per cent of girls were married by the age of fifteen (cf. Mehta 1970 : 20 & Sahai 1985 : XVII). The Marriage Act of 1978 allows a girl to be married only when she is eighteen years of age but a study conducted by the Family Planning Foundation in 1987 showed that 33 per cent girls in Orissa, 38 per cent girls in Uttar Pradesh, 48 per cent in Karnataka and 58 per cent girls in Madhya Pradesh had become married mothers before they were eighteen years of age. These under-eighteen mothers raised the national average of infant mortality rate in India to 105 a thousand, thereby making it one of the highest in the world (cf. Ind. Exp., 28 Dec., 1987).

Close on the heels of the notorious custom of child-marriage comes the heinous Hindu practice of widow-burning (sati). In a way, widow-burning and child-marriage are the two sides of the same coin. Motivated by the view of femininity, widow-burning has to be analysed in terms of the same scale of values as child-marriage. A girl is to be bound in early childhood to an adult male as her husband, otherwise she will give up her virginity and defile the family. Likewise, a widow must be disposed of along with her dead husband as she has already lost her virginity. As a wife, a woman has to surrender her virginity only to her husband and, having done that, she must remain totally tied down to him for ever, that is, both here and hereafter. Only the husband is authorized by Law Books to monopolize his wife's body and soul. A woman not monopolized thus by her husband is impure and sinful. Any Hindu female who has extra-marital sex relations, whether by choice or under compulsion, is a public woman. No other system on earth maintains such a rigid separation between the wife and the prostitute as orthodox Hinduism does. A woman, in its view, is either 'private' or 'public' property. There is no third category. Every woman has to be either a wife or a prostitute for life; the system does not visualize spinsterhood as a possible choice for a woman. But even in the binary division between private and public roles, a woman does not have any option. Whether a girl is going to be a wife or a prostitute is decreed by the male majority. Once decreed to be a wife, a woman must live for the husband and die with the husband because her survival after the husband's death is fraught with hazardous implications. This, in brief, seems to be the crux of the Hindu rationale for burning the dead man's wife on his pyre.

Many ancient peoples like the Chaldees, Celts, Gauls, Goths, Scythians, Slavs and Thracians buried or burnt a man's widows, slaves, horses and other cherished possessions with his corpse in order that he might have all that he loved and needed in the other world (cf. Basham 1967 : 188, Sengupta 1974 : 97 & Baig 1976 : 19). It is possible that ancient Hindus borrowed this custom from some of these peoples. But there is a basic difference between Hindu widow-burning on the one hand and widow-burning in these peoples on the other. Widow-burning for most of them was part of their prehistory whereas for Hindus it was part of their post-Vedic history. Vedic Hindus probably did not kill their widows. Then the widow used to be persuaded to marry her husband's younger brother or cousin. This custom was known as 'levirate marriage' (cf. De 1969 : 4-5). It was a common practice that the dead man's younger brother or cousin came to his bereaved widow and proposed: "Rise woman and come to the world of living beings. Come, this man near whom thou sleepest is lifeless, thou hast enjoyed the state of being the wife of thy husband, the suitor who took thee by the hand. ... Come, thou hast now entered upon the wifehood of this thy lord who takes thy hand to be thy husband and woos the" (Shastri 1969 : 20-21). Levirate marriage remained in vogue for quite some time. The *Arthashastra* mentions widow-marriage as prevalent among various castes (cf. Thomas 1964 : 73-74). That widows were allowed to survive is evident from the *Kamasutra,* although by this time they had ceased to enjoy the privilege of remarriage. Widow-burning may have started sometime in the fourth century BC. The earliest datable notice of the immolation of widows occurs in "Greek accounts of Alexander's invasion" (Basham 1967 : 189). Together with child-marriage, it appears to have been firmly established on a large scale during the post Smriti period. The prohibition of widow-marriage by the Sacred Law was logically followed up by the caste Hindu immolation of widows. Manu represents the consensus of his contemporaries when he declares: "Nowhere is a second husband permitted to respectable women" (V : 162). He clearly lays down that a man may marry after the death of his wife but a wife can never think of another man after the death of her husband (cf. V : 157 & 168). His advice to a surviving widow is: "Until her death let her be patient (of her hardship), self-controlled, and chaste, and strive to fulfil that most excellent duty which (is prescribed) for wives who have one husband only" (V : 158).

According to the Law Books, the highest religious duty of a wife was to see in her husband, alive or dead, her god and her ultimate salvation. Widow-burning followed as a natural corollary of such prescriptions and in course of time reached menacing proportions. A thirteenth century inscription, for instance, reads: "Those who do not bind her [*i.e.*, the widow] and throw her into the fire and kill her would get the sin of prostituting their own wives" (Thomas 1964 : 235). Six centuries later, Raja Ram Mohan Roy and his associates claimed in their representation against widow-burning that they had been eye-witnesses to widows having been "forced upon the pile, and there bound with ropes and pressed with green bamboos, were kept until consumed by the flames" and that those who tried to run away from the flames were "carried back by their relations and burnt to death" (*ibid.*, pp. 295-296). The worst part of this atrocious ritual was that the widow's son (or nearest kin in the absence of a son) had to set fire to his living mother tied to his dead father on the funeral pyre (cf. Sengupta 1974 : 70).

Historically speaking, the custom of widow-burning appears to have been practised on a selective basis for a fairly long time from Vyasa to Vatsyayana. The *Mahabharata*, for example, shows that some widows were immolated and some were not. Madri was immolated on Pandu's funeral pyre but Kunti was not. Devaki, Bhadra, Rohini and Madira were burnt with Vasudeva's corpse but his other wives were not. Similarly, Rukmini and seven other queens of Krishna were consigned to the flames along with their dead husband (Krishna) but Satyabhama and the other queens were not (cf. Lal 1980 : 84, 352-353 & 385). As time drew on, immolation of widows became increasingly rigid and regular. It was, however, during the Perso-Arabic period that it acquired the status of a ritual with all the sanctions of the hoary tradition. To prevent her escape from the raging flames, the widow was usually surrounded by men armed with sticks who goaded her to her destination by physical force. Describing his decision to abolish sati by law, William Bentick wrote: "To consent to the consignment, year after year, of husbands of innocent victims to a cruel and untimely death, when the power exists of preventing it, is a predicament which no conscientious man can contemplate without horror. ... I should be guilty of little sort of the crime of multiplied murder if I could hesitate in the performance of this solemn obligation" (Thomas 1964 : 263). Sati was not totally abolished immediately after Lord Bentick's Edict, proclaimed on 5 Dec. 1829. Writing in 1911, Edward Thomson points out: "The number of women burned alive at his funeral had in many states been the criterion of a Prince's success in life. Eighty-four women died with Raja Budh Singh of Bundi, sixty-four with Raja Ajit Singh of Jodhpur, and numbers in the neighbourhood of twenty were usual" (Baig 1976 : 20).

To think about sati is to be filled with horror and shame, astonishment and indignation. Sati was, in most cases, the cold blooded and brutal public murder of a lone and helpless widow by the males of the family and locality. All religious or doctrinal rationalizations of this custom are hideous and barbaric. Most Hindu texts contain motivated interpolations and distortions but no distortion is so disasterous and demoralizing as the one which converts a marriage ritual into a death warrant. The Rig-Vedic instruction for the widow originally read: "Let the woman advance to the altar first" (*i.e.*, Arohantujanayo yonim *agre*). This line refers to the Vedic custom in accordance with which the widow had to ascend the funeral pyre of her husband only to be led away by his younger brother or cousin for her marriage with him. The post-Vedic Brahmanas replaced the last but one letter of the line (*i.e.*, `r' with `n' so that `agre' became `agne') and it read: "Let the woman advance to the womb of fire" (*i.e.*, Arohantu janayo yomin *agne* cf. Mangalwadi 1987). The replacement of `r' with `n' turned `to the altar' into `to the fire' which converted `widow-marriage' into `widow-burning'. Max Muller rightly describes this vicious replacement as "the most flagrant instance of what can be done by an unscrupulous priesthood" (*ibid.*).

It was a rare moment in Hindu history that a crusader like Raja Ram Mohan Roy vowed to fight against this most sinful custom.

Started in 1818, his campaign achieved historic success on 5 Dec., 1829 when Lord Bentick passed his Edict banning widow-burning throughout British India. By 1862 sati was banned throughout India, including the native states. In spite of this, stray incidents of widow-burning continued to occur from time to time. Roop Kanwar's consignment to flames on 4 Sept., 1987 at Deorala in Rajasthan is the most recent public incidence of widow-burning. In spite of incidents like these and a great deal of obscurantism around (cf. Ind. Exp., 13 April 1988), it would not be wrong to say that widow-burning stopped (almost totally) by 1862 itself.

Once widow-burning was abolished, the number of widows suddenly shot up. In a few decades the population of widows, including a large number of child-widows, ran into millions. The widow-marriage act of 1856 and the Hindu Code Bill of 1954 have not achieved any tangible results. Besides, obscurantist slogans like 'once a widow, always a widow', further add to the ever-increasing widow-population. Looking back over a century and a half, we clearly realize that the legal abolition of widow-burning was one thing, while the legal amelioration of widowhood is quite another. The death of the husband even today means for an average Hindu wife a further worsening of her position in the family.

For a Hindu wife widowhood traditionally means one of three things: immediate death (whether murder or suicide), life long condemnation to segregation and drudgery, and subjection to clandestine sexual exploitation by the males of the family and/or locality. It is probable that in days of old widows at times themselves preferred a painful death to a dreary life of "hunger, scorn and domestic servitude" (Basham 1967 : 190). Forced to refrain from all that was good, healthy and auspicious in life, the widow had to have her head clean shaven as a punishment for her past sins causing the death of her husband and as a vow of chastity to ensure reunion with her husband in her next life. Presumably large chunks of Hindus believed in the cathartic efficacy of the endless persecution and torture of widows. Always watched by the parents and relatives of her dead lord, lest she broke her vows and imperilled the dead man's spiritual welfare, and shunned as unlucky even by women and servants of the family, the life of the widow was (and is) miserable in the extreme. In the wake of the public uproar against the Deorala outrage, a woman social worker from Rajasthan told a journalist: "At the very moment a dead man's body is removed from the house for crema tion, a black sheet is drawn around the widow. For a year she is not to be seen by males or married women. She sits on the floor within this black cubicle, with knees pulled to the chest and the head touching the knees. For ablutions and bath she leaves the cubicle at night. Saltless food is brought to her. Before a meal, she must cry because food is the basis of life, and as a widow she is deemed to have lost her moral right to life after her husband's death. She must cry before eating, also to express her guilt" (Singh 1987). Sitting on knees twelve hours a day, forced to live on insipid and scanty food, shunned by people and surrounded by so much condemnation, the widow soon loses her will to live, takes ill and succumbs to death in a few months or years.

The Hindu widow, on the one hand, is ostracized and required to observe a vow of continence and chastity, while on the other, she is often seduced or sujected to sexual exploitation by starving males around. The widow, like the unwed woman, is forced to contraception and abortion. In case, she bears children, they are illegitimate and they make her more scornful but not less vulnerable. It is astonishing that the sexual abuse of widows is sometimes recommended or appreciated. The *Kamasutra* describes a widow as a sexual object. As there is no regular marriage for the widow, she is exorted to ally herself to a seeker after pleasures (bhogin) and make the best of her life. Vatsyayana's term for such a widow is *punarbhu*, that is, 'a woman allied to a man for a second time'. He places the punarbhu between a maiden (kanya) and a prostitute (Veshya). She is just a mistress. She is allowed a degree of freedom unknown to the wife but she is also denied the privileges of wifehood (cf. De 1969 : 97-98 & Chakladar 1976 : 181-182). How unfortunate it is that most widows are still shunned and sought for wrong reasons and yet they cannot enjoy even the kind of 'acceptability' that was available to Vatsyayana's contemporaries !

4

STRATEGIES OF EXPLOITATION

4.1 Tightening the Grip

"Day and night women must be kept in dependence by the males of the family."

—*Manusmriti*

The religious literature of the Hindus consists mainly of the Vedas, Brahmanas, Aranyakas, Upanishads, Puranas, Dharmashastras or Smritis, Grihyasutras and the Itihasas. Each of the four Vedas (generally believed to have been written before one thousand BC) is a collection of hymns and oblational verses called *Samhitas*. The earliest and foremost collection of such sacred hymns and oblational verses is known as the *Rig-Veda*. The *Yajur-Veda* is a collection of sacred formulas (*mantras*) and sacrificial verses, the *Sama-Veda* is a collection of melodic recitations and oblational verses, and the *Atharva-Veda* is a collection of hymns, magic spells and incantations. Most of the Vedic hymns extol deities who personify natural and cosmic phenomena such as fire, sun, rain, war and divine authority. These hymns have three notable characteristics: (i) They extol a number of male gods such as Agni, Varuna, Indra, Rudra, Soma and Surya but the last one seems to be the most important. He is also called Vishnu and Savitar. The most sacred verse of the *Rig-Veda*, 'Gayatri', is called the mother of the Veds (Veda-mata) and is addressed to the Sun-god. It says: "Let us dwell on the glory of the sun-god so that he may inspire our minds". Every member of the three higher castes, Brahmana, Kshatriya and Vaishya, is required to recite this mantra twice a day. (ii) The Vedic people called themselves 'Aryans'. Throughout the Vedas they are depicted as constantly fighting against the snub-nosed and dark-skinned 'Dasyus' (or 'Dasas'). (iii) The Vedas do not contain any significant female god (cf. Roy & Gidwani 1984 : 126-27, 1985 : 274-75 & 1986 : 262).

Vedic Samhitas are followed by elaborate expositions intended for the instruction and guidance of sacrificial priests and later scholars. These expositions are broadly known as *Brahmanas*, usually divided into three parts, the first part being the *Brahmana* proper, the second part being the *Aranyaka* and the third part being the *Upanishad*. Most of the *Brahmanas* are now lost. Of the thirteen that survive, two are attached to the *Rig-Veda*, *Aitareya* or *Ashvalayana* and *Kaushitaki* or *Shankhyayana*, two are attached to the *Yajur-Veda*: *Taittiriya* and *Shatapatha*, one to the *Atharva-Veda*: *Gopatha*, and eight to the *Sama-Veda* : *Panchavinsha* or *Tandya*, *Shadavinsha*, *Mantra*, *Talavakara* or *Jaiminiya*, *Samvidhana*, *Daivata*, *Arsheya* and *Vansha*. Of the *Aranyakas* only four are extant: *Brihada*, *Taittiriya*, *Aitareya*, and *Kaushitaki*. They are appended to the *Shatapatha-Brahmana*, *Taittiriya-Brahmana*, *Aitareya-Brahmana* and *Kaushitaki-Brahmana*, respectively. These Aranyakas contain directions for the rituals of the Brahmanas as well as philosophical explanations of the nature of God. As the concluding portions of the Vedas and appendices to the Aranyakas, the Upanishads (*i.e.*, 'Secret Instructions') are also called *Vedanta*. A large number of Upanishads are extant but only thirteen of them are considered genuine and important, all of which are assigned to a period preceding six hundred BC. They are: *Ishavashya*, *Kena*, *Katha*, *Prashna*, *Mundaka*, *Mandukya*, *Taittiriya*, *Aitareya*, *Chhandogya*, *Brihadaranyaka*, *Kaushitaki*, *Maitrayaniya* and *Shvetashvara* (cf. Hume 1949 & Maladevan 1975).

The basic springs of Indian Philosophy, the Upanishads are sublime philosophical speculations upon the nature of God. They are the earliest records of the Aryan attempt to construe the world of experience as a rational whole and they have continued to be widely accepted as authoritative documents of the Aryan philosophy of life. All later texts are formulated in conformity with the central thrust of the Upanishads. Paul Deussen's remark is noteworthy: "To every Indian Brahmana the Upanishads are what the New Testament is to Christians" (cited in Hume 1949). We should also remember that the *Samhitas*, the *Brahmanas*, the *Aranyakas* and the *Upanishads* are collectively known as the *Shruti, i.e.*, 'that which is spoken and heard', the revelations or the Holy scriptures, as they are believed to have been spoken by the Absolute himself (*i.e.*, God) and heard and remembered by the holy ones. These scriptures are said to have been orally transmitted from generation to generation till such time as they were committed to writing.

The Dharmashastras are those religious texts which lay down civil and criminal laws and the inventory of rights and duties of the people. To distinguish the texts from the commentaries attached to them, the Dharmashastras are generally called *Smritis*, that is, Law Books or Codes. The actual number of these Smritis is uncertain but twenty of them are widely known and generally accepted as authoritative. They are named after their authors *viz.* : Manu, Atri, Vishnu, Harita, Yajnavalkya, Ushanas, Angiras, Yama, Apastamba, Samvarta, Dakshya, Gautama, Shatatapa, Vashishtha, Vyasa, Shankha and Likhita. Posterior to the *Shruti*, the *Smritis* are looked upon as the foundations of popular Hinduism. As the Smritis deal with the social life of the people, the *Grihyasutras* (*i.e.*, 'Aphorisms on the observances of domestic life') spell out the rights and duties of the people for their day-to-day life in the family. Thirteen Grihyasutras are generally regarded as authentic. They are also named after their authors *viz*: Sankhyayana, Ashvalayana, Gobhila, Khadira, Paraskara, Apastamba, Hiranyakeshin, Baudhayana, Manava, Kathaka, Bhardvaja, Vaikhanasa and Kaushika.

The Puranas (literally 'Ancient Traditions') are those religious texts which teach religion, cosmogony and laws through an elaborate network of tales and legends. According to the *Amarkosha* (the lexicon), every *Purana* should ideally deal with five subjects: creation (*Sarga*), cycles of dissolutions and renewals of the world (*Pratisarga*), genealogy of gods and seers (*Vansha*), the great periods, each of which is headed by the primal ancestor (Manu) of the human race (*Manvantarani*) and the history of the great dynasties whose origins are ultimately traced back to the sun and the moon (*Vanshanucharita*). However, not all the Puranas deal with these five subjects nor are all of them confined only to these subjects. Some scarcely touch upon any one of these subjects, while some contain much more than these subjects. Like the *Smritis* and the *Grihyasutras*, the *Puranas* have continued to be indispensable to the mainstream (*i.e.*, Brahmanic) Hindu thought through the ages. They are traditionally believed to be eighteen in number, all composed by Vyasa. They are: *Brahma, Padma, Vishnu, Shiva, Bhagavata* or *Shrimad-Bhagavata, Naradiya, Markandeya, Agni, Bhavishya* or *Bhavishyat, Vaivarta, Linga, Varaha, Skanda, Vamana, Kurma, Matsya, Garuda* and *Brahmananda*. Contemporaneous with the Smritis and the Grihyasutras, the Puranas may have been written between 300 BC and 500 AD.

Closely allied with the Puranas are the two epics which are sometimes called *Itihasas* ('histories' or 'tales of thus it happened'). Mainly concerned with the two great dynasties, the lunar and the solar, the *Mahabharata* and the *Ramayana* respectively also present interesting accounts of the socio-religious and political life of people in ancient India. They are literary classics no doubt but the average Hindu sees them as part of his scriptures. They certainly contain a good deal of religious thought and may fittingly be considered indispensable to the sacred literature of the Hindus. In a sense, the two classical monuments of secular writing, Kautilya's *Arthashastra* and Vatsyayana's *Kamasutra* are also religious texts. They are clearly far more liberal than the general run of orthodox writings but it is undeniable that they also share the central tenets of doctrinal thinking on almost all important matters.

As all the principal texts of Hindu orthodoxy are written by men, it is not surprising that they lay down guidelines, precepts, laws and rituals which are male-centred. Religion or dharma, for all these texts, means the way of life which suits an Aryan male and enables him to establish and maintain his indisputable sway over the female. It is no mere coincidence that all these texts prescribe in a chorus more or less the same set of duties and obligations for women. Nor is it an accident that these texts in one way or another seek to confine women to sex and drudgery; that they indulge in the ruthless vilification of women; that they discover in women the genius of evil. The entire corpus of Hindu literature from the *Rig-Veda* to the *Kamasutra*—should be seen as a careful stockpiling of strategies to convert woman into a machine which can be used or abused at the pleasure of the male and without any regard to her working capacity. Every succeeding text of this gigantic corpus drives a fresh nail into her coffin so that the woman who appears before us at the time of the earliest Perso-Arabic invasion of India is a mere lump of flesh punctured on all sides and in all respects. The history of the Perso-Arabic rule in India begins with a profusely bleeding woman, standing alone in a crowded and hostile city. There is no help, no succour, and no consolation in this city for this pathetic female. Everyone around pokes her in her wounds, throws stones at her and makes a laughing-stock of her. Punctured, spurned and ridiculed, the lonely female loses all faith, all hope, all purpose. She has no use for God or Religion or Ethics. Each of these binds her, tortures her, and scoffs at her.

No other history presents to an impartial reader so shocking a record of the increasing colonization of woman as the Hindu history does in its long stride from the Rig-Vedic times to the Perso-Arabic conquest of India. The society depicted in doctrinnaire literature reflects a strong system of patriarchal values and a rigid code of conduct for women. Institutions, practices and beliefs like marriage, prohibition of widow-marriage, widow-burning, the son's ability to deliver parents from hell, the undesirability of daughters, the impurity of women during menstruation, pregnancy and child-birth, the physical correction of women, religious values attached to the gift of daughters in marriage, the three aims of marriage, disqualifying girls from religious rites and samskaras and identification of women with Shudras are some of the devices used to force women into the systematic and ever-tightening grip of men. It is not only that women have no share in the social economy or the body politic; they are pushed into endless slavery again and again. The husband is the absolute master and the ultimate judge of his wife. His control over his wife's duties and obligations towards him is despotic. From the nuptial hymns in the Vedas it appears that a girl is transferred from the father to the husband like a commodity. While formally releasing her from his authority and transferring her to the power of the husband, the Rig-Vedic *pater familias* tells his daughter at the conclusion of the wedding ceremony: "I set thee free from hence, but not from thence : I place thee there firmly bound" (cf. Thomas 1964 : 51). The *Manusmriti* decrees: "Day and night women must be kept in dependence by the males of the family .... her father protects her in childhood, her husband protects her in youth and her sons protect her in old age; a woman is never fit for independence" (IX : 2-3). The *Mahabharata* repeats this decree almost verbatim: "There is no independence of woman; women are indeed dependent: the father protects a woman in her childhood, the husband in youth, the sons in old age, a woman does not deserve independence" (Banerji 1976 : 23 : 14 & 18). Likewise, in the *Ramacharitamanasa* Rama, the best of men (*Purushottama*), confides to his faithful younger brother, Lakshamana, at a time when both of them are lamenting Sita's abduction by Ravana: "As the borders of the field are broken asunder by a heavy downpour, so is a woman spoilt by independence" (Kishkindha Kanda : Chaupai 15). One finds it difficult to believe that even a secular text like the *Arthashastra*, written at a time when brothels were managed by the State and regularly visited by married men, should ordain: "If a woman is found conversing with another man in a suspicious place, then a Chandala has to give her five lashes on each side of her body" (cf. Basham 1967 : 181). The worst part of such multi-layered confinement of woman relates to the philosophy that treats her, at once, as a slave and a storehouse of evil.

The *Maitrayani Saṃhita* places woman on a par with dice and drink and describes her as one of the major evils in society, while the *Shatapatha Brahmana* ordains that a wife must take her meals after her husband has finished his, that she must not disagree with him even under grave provocation and that the disobedient wife should be taught obedience by using physical force, if necessary (cf. Thomas 1964 : 58-59).

The Aryan obsession with conjugal fidelity is never applicable to the husband. It is only the wife who has to guarantee absolute devotion to the husband even if he hobnobs with other women. In a nuptial verse in the *Paraskara Grihyasutra* the husband vows: "With thy breath I join my breath, with thy flesh my flesh and with thy skin my skin" (cf. Shastri 1969 : 179) and yet he is not prepared to take back his wife once she is abducted or raped by someone. A moral wreck is adorable as a husband but a single blot forced on a wife by another wreck is considered fatal for her. She is immediately spurned by her husband and family. A woman once captured or raped is reduced to hanging between suicide and defilement for the rest of her life. It is not for nothing that not a single woman forced into a Muslim harem in India ever tried to return home. The story of the queen of Bhima (Gujarat) is highly instructive. Kamaladevi was abducted by and married to Alla-ud-din of Khilji. She not only reconciled herself to her destiny, she conspired with her new husband to have her own daughter abducted and married to the Crown Prince (cf. Altekar 1956 : 310-12).

4.2 Mandatory Husband-Worship

"Commend me to my kind lord."

—*Othello (V : II : 126)*

A man needs a woman just as a master needs a slave. From the master's point of view, it would be sheer absurdity to try to find out whether someone likes to be a slave or to be a slave in a certain way or for a certain period of time. Similarly, from the man's point of view, it would really be ridiculous to try to ascertain whether a girl likes to marry him or marry him in a certain fashion or for a specified period of time. As someone inferior but desirable, the slave or the wife has to be acquired and owned by a man who is going to be her master for ever. It is entirely a man's privilege (so he thinks) to decide to acquire and own a woman as a wife or otherwise and for as long as he pleases. In an equation like this, the man is the master and the woman the slave. It is the master's prerogative to determine the form and function of the relationship whether it is marriage or any other sort of bond. As a matter of fact, this man-woman relationship, particularly as a marriage in Hinduism, has often been used as a powerful tool to possess and use woman for a variety of individual and social functions which do not require the participation of her heart and soul or mind and spirit.

Defined and structured by chauvinistic males, all patricentric and acquisitive marriages treat women as slaves who have not only to put up with their thoroughly possessive, dehumanizing and crippling husbands but also to revere and adore them as a matter of daily routine and as the only way to salvation. Wholly uprooted from their home and parents and completely chained up to the whims of their autocratic husbands, brides are exorted again and again through endless doctrination to strictly abide by the rules of the game euphemistically labelled as "marriage". Once married, these brides gradually come to realize at their own expense that men are born to rule and women to obey. The divine decree enunciated in the *Genesis* very clearly tells the wife: "thy desire shall be to thy husband and he shall rule over thee" (3 : 16). The Quranic injunction leaves no room for interpretation: "Men are incharge of women, because Allah has made the one of them excel the other. ... So good women are the obedient" (Pickthall 1924 : IV : 34). In the concluding incantation of the marriage ceremony, the Rig-Vedic bridegroom assures his bride :

"I take thy hand for good fortune that thou mayst attain old age with me, thy husband; the gods have given thee to me that I may be the master of a household" (cf. Shastri 1969 : 13).

Patriarchal traditions of thought consistently project an ideal wife as a woman who always and ungrudgingly carries out the instructions of her husband, whatever be these instructions. The last wish of dying Desdemona is to be commended to her 'kind lord'. In life Desdemona assures Othello: "I wonder in my soul/What you could ask me, that I should deny" (III : III : 69-70). Desdemona's commitment to Othello is absolute: "whatever you be, I am obedient" (III : III : 90). A wife, Desdemona or any other, cannot think of life without her husband. In Milton's Epic, the first woman has this to say about the first man: "So dear I love him, that with him all deaths/I could endure, without him live no life" (*Paradise Lost* : IX : 832-833). At a moment of sheer blissfulness, Eve assures Adam : "My author and disposer, what thou bidst/Unargued I obey; so God ordains/God is thy law; thou mine: to know no more/Is woman's happiest knowledge and her praise" (IV : 635-638). An ancient Greek treatise on `Advice to a young lady', mischievously attributed to a woman named Perictione (not Plato's mother), says: "A woman must bear all that her husband bears, whether he be unlucky or sins out of ignorance, whether he be sick or drunk or sleeps with other women. ... A woman must preserve the law and not emulate men. And she must endure her husband's temper, stinginess, complaining, jealousy, abuse, and anything else peculiar to his nature. And she will deal with all of his characteristics in such a way as is congenial to him by being discrete. For a woman who is affectionate to her husband and treats him in an agreeable way is a harmonious woman and one who loves her whole household and makes everyone in it well disposed. ... And if her husband thinks something is sweet, she will think so too; or if he thinks something is bitter, she will agree with him. Otherwise, she will be out of tune with her whole universe" (cf. Pomeroy 1975 : 135-36).

Far more rigidly defined and firmly entrenched than any other patriarchal system, Hinduism has such meticulous and demanding views on the duties and obligations of a wife as no other set of socio-religious beliefs can ever have. From the beginning it has been dinned into the ears of Indo-Aryan wife that her whole world is centred in her husband, that he is the highest stage (*ashrama*) of her life and her only place of pilgrimage (*tirtha*), and that therefore she ought to consider him, as an inviolable duty (*dharma*), her only Lord and God (*Ishvara*). The majority of sacred Hindu texts dealing with husband-wife relationship ordain again and again that a wife must associate herself only with her husband's religious acts and that she must not do anything for her own spiritual benefit except the adoration of her lord. The *Matsya Purana*, for example, enjoins on a wife that she should worship her husband as God (cf. Baig 1976 : 10). The Law Books explicitly state that a wife's duty it is to wait on her husband, to fetch and carry for him, to rub his feet, to rise before him and to eat and sleep after him (cf. Basham 1967 : 182). The famous Law-giver, Atri, lays down that all that a wife has to do to attain religious merit is "to wash the feet of her husband and drink the water" (cf. Thomas 1964 : 222). The *Manusmriti* defines a wife's duty in these words : "Though destitute of virtue or seeking pleasure (elsewhere), devoid of good qualities, (yet) a husband must be worshipped as a god by a faithful wife. No sacrifice, no vow, no fast must be performed by women apart from their husbands, if a wife obeys her husband, she will for that (reason alone) be exalted to heaven" (III : 154-155). It further says that a virtuous wife who "never slights her lord in thought, word or deed is blessed but one who violates her duty to her husband enters the womb of a jackal after death and is perpetually tortured in hell" (III : 164-166).

The *Mahabharata* is a puzzling book as far as its views on women and womanly obligations are concerned. It is full of contradictory laws, customs, morals and practices. Polygyny, levirate marriage, pre-marital maternity, extra-marital maternity, wife-sharing, marriage by capture, marriage by purchase, marriage by contract and the like are mentioned with approval and yet tediously long sermons on wifely duties are put into the mouths of great wives. Wives themselves are made to lecture on the duties and constraints of a wife mainly with a view to carrying conviction with the readers/listeners as well as showing that these duties and obligations are chosen by women themselves and not imposed on them by the males of the family. An illustrious wife like Shakuntala, for instance, assures her husband: "The wife is the constant companion of her husband; in exile she follows him into the forest, in adversity she is always beside him. In death the devoted woman joins him in the grim regions of Yama" (cf. Thomas 1964 : 151-152). Shakuntala's foster father says goodbye to her with the following instruction : "Be friendly towards the ladies of the palace/never be angry with your husband, no matter what happens. In everything be humble. These qualities make a woman; those without them are like black sheep in their families". To this Gautami adds: "A bride needs nothing more" (Lal 1964 : 44-45). In her speech on this topic, Shiva's spouse, Uma, says: "A woman who conducts herself by prescribed ordinances is truly chaste and religious: she should observe all the vows of her husband, should wait upon him and serve him as her god; surrendering her own will to that of her husband, she should always appear cheerful and should not, even in thought, entertain any man except her husband. Devotion to the husband is the great virtue of a married woman; it is her penance and salvation. The husband is the god a woman has. He is her friend and refuse. Women have no greater refuse, no greater gods than their husbands. The husband's grace and heaven are alike to a woman. If a husband, poor, diseased, distressed, fallen among foes or afflicted by the curse of a Brahmin, were to command his wife to do anything that is improper or unrighteous or anything that might even lead to loss of life itself, the wife should, without hesitation, accomplish it bearing in mind the code of conduct by the law of distress" (Thomas 1964 : 152-153). Satyabhama, one of the favourite wives of Krishna, asks Draupadi : "How do you manage to please your husbands so well?" Draupadi's reply is as follows : "Let me tell you what my ways are : I put aside my ego, I try not to be jealous, I strive to be modest and gracious, I neither beg nor eat nor sleep till my husband has; till, in fact, my servants have. When he returns from the town or the forest, I have water and seat ready for him. I do the household chores, cook and clean at the right time, I don't dawdle at the gate, I don't laugh unless the joke is really good. I see that things which don't appeal to him don't appeal to me either. A husband is a god to his wife. ... A husband gives us children, a husband gives us beds and sheets, dresses and perfumes and garlands, even fame in society and happiness. ... When he orders a maid to get something, get up and fetch it yourself. When he is at the gate, be ready to give him your seat and offer to wash his feet. Shun his enemies. Don't be careless and frivolous when other men are present; be silent about what you think; don't be alone too much even with your sons. Avoid women who drink, shout, steal, gorge and gossip. And learn how to make yourself attractive with ornaments, perfumes and unguents" (Lal 1980 : 158-159).

A number of husbands in the *Mahabharata* are polygynous and libidinous, often with a sense of bravado, but verses like the following enjoin on married women to be loyal and worshipful towards their husbands: "O Yudhishtira, she always eats the remnants of her husband's food, and acting in accordance with the husband's mind, looks upon the husband as god.

That woman is pious whose longing for objects of desire, enjoyment, prosperity and happiness, is not so much as for the husband.

Of a woman there is no sacrifice, no *shraddha*, nor fast. Her *dharma* is the service of the husband; thereby she wins heaven.

That woman is devoted to the husband who, though harshly spoken to and looked at with a cruel eye, has a delightful face towards her husband.

Whatever, O Princess, the husband says, be it lawful or unlawful, should be done accordingly by the wife; those who are versed in *dharma* say so.

It is the highest tribute to a woman that she obeys the husband; she gets the highest state before the husband" (Banerji 1976 : 111-113).

Considered from the sociological point of view, the *Ramayana* is a far more conservative book than the *Mahabharata* in its philosophy of man-woman relationships. Valmiki stands for absolute dependence of women upon men. He can't even think of any degree of independence for women. He is there to reinforce the doctrine that a woman has no salvation except through her husband who is a god. On the eve of his departure to the forest Sita appeals to her husband to be allowed to accompany him. "My Lord", she pleads with Rama, "father, mother, son, brother, daughter-in-law, all of them reap the consequences of their own acts; it is wife alone that shares in the fate of her husband. ... Not to speak of other relations, woman cannot save herself: husband is her mainstay in this world as well as in the next. A woman should always take shelter at the feet of her husband, though he may be deprived of heaven. ... take me with you as the travellers take the remnants of their drink along with them" (Sen 1976 : 165-66).

The *Ramayana* abounds in anecdotes which mention a number of elderly and pious women lecturing on the duties of a wife. One of such venerable women is Kausalya, Dasaratha's eldest queen and Sita's mother-in-law. Reminding Sita of her duties towards Rama, particularly during his forest life, Kausalya tells Sita: "My daughter, the woman ... who fails to serve her husband in adversity is reckoned as unchaste, ... Fickle minded women do not care for rank or lineage; they are worn over by ornaments or dress; they are ungrateful, and have little regard for righteousness, and they never acknowledge their faults even when pointed out. But those who are obedient to their superiors, truthful and pure, regard their husbands as the supreme agents for moral and spiritual well-being" (*ibid.*, p. 187).

Despite her unwavering loyalty and exemplary goodness to her husband, Sita is banished by her king husband in the most cruel circumstances. But Sita's valedictory address reads like this: "O Lakshmana! Certainly I would have drowned myself in the Ganga if Rama's child was not within my womb. ... But let me tell you ... tell my royal lord that I am thoroughly devoted to him and my character is stainless. ... He is the highest goal of my life. ... Her husband to a woman is her highest lord, friend and preceptor. A woman should even sacrifice her insignificant life for the good of the husband" (*ibid.*, pp. 427-28).

The celebrated author of the *Ramacharitamanasa*, however, remains to this day, perhaps the most orthodox Hindu writer on conjugal obligations of the wife. The Bible of the Hindi-speaking Hindus, the greatest Epic in Hindi literature and the most popular version of the Rama-Ravana legend, the *Ramacharitamanasa* contains God's plenty, as far as obscurantism regarding wifely duties is concerned. The rigidity of its doctrinaire prescriptions of what a married woman must and must not do is matched only by the ruthlessness of its denigration of women as a class. One can easily cite any number of extracts from the text to illustrate such generalizations. But within the limited scope of this study, it may be sufficient to cite just a few relating to Sita and Parvati, the two greatest women in Hindu history.

Abandoned by her husband and rejected by her father, Sati (Shiva's spouse) commits suicide by immolating herself in fire raged through her yogic powers. She is reborn as Parvati (or Girija), the Himalaya's daughter. But once again she has to do penance for thousands of years to regain Shiva as her husband. Tulasidasa's description of the penance defies critical evaluation: "Uma [*i.e.*,

Parvati] laid on her heart the feet of the lord of her life, and went to the forest and began to practise penance. Her delicate frame was not made for penance, yet she thought on the feet of her lord and abandoned all delights. Day by day her devotion to his feet was renewed, absorbed in penance, she took no heed of her body. For a thousand years she ate roots and fruits, and then she spent a hundred years living on vegetables. For some days she fed on water and air; for some days she kept strict fast. Then for three thousand years she ate dry leaves that fell to the ground from wood-apple. Then she gave up eating even the dry leaves. ..." When Brahma saw that Uma's body was emaciated by penance, his solemn tones were heard in heaven: "Hearken, daughter of the king of mountains! your desire has born fruit". Rama also requests Shiva to marry Parvati. There are further entreaties made by Parvati's mother. Finally, he agrees to marry Parvati but she has to make this declaration: "I am your servant in thought, word and deed" (Hill 1952 : 39-53).

Sita's parents are as apologetic about their daughter and as solicitous to please their son-in-law as Parvati's parents are. With folded hands and bowed heads, Janaka, his wife and his brother beg Dasaratha and Rama to treat Sita with "Compassion" (*ibid.*, p. 146). Much after the marriage, Rama, is ordered into exile for fourteen years. He is getting ready to go. Sita wants to accompany him. Rama does not want to take her with him.

Pleading with Rama why he should take her with him, Sita says: "Lord of my life, home of compassion, fair giver of bliss and wise. ... Heaven without you would be hell! Mother, father, sisters, and dear brothers, the loved ones of the family and the circle of friends, the mother and father of her lord, the guru, relatives and helpers, fair sons and noble who bring happiness, nay all there is of love and kinship, O my husband, is to a wife, without her lord, a grief that burns even more fiercely than the sun. ... Lord, without you pleasure would be sickness, ornaments a burden, the world as the tortures of the god of death. ... As a body bereft of life, as a river that has no water, so, lord, is a wife without her husband. With you, my husband, all is happiness" (*ibid.*, p. 188). Incidentally, the last lines here share Eve's feelings to Adam in *Paradise Lost* (IV : 639-40):

"With thee conversing I forget all time, all seasons and their change, all please alike."

Moved by her entreaties, Rama takes her with him on that long journey. When he reaches the river, he asks her to get back home. But Sita sticks to her resolve and says again: "Can a shadow exist apart from its substance?" (*ibid.*, p. 201). In the forest Sita visits a number of holy men and women with Rama and Lakshmana. In course of time she meets Anusuiya, the wife of Atri. Now Anusuiya, one of the most revered women in the epic, educates Sita on what a devoted wife should do: "Hearken, Princess! Mother, father and brother are all friendly helpers, but the happiness they give is limited; there is no limit, Sita, to the happiness a husband can afford, and base is the wife who does not pay him reverence. ... Though a husband be old, diseased, stupid or poor, blind, deaf, bad tempered, or in great distress yet if the wife treats him with disrespect, she will suffer all the tortures of hell. This is her one religious duty, her one vow and observance: devotion in thought, word and deed to her husband's feet. ... The wife who honestly fulfils her wifely duty wins salvation with the greatest ease; but she who is disloyal to her husband, whenever she be born, becomes a widow in her early youth. Woman is inherently impure, but if she serve her husband faithfully, she wins highest bliss" (*ibid.*, pp. 297-298).

Coming across injunctions, admonitions and decrees such as those referred to in the foregoing paragraphs, one would like to know if there is anything like this on husbandly duties towards the wife. It cannot be a matter of chance that there is nothing like that in the *Ramacharitamanasa* or perhaps in any other Hindu text. The husband has no duties to his wife, whatsoever. Even secular thinkers and writers do not require husbands to be dutiful or affectionate to their wives. They do instead toe the obscurantist line on wifely duties. Vatsyayana for example, decrees that a virtuous woman should "act in conformity with his wishes as if he were a divine being, and with his consent should take upon herself the whole care of his family" (Archer 1963 : 197). Elaborating his views on the subject, Vatsyayana says: "When she hears the sound of his footsteps coming home, she should at once get up and be ready to do whatever he may command her, and she either orders her female servants to wash his feet or wash them herself. ... She should always sit down after him and get up before him and should never awaken him when he is asleep. ... She should avoid bad expressions, sulky looks, speaking aside, standing in the doorway, and looking at passers-by, conversing in the pleasure groves, and remaining in a lonely place for a long time; and finally, she should always keep her body, her teeth, her hair, and everything belonging to her tidy, sweet and clean" (p. 198. Take note of the striking similarity that this passage has with Draupadi's speech cited earlier). A tireless advocate of male revelry and licentiousness, Vatsyayana prescribes that the wife must be wholly devoted to her husband while the husband is free to marry again if he is unhappy with his living wife or if he is looking for new pastures" (p. 201). He further lays down that "from the very beginning, a wife should endeavour to attract the heart of her husband by showing to him continually her devotion, her good temper and her wisdom. If, however, she bears him no children, she should herself tell her husband to marry another woman. And when the second wife is married and brought to the house, the first wife should give her a position superior to her own ... and should not mind all the husband's favour being given to her" (p. 202). In matters relating to the duties of a wife, Vatsyayana is clearly as orthodox as a Valmiki or a Vyasa:

4.3 The Proprietary Attitude

> According to the laws of Romulus "husbands ruled over their wives as possessions."
>
> —*Dionysius of Halicarnasus*

Men have not moved very far from Manu's or Aristotle's notion of femininity. Aristotle held the view that women lacked many qualities and were deficient in many respects: "We should regard the female nature as afflicted with natural defectiveness" (cf. Amundsen 1971 : 114). For the same reason Manu decrees: "A girl, young woman or a matron must do nothing according to her own pleasure even in her own dwelling place"(cf. Sengupta 1976 : 67). Allegedly devoid of intelligence and the power of judgement, the sons of Manu still believe that women need a good deal of leading by the nose. Not too long ago, US Vice-President Agnew had this revelation to make: "Three things have been difficult to tame—the ocean, fools and women. We may soon be able to tame the ocean; fools and women will take a little longer" (cited in Amundsen 1971 : 114). It is no wonder therefore that women are still treated as domesticated animals by a vast majority of males and judged according to the work they do. And the work assigned to them is seldom in recognition of their ability or choice.

In India, more than anywhere else in the civilized world, women are still made to work like voiceless slaves. They are obliged to provide their bodies, give children and faithfully offer unpaid services on a non-leave, non-stop basis to maintain the home (cf. Baig 1976 : 31). The point being made here is not that women elsewhere live blissfully. According to a survey report published in a Women's Lib Book, working women in the West have to put in 96 hours of hard work a week or 14 hours day, while working men have to put in only 40 hours a week, that is, less than 6 hours a day (*ibid.*, p. 36). These women do what only slaves are required to do in a barbaric system. A woman writer puts it so aptly: "Millions of our female species conglomerate behind millions of sinks where they wash millions of nappies a million times over" (Trench 1971). Statistics like these clearly illustrate the unenviable position Western women are in. But the point at issue here is that if we look at the position of women in India from the Western point of view, we can easily realize the abjectness of their plight. For a majority of Indian women, there are not even "nappies and sinks", sometimes not even water, and yet they have to work without end, without rest, without remuneration and without appreciation.

The doctrine of the perpetual tutelage of woman, as advocated and practised in India, is derived from the general male consensus that women have to be owned as possessions and treated as slaves because they are allegedly both inferior and vulnerable. Many ancients were convinced that as they were deficient in understanding, judgement and virtue, they required to be controlled and led through in every sphere of life. The society depicted in the *Iliad* and the *Odyssey* viewed women, symbolically as well as literally, as 'property'. Dionysius of Halicarnasus, the remarkable chronicler of the reign of Augustus, explicitly states that according to the laws of the time wives were treated as "possessions" (cf. Pomeroy 1976 : 153). A modern scholar points out that in ancient Greece and Rome, woman was defined "not as a person but as a thing" (Kidwai 1976 : 4). In India, Valmiki's society considered women as vicious, untrustworthy and devoid of the power of judgement and therefore treated them as "chattels" (cf. Sharma 1971 : 109, 110 & 115). With the establishment of the priestly oligarchy and caste-system, mainly owing to the law books, the status of women deteriorated so much that the shades of the prison-house began to close in on them and they came to be subjected to a form of feudal ownership of men (cf. Sengupta

1974 : 66). As rulers and owners of their daughters and wives, Hindu males in post-Puranic India loved to enjoy their new privileges and prize their new possessions in a way and to an extent that their ancestors could never do in any earlier period nor could their contemporaries claim in any other part of the world.

A Midsummer Night's Dream refers to a very interesting law among the ancient Athenians. Hermia wants to marry Lysander. Her father, Ageus, wants her to marry Demetrius. Hermia does not agree. Ageus, therefore, comes to Theseus, Duke of Athens, and makes the following appeal:"

"I beg the ancient privilege of Athens:
As she is mine, I may dispose of her,
which shall be either to this gentleman
Or to her death, according to our Law
Immediately provided in that case" (I : I : 41-45).

The sole owner and master of his daughter, the father, whether Athenian or Indian, ancient or modern, has (or he believes) a rightful claim to the disposing of his daughter. Once a girl is formally handed over to a man as her husband, she becomes the 'property' of her husband. Such beliefs and customs enable the father or husband to stake and exercise 'his right to property' in regard to his daughter or wife, as the case may be. This is the proprietary attitude to woman. The proprietary philosophy derives from the male's refusal to see or recognize any shred of individuality or humanity in the female. This philosophy converts a human female into a thing, possession or object which is definitionally incapable of self-awareness and, therefore, ineligible for any right to self-determination.

Several customs and practices traditionally define a Hindu woman as a thing. According to Hindu texts, three values are related to girls. A girl is for gift, sale or abandonment (cf. Baig 1976 : 89). Vatsyayana quite earnestly advises parents and relatives of a marriageable girl to array her in a smart dress and to take her to wherever there may be a gathering of people so that they may find a suitable bridegroom for her. A marriageable girl, Vatsyayana explicitly states, is "of the nature of an article of trade" (cf. Chakaladar 1976 : 123). As in Greece, girls in India were frequently abandoned, killed, sold or gifted to temples. Sold or gifted girls were to become slaves, wives or prostitutes. Notorious customs like polygyny, prostitution, concubinage and wife-sharing emanated from the perception of woman as a barter, as an article of trade. It boggles the mind to read that passage in the *Mahabharata* where Pandu coerces his wife, the famous Kunti, into coupling with other men to beget sons, in spite of his awareness of the universal and age-old Hindu insistence on the marital chastity of wives. Pandu has no qualms of conscience when he induces his wife to commit blatant adultery: "And even Manu says that husbands without offspring should obtain the services of others for their wives, because sons bring the highest merit. I command you, Kunti, to give me sons from someone either equal or superior to me. You know such an act was done by the daughter of Saradandayana at the order of her husband. Do likewise for me" (Lal 1989 : 80-81 cf Pomeroy 1975 : 37 & Baig 1976 : 60 & 70).

Of the eight types of marriage enumerated in religious texts, three types related to using woman as commodity. Interestingly, these three types were known as Daiva Vivaha, Asur Vivaha and Rakshasa Vivaha. In Daiva form of marriage a girl was given by her father or guardian to a priest as part of his fee. Such marriages were prevalent even among Brahmanas (cf. Basham 1967 : 169-70). In Asur marriage the bride was bought from her father or guardian to become somebody's wife. Such marriages were prevalent even among Kshatriyas. Pandu's marriage to Madri is an illustrious example of marriage by purchase. Even Bhishma considers it "honourable and virtuous" (cf. Lal 1980 : 77). As regards Rakshasa Vivaha or marriage by capture, it is worth noting that in ancient India (as in ancient Greece) quite legitimate it was to carry away a woman, whether unmarried, married or widowed, for marriage. The etymology of the word *Vivaha* itself (as already noted), refers to carrying away or abduction of the bride. Greek mythology celebrates references to those heroes who kidnap women, whether for marriage or for other purposes. During one of his twelve most heroic adventures, Hercules kidnaps Iole and her two sisters to cook and scrub floors (cf. Graves 1960 : 102). The *Mahabharata* mentions a number of anecdotes in which venerable heroes abduct women as prizes of contests, spoils of war or monuments of invincible power (cf. Thomas 1964 : 145).

One of the worst corollaries of the proprietary attitude to woman manifests itself in the form of sexist institutions and ideologies which consider male domination normal and woman's inferior assignation proper. The modern woman's self-concepts are largely derived from such chauvinistic differentiations of male and female roles and functions. If a woman thinks today that she cannot compete with man, she manifests only the patriarchal indoctrination of her thinking for ages. Kenneth Clark, the eminent American scholar, rightly holds that one of the most debilitating effects of prolonged racist/sexist domination is that the victims "come to believe in and even cherish their inferiority" to the dominant group (cf. Amundsen 1971 : 107). Men preserve and protect women as their property. What will men do if women—wives and daughters—refuse to be their property?

4.4 Subjection to Sex and Violence

> "The sexuality of most men shows an admixture of aggression, of a desire to subdue."
>
> —*Freud*

Apart from certain microscopic forms of life, every organism, as an organism, has two innately specified basic urges or drives: the urge for the survival and preservation of the self and the urge for the survival and preservation of the species. The organism has to satisfy hunger so that it survives and grows. It has to have sex so that the species survives and grows. Evidently, the purpose of eating is self-preservation as the purpose of sex is species-preservation. These two types of preservation are interdependent: the one cannot take place without the other. Besides, these preservative drives are common to and obligatory for all organisms. No organism can dispense with them. These drives are therefore amoral, organism-specific and organism-uniform. There is absolutely no dividing line between the non-human and the human in the twin realms of hunger and sex, survival and preservation.

When we talk about sex, we may distinguish between two forms of this drive: the one that is common to all organisms as transmitted genetically from one generation to another, and the other that is peculiar to the *homo sapiens* as culturally transmitted from generation to generation. For want of a better set of terms, we may call the genetic form 'sex' and its cultural variant 'sexuality' (cf. Sharma 1986). As non-humans do not have 'culture', they are innocent of sexuality which is a clear gift of human evolution.

Sex and sexuality are as different from each other as is light from darkness, even though they share a common frontier. Sex is necessary, benign and pure because it is procreative while sexuality is superfluous, malignant and amorphous because it is recreational. Both structurally and motivationally a hybrid product of psychology and physiology, sexuality is by nature volatile, insensible, chameleon—like and satanic. Not connected with procreation and therefore preservation, sexuality is ever-demanding, aggressive and masculine. In respect of sexuality the female is a dupe, an unwilling partner or a helpless victim. The most pernicious aspect of sexuality is its psychic determination. As a necessary product of civilization, sexuality is essentially a psychic demand for and a psychic act of 'recreation.' Its physical concretization emits only the stink of the ever—hungry monster which lies hidden in the male psyche.

In his analysis of human sexuality, Freud draws a clear line between what he calls the sexual aim and the sexual object (cf. *ibid.*). There are, he posits, many forms of sexual behaviour which deviate from the norm in aim, in object or in both. The normal sexual aim is 'coitus', while the normal sexual object is an adult 'female', but as far as human sexual behaviour goes, there is no logical connection between the sexual object and the sexual aim. A man can choose for his sexual object, an adult of his own sex (homosexuality), a minor of either sex (paedophilia), himself (autosexuality), an animal, a dead body, urine, faeces or inanimate objects (perverted sexuality) and even a symbol or an idea (pornography). Similarly, a man can use the normal sexual object to realize any aim, *viz.*, seeing or showing nakedness, quarrelling, brain-washing, ridiculing, harassing, kissing, biting, causing pain or killing. Male ingenuity is nowhere as evident as in the domain of sexuality. Freud makes it quite explicit in his famous essays on sexuality that even the most normal sexual act involves a certain degree of perversion. The sexuality of the human male, Freud would argue, shows a basic urge to subdue and involves a certain degree of aggression (cf. *ibid.*).

Male sexuality is both possessive and destructive. It is never a shared activity between a male and a female. It is never motivated by a desire for reproduction. It is never initiated by the female. To demand and provide the satisfaction of the sex urge in a civilized society should ideally be the mutual right and obligation of both partners, the female and the male, the wife and the husband. But it is not so. No sexual relationship defined and established by the male can ever recognize the independence and equality of the female. As a sexual relationship, marriage itself is an excuse for subjugating and possessing the female. Wife-battering, says Schechter, author of *Women and Male Violence*, is "a pattern of coercive control" (cf. Safran 1987). Male sexuality, of necessity, converts the female, both within as well as outside marriage, into a sexual object which can be used or discarded at will. As all sex relations between male and female are demanded and fixed by the male, the use of force or coercion becomes an inevitable part of acquiring a female, whether temporarily or for life. Man resorts to violence to destroy resistance and to ensure compliance by woman.

It is sometimes claimed that men "protect" women. But the question is: Do they? Or, who do they protect women from? Who are the molesters, the seducers, the rapists, the swindlers, the humiliaters, the exploiters, the batterers and the slayers of women? Some people might say that men protect their wives and daughters. Here again the same question poses itself. Do men protect their wives and daughters? Or, should a wife or a daughter need protection from her husband or father who should she go to? The whole question of protection is based on a manipulation of words or on a vicious circle. Protection of women by men, for men and from men does not and should not mean anything for the protected. Men could as well give up the whole game of "protection" and let women alone.

The use of force against women is part of the patriarchal culture, The patriarchal ideology derives from the basic construct that women must be subdued, by using force, if necessary. An ancient proverb in China, for example, proclaims: "A wife is like a horse. You can order her about or beat her as you please" (cited in Baig 1976 : 43). The Italians believe: "As a horse, whether good or bad, requires spurs, so a woman, good or bad requires thrashing" (cited in Kidwai 1976 : 8). A verse in the *Quoran* lays down: "So good women are the obedient. ... As for them from whom ye fear rebellion, admonish them and banish them to beds apart, and scourge them" (Pickthall 1924 : IV : 34).

According to a survey, a woman in America is battered by her husband or boy-friend every 18 seconds. And every year more than a million of such women need medical help. On an average, four battered women die every day. The survey reveals that in the majority of cases the batterer feels that he has a right, even a duty, to control his wife or girl-friend. Between beatings, therefore, he often controls her with shouting, name-calling, intimidation and other emotional blows. A Boston school teacher who is a habitual wife-batterer explains his attitude to such violence in this way: 'If I said, "Jump" and she did, then I'd say, "jump higher". This goes on till the wife fails and he has a chance to beat her again. Another wife-batterer threatens his wife: "If you try to leave, I'II find you and kill you". A victim of regular violence from her husband reports: "He beat my face to a pulp. Then he pushed me in front of the mirror." "Look at yourself", he shouted. "Who else would have you"? Wife-battering is a culpable offence in the United States, as it is in several other countries, and yet the American Police often hesitate to take action against wife-batterers, even when the complaint is formally lodged on the ground that it is "a private matter" (cf. Safran 1987).

We do not have in India such readily available statistics about wife-beating, even though it is much more fashionable here than it is in America. The absence of statistics, however, need not baffle or embarrass us. Statistics or no statistics, we Indians are far ahead of the Americans in areas like these. As is so well known, we have a history of culture, much longer than they have. We have been far more considerate in our social or familial behaviour than they have been. We have a much larger body of religious writings than they have. It is only natural, therefore, that we outdo the Americans in our cruelty to women. Our mythology is galore with tales of how our ancestors treated their wives and daughters. The great sage Jamadagni suspected his middle-aged wife, Renuka, of having entertained sensual thoughts about another man. He ordered his son, Parashurama, one of the incarnations of Vishnu, to kill her. Parashurama immediately chopped off his mother's head. The story of Ahalya's alleged pollution and conversion into stone is another example of how even innocent women were treated by their husbands. The *Ramacharitamanasa* contains picturesque accounts of how women are dealt with: elderly Manthara and Lankini are hit with blows; rebellious Surpanakha is mutilated; Taraka and Trishira are just done to death. During the war in Lanka, Rama's soldiers barge into Ravana's palace and drag the women out to force Ravana to give up the sacrificial performance: "They seized his wives by the hair and dragged them out of the palace while they screamed with pain" (Hill 1952 : 407). Tulasidasa, like many other eminent Hindu sages and philosophers, recommends wife-battering as a necessary part of managing the family and the state: A drum, a village boor, a Shudra, a beast, and a woman, all these are fit for beating. Women and Shudras cannot expect a better deal from a people whose entire ethic is so explicitly oriented in favour of the males of a certain racial stock. The most disastrous consequence of the theology of violence has manifested itself in the attitudinal behaviour of women towards men. Steeped in sado-masochism and self-hatred, most women turn survilely to their men and cruelly to other and younger women. Women's involvement in bride-burning cases is a recent manifestation of the culture of cruelty injected into the feminine psyche through the ages. Most victims of male savagery do not even realize that it is unkind of men that they should resort to violence against women (cf. Wiser & Wiser 1963 : 80).

The gendered use of force obviously derives from the perception of woman as subordinate, weak-kneed and mischievous. Apart from usual beatings of wives and daughters, masculine violence against women includes such social phenomena as widow-burning and bride-burning. There used to be a time when widows were consigned to flames by the men of the family and the neighbourhood as a matter of compulsory family ritual. One can only hope that this atrocious custom has now practically stopped. But of late, widow-burning has come to be replaced by what is popularly known as "bride-burning" or "dowry-death". Such burnings or deaths have long been culpable offences in India. The Dowry Prohibition Act was passed in 1961 while the Amended Dowry Act was passed in 1984. But the incidence of bride-burning has been rising from year to year. There was a time when even a single case of bride-burning would spark off protests, demonstrations and letters to editors. But now bride-burnings even in the national capital can go without a murmur of protest. If such burnings continue to rise in number from year to year, we would soon reach a social situation, in spite of law-enforcing agencies and feminist organizations, in which bride-burning becomes a regular family ritual and a symbol of heroic masculinism in the family and the neighbourhood.

As of today, a majority of dowry deaths are not reported to the police. Those which are, do not result in the conviction of the guilty. In cases where the victim dies on the spot, the complaints are lodged by her parents or relations who do not succeed in supporting their allegations. In cases where the victim makes a dying declaration, sufficient evidence is not provided by those who stand for the trial. In either case, the persecution charge is weakened and the guilty manage to get away from possible punishment. Besides, voluntary organizations do not often succeed in getting relevant information and the necessary staff to fight out the case on behalf of the victim. The police is not sufficiently trained to handle such cases nor is it honestly sensitive to women's problems (cf. Subramaniyam 1988). It remains a man's world. Bride-burnings take place mainly because most people, including the police, still work on the presumption that women are not to be taken seriously and that what happens to them happens because of their own faults or failings. The masculinist strategy of success also draws its impunity from the conditioned participation of the mothers-in-law and the sisters-in-law in the sordid drama of bride-burnings. If women could stand united, this drama would stop immediately. The only hope of success lies with women themselves. Men are not going to oblige them now or ever.

When we try to account for the practice of violence against women, we feel that there is probably an inevitable nexus between progress and cruelty against women. As there are louder claims for more security and freedom for women, there are matching and pervasive crimes against women. Women want security against men. Men turn out to be more threatening to them. Never in the past have women been subjected to harassments and indignities on a scale as they are at the present moment. It is therefore imperative that women call a halt to such nonsense once for all in a concerted and careful manner on the national scale.

Crimes against women have been on the rise from year to year in the recent past as never before for the simple reason that only a shortwhile ago women in India began to voice their protest against traditional discrimination and male chauvinism and to assert themselves in various fields. Indians, Hindus in particular, having been brought up on a traditional ideology of superiority to women as a class, have found it difficult to accept that women are equal to them. The recent cult of violence emanates from their outrage at the challenges posed by women. Their increasing violence is clearly relatable to their increasing sense of panic. But there is also the traditional history of their perception of woman as weak and vulnerable.

Unless there is a miraculous change in the masculinist perception of femininity, man would consider woman a thing of joy and subjection for as long as he possibly could. He has always done that and he would love to do that for all time to come. Man looks on woman and he thinks of invasion and conquest. It is characteristic of Theseus to recall his pristine feelings of ecstasy when he loved to possess the Amazon: "Hippolyta, I woo'd thee with my sword/And won thy love doing thee injuries" and the next moment he assures her: "But I will wed thee in another key/With pomp, with triumph, and with revelling" (A Midsummer Night's Dream I : I :16-18). The moment Dushyanta looks on Shakuntala, he makes up his mind: "This is not fire, but a gem/I must shape her and make her mine" (Lal 1964 : 20).

Man's love for woman is full of contradictions. Othello loves Desdemona, weds her, suspects her, kills her and patronizes her: "I kiss'd thee ere I kill'd thee" (V : II : 357). Man loves woman. He hates her. He enjoys her. He destroys her. He loves to hate. He enjoys to destroy. His love is sex. His sex is possession. His possession is victimization. Love and hate, sex and violence, possession and victimization are his prerogatives. The target of his love and hate, sex and violence, enjoyment and ravishment is a mere recipient, slave, victim, object, thing. Man feels proud of his power to possess, humiliate, enjoy and destroy woman who might (unless ready to fight back) invoke Gloucester's incantation to define and articulate her experiences of the god-like man or men: "As flies to wanton boys are we to the gods/They kill us for their sport" (*King Lear* IV : I :37-38).

Why does Othello kill Desdemona? A simple answer to this question is this; Murder is a desperate attempt to retaliate and control. But the question now is: "What is there in Desdemona that provokes Othello to retaliate and control? Desdemona is so simple, meek, full of love and submissive. But there is something in her which is, again very simple and yet very subtle and therefore powerful. Desdemona has the power to hurt, to remind Othello that he is a creature of the flesh and that there is a limit to what he can do. Desdemona can easily puncture his ego and expose his inner hollowness. It is this power in Desdemona that Othello seeks to eliminate by ending her life (cf. Gohlke 1980).

Man's vision of woman as an object worth possessing inevitably leads to an obnoxious combination between sex and violence. It is no mere vulgarity or just violence that the *Kamasutra* refers to the popular Hindu custom of striking women so as to cause marks on their body, with a wedge on the bosom, with scissors on the head, with piercing instruments on the cheeks and with pincers on the breasts (cf. Archer 1963 : 156). There is much more to it. For a fuller view of violent male sexuality we can turn to the sixth chapter of the *Brihadaranyaka Upanishada* which represents, through powerful visual images, a meticulous description of that erotic process which begins with man's craving for woman and concludes with his decisive triumph over her: "Woman, verily, is a sacrificial fire, the sexual organ, in truth, is its fuel; the hairs, the smoke; the vulva, the flame; when one inserts, the coals; the feeling of pleasure, the sparks" (VI : II : 13). Again,

"Her lap is a sacrificial altar; her hairs, sacrifical grass; her skin, the soma-process. The two labia of the Vulva are the fire in the middle. Verily, indeed, as great as is the world of him who sacrifices with the *Vajpeya* (strength-libation) sacrifice, so great is the world of him who practises sexual intercourse, knowing this, he turns the deeds of women to himself" (VI : IV : 3). Again,

"Now, if one should see himself in water, he should recite over it the formula : "In me be vigour, power, beauty, wealth, merit"!

This verily, indeed, is loveliness in woman: when she has removed the clothes of her impurity and is beautiful, one should approach her and invite her. ... If she should not grant him his desire, he should bribe her. If she still does not grant him his desire, he should hit her with a stick or with his hand; and overcome her, saying: "With power, with glory, I take away your glory"! Thus she becomes inglorious (VI : IV : 6-7). And finally,

"The woman whom one may desire with the thought `May she enjoy love with me'!—after inserting the number in her, joining mouth to mouth, and striking her lap, he should mutter:

Thou that from everything art come, That from heart are generate, Thou art the essence of the limbs! Distract this woman here in me, as if by poisoned arrow pierced" (VI : IV : 9).

Of all forms of atrocity against woman, rape is certainly the worst. It is the most notorious and vulgar manifestation of man's essential ambivalence towards woman. It is the most inhuman form of male violence against the female. It is a sort of murder which picturizes a helpless victim in the clutches of a heartless brute. The female flesh is seen as a passive microcosm. The feminine physique blooms and swells only to be pressed and polluted by a male who speaks like an angel and acts like an agent of the devil. As a woman writer remarks: "When a man pursues, besieges, and batters a woman's body, he assaults a total world" (Stimpson 1980).

The sexual terror of the rape victim stands for the difficulty of her sex. Man who has more power than woman abuses it and woman who has less power than man absorbs the abuse. The horrors of rape are seldom better described than in Shakespeare's *The Rape of Lucrece*. Coppelia Kahn reads it as the poetic version of an ideology that justifies the male power through imputing "a sort of inevitability between men and women as the relationship between the strong and the weak" (*ibid.*). Nevertheless, it may be useful to have a detailed look through Shakespeare's longest poem.

Every rapist is a Tarquin—immoral, hypocritical, brute-like. Every victim is a Lucretia—simple, helpless, lamb-like. Every rape victim, (perhaps every woman who has physically known a man), knows only too well that the man who seizes and subdues her has nothing in common with the man who lectures on morality and metaphysics, and yet, the two are the one and the same man. The brigand who apparently passes for a gentleman is the creature who puzzles every woman who has had experiences of the sex act. The woman is baffled to find that openly the man subscribes to the ideals that secretly he ignores or flouts. She fails to define her attitude to the pervert she has to put up with in a lonely corner or in bed who suddenly becomes so fussy about the values of civilization and culture. The woman learns to her cost that no sex-doing male (not to speak of a rapist) can ever be *truly* noble because she knows that nobility and sexuality never fuse into each other to form an integrated whole—at least as long as they belong only to the male.

The rape of Lucrece offers a graphic account of the ingredients of rape. Tarquin steals into Lucretia's bed to find her fast asleep. He gazes at her body. He is engulfed by a death-in-life sort of vision the moment his eyes fall on her naked breasts:

"Her breasts, like ivory globes lined with blue.

A pair of maiden worlds unconquered" (407-8).

The breasts swell only for Tarquin to press and conquer them. Suddenly seizing them, he announces:

"The colour in thy face ...
Shall plead for and tell my loving tale
Under that colour am I come to scale
Thy never-conquer'd fort" (477, 80-82).

Lucretia is shocked and frightened. She makes a fervent appeal to the aggressor:

"If man were ever moved with woman's moans
Be moved with my tears, my sighs, my groans" (567-68).

Several questions torture Lucretia's mind and outrage her sensibility: Is it the Prince Sextus Tarquinius who is her guest and to whom she has been so nice? Is it a heartless brute out to ruin her? How can the Prince be a brute like this? How can the brute like this be the Prince? Isn't a Prince like a god who protects women's chastity? How can the protector suddenly become a destroyer? Is it all a bad dream? Isn't there a real threat to her chastity from the Prince and guest who has ridden on her? In thé midst of such nerve-breaking questions, she makes an appeal to his conscience.

"Thou are not what thou seem'st; and if the same
Thou seem'st not what thou art, a god, a king" (600-601).

Lucretia is thoroughly disappointed and hopeless. Tarquin has no use for his family name or for his public image. He is instead hellbent on ravishing her:

"... by heaven, I will not hear thee !
Yield to my love, if not, enforce hate
Instead of love's coy touch, shall rudely tear thee" (667-69).

After this Tarquin performs the unperformable: "The wolf has seized his prey, the poor lamb cries" (677). He ravishes and tears her past from her future:

"She has lost a dearer thing than life
And he hath won what he would lose again" (687-88).

And then he

"like a thievish dog creeps sadly thence
She like wearied lamb lies panting thence....
He thence departs a heavy convertite
She there remains a hopeless cast away" (736-37 & 743-44).

The consequences of rape are sordidly discriminatory against the victim:"

"The patient dies while the physician sleeps

The orphan pines while the oppressor feeds

Justice is feasting while the widow weeps;

Advice is sporting while infection breeds' (904-907).

The 'private pleasure' of the oppressor becomes the 'public shame' of the victim (line 890). The brutish male makes a helpless female a 'tenant' to his 'shame' (cf. line 1260).

An obscene combination of sexuallity and cruelty, rape is committed on little girls, adolescent girls, unmarried women, married women, widows and even elderly women. It did not take place only in the Archaic period in Greece, the Augustan age in Rome or the Puranic times in India; it has always occurred and it has not yet become a thing of the past. It is rather taking place today on an increasingly larger scale. Modern men have gone much farther than their ancestors. Perhaps never before was a woman gang-raped. It is only in our times that rapes are committed by groups of males on single females. Not too long ago did Hubert Selby record the tragedy of a helpless woman who was stripped, gang-raped, mutilated, murdered and dumped by the road-side in *Last Exit to Brooklyn* (1966). A gang of woman-eaters caught hold of the lonely Tralala, denuded her and rode on her one by one. And then "more came 40 may be 50 and they screwed her and went back on line and had a beer and yelled and laughed and someone yelled that the car stunk of cunt so Tralala and the seat were taken out of the car and laid in the lot and she lay there naked on the seat and their shadows hid her pimples and scabs and she drank flipping her tits with the other hand and somebody shoved the beer can against her mouth and they all laughed and Tralala cursed and spit out a piece of tooth and someone shoved it again ... and the next one mounted her and her lips were split this time and the blood trickled to her chin and someone mapped her brow with a beersoaked handkerchief and another can of beer was handed to her and she drank and yelled about her teats and another tooth was chipped and everyone laughed and she laughed and she drank more and more and soon she passed out and they slapped her a few times and she mumbled and turned her head and they couldn't revive her so they continued to fuck her as she lay unconscious on the seat in the lot and soon they tired of the dead piece and the daisychain broke up and they went back Willis the Greeks and the base and the kids who were watching and waiting to take a turn took out their disappointment on Tralala and tore her clothes to small scraps put out a few cigarettes on her nipples pissed on her jerked off on her jammed a broomstick up her snatch then bored they left her lying among the broken bottles, rusty cans and rubble of the lot and Jack and Fred and Ruthy and Annie stumbled into a cab still laughing and they leaned toward the window as they passed the lot and got good look at Tralala lying naked covered with blood urine and semen and a small blot forming on the seat between her legs as blood seeped from her crotch..." (cited in Greer 1973 : 257-58).

Needless to add, this extract is a telling commentary upon the progress of human civilization based on the ideological supremacy of male values.

A religious ordinance known as Hudood and dealing with offences like adultery, rape and fornication was confirmed as law in a neighbouring country in 1985. According to the provisions of this law, the onus of proof in a rape case lies on the victim. If the victim is unable to prove the charge in a court of law, her allegation is considered a confession of her guilt. She is then charged with having seduced the man and is therefore liable to prosecution and punishment. This law naturally aggravates the incidence of rape because men feel sure of getting away. Hudood has been responsible for a number of unbelievable convictions. In July 1983, a nineteen-year-old-blind girl had been allegedly and repeadely raped by her landlord and his son. She became pregnant. The matter came to court. The court sentenced her to be flogged in public and then sent to prison for three years. The accused were let off as the blind victim had failed to identify them. A similar fate awaited a thirteen-year-old orphan who had been allegedly and repeatedly raped by her uncle and his son. She became pregnant. The matter came to court. The court held her guilty of seduction of two innocent men and therefore sentenced her to imprisonment. This orphan had also failed to prove her charge. There are hundreds of such helpless victims in jails (cf. *Ind. Exp.*, 14 Dec., 1987).

In India more than five thousand cases of rape are annually reported to the police. Thousands and thousands of cases are not reported to the police because of the social stigma attached to a girl or woman having been defiled. In addition to the steep rise in the incidence of rape, other crimes against women have also been on the increase from year to year. Taunts, abuses, threats, molestations and the like are seldom considered worth reporting, even though a majority of repeated threats or abuses escalate into beatings, abetments to suicide or murders. In cases which are reported to the police, there is hardly any effective pattern of punishment. More often than not, the accused even in cases like rape and murder are acquitted for want of convincing evidence. Since rapes and murders generally take place in lonely places or of lonely women, it is difficult to provide incontrovertible evidence of the crime committed.

One of the worst forms of cruelty to women in today's Hindu society relates to wives being regularly battered by their husbands. Such occurrences are viewed by the police as unavoidable outbursts of domestic skirmishes and by society as instances of normal confrontations between men and women. A survey conducted by the Centre for Social Research shows that in 78 per cent of the sample cases, the young wife is assaulted every alternate day or in 57 per cent cases wives are threatened to be killed and in 71 per cent cases to be deserted or thrown out (cf. *Ind. Exp.*, 24 April, 1988). With no effective sympathizer in her parents' home, the wife is obliged to put up with the almost daily ritual of psychological and/or physical tortures which she is subjected to in her husband's home. The predicament of such unlucky women accrues from the faith in marriage as a panacea for the economic, social, cultural, biological and emotional crises of woman.

The stereotyped masculinist slogan that 'woman is the enemy of woman' needs to be examined very critically. The myth that women work against women or that women themselves impede the freedom of women must not be taken as a gospel of male wisdom. Such slogans and myths and bogeys have been there since the beginning of civilization so that men have continued to maintain their grip on women as well as to make them feel guilty of their own complicity in the trade-off. The system that plays one woman off against another must be challenged, replaced or destroyed if sensitive people are genuienly concerned about women welfare.

5

SAGA OF SEXUALIZATION

5.1 The Secular Picture

> "Throbbing breasts, aching for loving embrace, are hard to touch!
>
> Rest these vessels on my chest ! Quench love's burning fire!"
>
> —*Gita Govinda*

Freud's identification of man as *homo sexualis* is obviously based on his observation and understanding of the multitudinous manifestations of masculine sexuality. His obsessive insistence on viewing every male activity as an attempt to satisfy some sexual craving, whether conscious, preconscious or unconscious, is not a figment of the imagination nor a wicked concoction; it is certainly justified and validated by what most normal men do in their day-to-day life. To the utter dismay of the self-righteous, Freud propounds the theory that all human behaviour (*i.e.*, male behaviour) is *motivated* and *goal-directed*, the motivating force being sexuality and the goal being the optimal satisfaction of the sexual drive (cf. Sharma 1986). As a psychic function, Freud tells us, sexuality is uniformly operative in *all* human beings (*i.e.*, all men), including the good and the great. We may not go the whole hog with Freud but we have to admit in any case that his generalization holds true of most men.

Once sex ceases to be just a natural urge, a purely somatic function necessarily linked with reproduction, it acquires the degree of devilry which is as dangerous as amorphous. Reproductive 'sex' gives way to recreational and possessive 'sexuality' which enters into the inner domain of the psyche and sexualizes the whole mechanics of thinking—the most baneful development in the evolutionary history of the human male. When sex couples with intelligence to become a psychic demand and a psychic function (*i.e.*, sexuality), it acquires the power of assuming an infinite variety of forms to draw satisfaction in all possible ways. As Don Juan tells Anna in Shaw's *Man and Superman*: "Do you know that where there is a will there is a way? That whatever man really wishes to do he will finally discover a means of doing" (*ibid.*).

As a poisonous growth, sexuality first pollutes the possessor and then infects and distorts the possessed. All-pervasive and all-consuming, as it is, sexuality is a perpetual degeneration which so debauches the male spirit that recovery to health becomes almost impossible. It is significant to note here that the physical manifestation of sexuality, however devilish and stinking, is only the tip of the iceberg which lies hidden in the innermost depths of the psyche—the agency that determines and monitors what the body does. A verse in the Gospel warns: "Ye have heard that it was said by them of old time. Thou shall not commit adultery. But I say unto you, That whosoever looketh on a woman to lust after her hath committed adultery with her already in his heart" (St. Mathew : 5 : 27-28). A man is what he thinks and he does what he thinks. A man guilty of physical sexuality is only an aberrant fool; the real criminal is the one who, operating behind the scenes, entertains and seeks satisfaction for psychic sexuality in all sorts of possible disguises. Whether a man is correct or corrupt largely depends on what he does within his psyche or on what his psyche does: "There is nothing from without a man that entering into him can defile him but the things which come out of him, those that defile the man" (St. Mark 7 : 15). A verse in the *Gita* puts it like this: "As the waters of different rivers enter the ocean which, though full on all sides, remains unperturbed; likewise, he, in whom enter all types of (sexual) cravings (from outside), attains peace, not he who hankers after these (sexual) cravings (emanating from inside) ... (my translation cf. Radhakrishnan 1993 : II : 70). As the only animal who thinks, man must be judged by what comes out of him rather than by what goes into him, by the structure of his thoughts rather than by the variety of his physical doings.

When we think of the psychic determination of male sexuality, we are naturally reminded of the prophet of the unconscious. It was he who showed us that most of what we are conscious of is not real and that most of what is real is not in our consciousness. Centuries before Freud, Plato had noted: "The virtuous man contents himself with dreaming what the wicked man does in actual life" (cited in Sharma 1986). In the following pages an attempt will be made to show how the wicked and the virtuous fuse into one another to evolve human males as woman-eating monsters in whom the former display their crudity while the latter retain their finesse.

From very early times, man has shown deep erotic attachments-sometimes to himself and sometimes to the other members of his own class. That is, man has been both autosexual and homosexual. But such by-ways of his erotic pursuits have never succeeded in dissuading him from going along the gendered highway. Woman has been the main target of his eroticism, *i.e.*, his sexuality. The human male continues to remain very largely female-oriented (*i.e.*, heterosexual), not out of his concern for or commitment to the preservation of the species but mainly because his being so is more convenient and gratifying. In addition to drawing satisfaction for his libido, he achieves fulfilment for his will-to-power by pursuing and possessing the female. He could not have achieved such sublimity or fulfilment by choosing and enjoying another male nor could he have done so by centring on and enjoying himself. Whatever it may be, no one can deny the credit due to the human male for having been able to *foresee* the benefits of owning the female even in the infancy of his civilization. Looking back over the millenia, he congratulates himself today that even in the dim light of pristine history he had the requisite insight to plan and execute his strategies vis-a-vis the female so effectively that he had no regrets in later times. On the contrary, all later generations of males have acknowledged their indebtedness to him for his yeoman service to their gender. History has paid glowing tributes to him for his prophetic visions of a stable culture. Numerous classics have glorified his heroism and wisdom. All such eulogies have helped to shape his attitude to history, civilization, culture and morals. Today he lords over everything past and present and is gleefully looking forward to a prosperous future for *his* species.

It is only natural for such a privileged, resourceful and bemused male to visualize the female as an embodiment of sexuality and to insist on squeezing gratification for his sexual drives from every bit of the female flesh. There is no doubt that it is the masculinist vision of the female as the sexiest of all feminine creatures that motivates his sexualization of the human female. As a matter of fact, all nude paintings, obscene sketches and pornographic descriptions (whether literal or symbolic, overt or covert, crude or sophisticated, secular or sacred) unhesitatingly stand as monuments of male voyeurism. Historically speaking, the human female has been so much cajoled, scorned, ridiculed, X-rayed, falsified, brainwashed, hunted, waylaid, torn, ground, sifted and scrutinized that there is not a cell in her body nor a tissue in her brain that has not been detected, examined and reported. She should long have been dead, buried and forgotten. But it is only a miracle that she can still sometimes rise from the debris phoenix—like and claim sexist attention, love and hate.

Love, like many other words in masculinist vocabulary, is a bad word. Notwithstanding what the high priests of masculinism claim for it, love is a smokescreen or camouflage to deceive and exploit the female. No acquisitive system, whether Aryan Hindu or any other, does recognize the autonomy of the female and it cannot therefore allow the semantics of love to emphasize an unqualified sharing of certain feelings and experiences between equal heterosexual partners. Every society is a product of its own history, ideology and perception of human relationships. A peoples' racial memory is much stronger than it is often thought to be. "Human behaviour", says Hunt, "is the product of an interesting complex of forces ranging from the individual's bloodsugar level to the ethos of his civilization" (1961). As an important aspect of human behaviour, love cannot but mean what its coiners want it to mean. It has so far been associated, throughout the history of civilization, with the sexual quest of the male. As a matter of fact, it is simply "a set of emotions contingent upon and appropriate to the sexual courting and pursuit" of the female by the male and this theory of love has been held not by the low-minded libertine but by the "high-minded evangels" of social ethics and moral philosophy (cf. *ibid.*). "The literature of Hindu India", writes Basham, "both *religious* and *secular*, is full of sexual allusions, sexual symbolism and passages of frank eroticism" (1967 : 172, italics added).

The pan sexualism of masculinist cultures like those of India and Greece is evident from their religious works and institutions. It is no mere coincidence that ancient sculptures in both cultures unabashedly stress the grossly sensual. The temples of Konark and Khajuraho, like the great monuments of Hellenistic sculpture, show women not only in the nude but also engrossed in coitus (cf. Sengupta 1974 : 91 & Pomeroy 1975 : 144). Any attempt to justify the crudity of such allusions with reference to mysticism or religious symbolism must be dismissed as disgustingly hypocritical. No one should be allowed to blow hot and cold at the same time or to have the cake and eat it too. These sculptural novelties along with the cave paintings of Ajanta and Ellora must be seen as concrete evidence of Indo-Greek male voyeurism.

To view woman as "cultivable land" or as "food" (in the literal sense of the term, as it were) is a characteristic peculiar to patricentric and possessive cultures. Eulogizing Cleopatra's rare beauty and erotic value, Agrippa exclaims in Shakespeare's masterpiece:

> "Royal wench !
>
> She made great Caesar lay his *sword* to bed.
>
> He *ploughed* her, and she *cropped*"
>
> (Antony and Cleopatra II : III : 230-32, italics added).

A verse in a holy book decrees: "Your wife is a tilth for you, then come to your tilth as you please" (cited in Baig 1976 : 55). Woman is for man a 'field' which he can 'plough' and 'sow' the way he likes and as often as he chooses to.

The 'phallus-plough' and 'woman-furrow' images are common symbols of a sexualist and possessive philosophy of woman. The Indo-Aryans seem to have borrowed such images from their agricultural predecessors. They go to the extent of worshipping these images in the *Rig-Veda* and the *Yajur-Veda*. In Vedic vocabulary, it is worth noting, Sita is the furrow, worshipped as a deity presiding over agriculture and fruit. In the epic period it becomes the proper name of Janaka's daughter but the story of her origin is interesting. According to Valmiki, Janaka is ploughing a field for a sacrifice when there springs from the furrow a girl who he takes as his daughter and calls Sita (cf. Hill 1952 : 528 & Sengupta 1974 : 29). The metaphor of woman as a field to be ploughed, sown and reaped is a commonplace in Indo-Greek literature. In the famous Sophoclean classic, named after him, Oedipus is described as "a ploughman of the woman's chamber" (Vickers 1973 : 516). Similarly, in Kalidasa's masterpiece Dushyanta has this to say about Shakuntala: "I left her like a field sown, watered—and abandoned at harvest" (Lal 1964 : 65).

In an interesting passage in the *Mahabharata*, the image of 'furrow' and 'sowing' is almost literally used. To convince his stepmother why she should have Vyasa perform sex on her widowed daughters-in-law, Bhishma refers to an ancient story: "You have heard of the sage Utathya and his wife Mamata. When Utathya's younger brother, Vrihaspati *lusted* for her, she refused him for she was already pregnant with Utathya's *seed*. `The child in my womb is learned and knows the Vedas', she said. `Your *seed* will go in vain. Leave me alone.' But still he *lusted*, and when he was about to *enter* her, the child in her womb addressed him: `Uncle ! There is no space for two. Your *seed* will go in vain'. But Vrihaspati would not listen, and clasped *tight* the lovely-eyed Mamata. Just as his *seed* was about to spurt, the learned child put out its feet and blocked the entrance, with the result that the *seed* spilled on the ground. Terribly angered, Vrihaspati cursed the child with perpetual blindness" (Lal 1980 : 72, italics added).

Another characteristic image of woman is that of food, eating or eatability. Emilia confides to Desdemona in *Othello*:

"Tis not a year or two shows us a man.
They are all but *stomachs*, and we all but *food*!
They *eat* us hungerly, and when they are full,
They *belch* us" (III : IV : 4-7, italics mine).

In *Antony and Cleopatra* Enobarbus visualizes Cleopatra in grossly sensual terms, using analogies of flowering and eating:

"Age cannot *wither* her, nor custom *stale*
Her infinite variety. Other women *cloy*
The appetite they *feed*,
But she makes most *hungry*
Where most she *satisfies*" (II : III : 240-43, italics mine).

Likewise Dushyanta's description of Shakuntala (in the play named after her) exceeds all limits of decent writing. With its images of plucking, nailing, squeezing, tasting and deflowering, the poetic vision merges into the pornographic: "Her faultless form is a flower not yet *smelt*; a delicate sprout not yet *plucked by nails*; a jewel not yet *perforated*; fresh honey whose flavour is yet *untasted*; as if the fruits of merit not yet *divided*; I know not whom the Creator will present as the *enjoyer* here" (*Abhijnanashakuntalam* II : 10 quoted in Dalal 1973 : 191, italics mine). Apart from such erotic visions in secular writings, the image of woman as `food' is sometimes used even in religious literature. No sensitive Hindu would remain unrufled if he came across the following remark attributed to Sita in the *Ramacharitamanas*: "Who can tell my lord of my distress? That an ass should devour the food of the sacrifice!" (Hill 1952 : 313).

If one were to look at the bulk of the religious and speculative literature of ancient Hindus, one might come to the conclusion that the ancient Hindu was a man wholly absorbed in pious meditation. But a conclusion like this would not be authentic. As a matter of fact, the ancient Hindu was as much a lover of dice, drink and dalliance as he was of meditation and speculative philosophy. Ancient India was not a land only of holy recluses, benign dreamers, great poets and pious philosophers; it was also, probably more clearly, a land of chasers and enjoyers of lovely objects. In ancient Hindu literature therefore there is "a frank recognition of the sex-impulse as one of the most powerful impulses of the human mind" (De 1969 : 85). One of the most speculative hymns of the *Rig-Veda* portrays Kama (the god of love) as desire with a specific emphasis on sex-symbolism: the cosmogenic principles are spoken of as male and female, as impregnators and receptive powers, as "energy above" and "energy below". There is little doubt that the symbolism of the sex act is applied to the act of cosmic creation. Besides, the act of consummation is openly described in the wedding hymns of the *Rig-Veda* (cf. *ibid.*, 85-86). Similarly, intensely erotic imagery is used in the Brahmanas and the Upanishadas. It is a commonplace in the Brahmanas to liken "the fire-altar to the yoni and the production of fire to generation, while the *Satpath Brahmana* enjoins that the "fire-altar, who is a woman (yosha), the fire being her man, should be constructed in shapely elegance, broad about the sides, narrow between the shoulders and contracted in the middle" (*ibid.*, p. 87).

In his celebrated 'Introduction' to Archer's edition of the *Kamasutra*, Pannikar remarks that in Hindu literature sex is considered "not only normal and necessary but also sacramental". It is conceived as the counterpart of creation and the religious symbolism of the Hindus emphasizes this at all levels. It is the union of Purusha (matter) with Prakriti (energy) symbolized as the union of Shiva and Shakti, that is said to create the world. The symbol of Shiva is the Lingam or phallus and the symbol of Shakti is the yoni (the female sex organ). It is for this reason that every aspect of the godhead in Hinduism is "represented with a female counterpart" (1963). He goes on to say that there are verses in the *Rig-Veda* and the *Atharva-Veda* which cover every aspect of sexual relationship. In the *Chhandogya Upanishada* the sex act is compared to a sacred sacrifice: "The woman is the fire, her womb the fuel, the invitation of man the smoke. The door is the flame, entrance the ember, pleasure the spark. In this fire gods form the offering. From this offering springs forth the child" (*ibid.*). Pannikar holds the view that in every sect of Hinduism, sexual union, in one form or another, is accepted as fundamental to life. The *Brihadaraṇyaka Upanishada* for example, loftily declares (IV : 422) that the sex-desire stands on the same level as any other noble desire and that the sex-act is perhaps the most enjoyable experience of life:"In the embrace of his beloved a man forgets the whole world—everything both within and without" (cf. Pannikar 1963 & De 1969 : 88).

On the basis of what has been noted in the foregoing paragraphs, one can justifiably assume that in Hindu thought the dividing line between eroticism and spiritualism is generally blurred. But here one must be cautious enough *not* to assume, as the self-righteous often do, that a noble Hindu achieves the transformation of his sexuality by raising it to the level of spiritual thinking and ritual sacrifices. Sexuality is sexuality, irrespective of its nomenclature. One cannot change its semantics or spiritualize its mechanics by virtue of a powerful rhetoric or a pious and persuasive symbolism. Invoking mysticism or the doctrine of the superconscious does not refine the crudities of male sexuality. If coition is a liberating experience, then why is it condemned in Hindu texts so often and in so many words? Why are innocent people required to abstain from it? Why are women vilified for (allegedly) tempting men to sexuality? Even if one agrees that ritual coition is a wonderful experience, what difference does this definitional shift (or philosophical camouflage) offer to the sex object *i.e.*, the human female, whether the male is thinking of or performing physical or sacramental sex? The simultaneity of sexualism and spiritualism in traditional Hindu thought in fact seems to mean that the latter is used as a camouflage for the former. It is not for nothing that Hinduism possesses the vastest bulk of religious writings as well as the largest number of erotic texts ever known in any part of the world. Perhaps no other community on earth has such a massive simultaneous collection of erotic and religious texts as Hindus have.

The average Hindu is a man of divided loyalties with regard to his sex ethics vis-a-vis his spiritual aspirations. He adores the Upanishadas and loves the *Kamasutra* at a time. He looks above and he looks below all at once. He seeks to achieve union with the god of light but he has an instinctive association with the god of love. He wishes to transcend all human limitations to become a superman but the earthly woman tempts and binds him. He tries to realize the delectation of a beatific vision but feminine charms keep haunting his solemn meditations. He is shaken and confused. He is bewildered and lost. He becomes sick of the dichotomies of his vision. And then, he suddenly sees a way out of his chronic dualities. He transfers the female to the domain of his pious meditations in order that he may combine the cravings of the flesh with the yearnings of the spirit and formulate a philosophy of life which is "true to the kindered points of heaven and home".

Now, the question is: Why should the average Hindu go in for such a far-fetched solution to an otherwise simple problem? He wants sex, let him have it. He wants light, let him have it. Why can't he feel free to have what he wants to have? Why should he feel guilty about what he wants? Why should he be apologetic about his needs and demands? Why does he consider it necessary to justify his demands, spiritualize his leanings or to rationalize his acts? To answer questions like these, one may have to fall back upon Freud once more. The Freudian paradigm may have suitable tools to analyse the Hindu view of sexuality.

As is so widely known, Freud does not believe in sexual continence. Absolute continence, he contends, is incongruous or incompatible with mental health. Within the Freudian frame of reference, genital sexuality is held to be necessary and desirable. A healthy man therefore is defined as a man who has energetic sexual needs and the capacity to fulfil them to his best satisfaction. Sexuality in Freud is desirable because it is natural and necessary. Freud clearly holds that as genitality cannot be permanently suppressed or successfully sublimated, it must achieve fulfilment in normal coition or at least in substitutes like dreams, jokes and artistic works and symbols. Since the undisguised and instantaneous satisfaction of genital drives is often incongruous with desirable social behaviour, the human mind takes recourse to a psychic mechanism known as *repression*, that is, a delibrate shifting of socially undesirable impulses from the conscious to the unconscious region of the individual psyche. But such shifting or transfer has its own constraints. For repression to take place there has to be a tacit agreement between the aggressive and demanding *id* and the peace-loving and the appeasing *ego/superego* so that the deeds of the former may be fulfilled in ways which do not interfere with the normal functioning of the latter. Repression is based on the temporary truce between the genital and the social/moral agents of the psyche so that the individual can maintain his public image and yet fulfil his libidinal demands. It is only by virtue of such *compromise solutions* that an avowedly pacific person can condemn all forms of sexuality/cruelty and yet remain absorbed with newspaper reports or learned accounts of sadism, violence and rape (cf. Sharma 1986).

The predominating bulk of embarrassingly sexual imagery in traditional sacred writings of the Hindus seems to have emanated from psychic mechanisms like repressions and compromise solutions in authorial psyches. Utopian ideals of celibacy and sexual continence entailed segregation between the sexes on a mass scale. Such systematic segregations led to an unnecessary starvation of sexual urges. Starvation ultimately paved the way for a mass upsurge of aggressive sexuality which flooded every field of intellectual and creative activity. A character in an Aldous Huxley short story very rightly suggests to another character: "Read Freud. Repressions are the devil" (cited in Sharma 1986). Prolonged starvations boomerang. Repressions invariably foster some sort of voyeurism in those who harbour them. An awareness like this can easily explain why such a large part of Sanskrit erotic literature is openly voyeuristic. But here one must take care to separate the repressive from the genuinely pious. There seems to be no valid reason for going the whole hog with Freud. Sexual continence may be a fact of authentic experience for some—at least for those who freely choose to transcend sexuality. People who go through their erotic experiences, whether actual or imagined, as witnesses unto themselves, ultimately realize the inner hollowness of such experiences as their minds are consistently geared towards discovering the genuine adventures of the soul. Those who live life self-consciously or pursue the life of the spirit as the highest goal of human development can and do achieve true sublimation. There are plenty of such illustrious examples in history. Individuals can achieve any goal. Individuals can do miracles. Hundreds of individuals have already demonstrated that transcending sexuality is a child's play. Sex-seekers can definitely become sex-dispensers. Fools can become angels. An ordinary mortal can become a prophet by a continual search and research in the soul and by consciously moving towards a fixed goal. Success in matters of spiritual evolution will depend on a free and conscious choice on the part of the seeker as well as on his determination to achieve his noble aim as the highest aim of his mortal existence. Spiritual realization cannot be a matter of duplicity or double-dealing. A real calamity befalls a community when double-dealers pose as spiritual leaders and impose their bogus visions on others as visions of the ultimate truth. No one has a right to force others to be spiritualists, particularly when the leader himself is not truly spiritual. The plethora of sexual imagery in Hindu literature may be seen as the contribution of fake spiritualists who happened to be writers.

Perhaps no other text represents the equivocal Hindu view of sex than the *Kamasutra* does. In the concluding section of his work, the author claims: "The *Kamasutra* was composed, according to the precepts of the Holy Writ, for the benefit of the world, by Vatsyayana, while leading the life of a religious student and wholly engaged in the contemplation of the Deity" (Archer 1963 : 292). To Pannikar, the *Kamasutra* is essentially a didactic work: "The didactic character derives from the fact that kama or the life of the senses is considered by the Hindus as a necessary and integral part of man's life, as much entitled to study as all other aspects of life" (1963). From the very time of its writing, the *Kamasutra* acquired "the position of an authoritative text which no later writer has even ventured to question" and Vatsyayana has been alluded to with reverence as Vatsyayana "the great seer" (*ibid.*). Many a traditionalist like Pannikar would claim that the secret of Vatsyayana's immense popularity lies in his successful harmonization of Dharma and Kama, Piety and Eroticism. Vatsyayana is great because it is he who shows, for the first time in Hindu history, that erotic satisfaction is "as necessary for the existence and well-being of the body as food" (Archer 1963 : 106). Such historical defence of Vatsyayana's timeless appeal to the Hindus calls to mind Dr. Johnson's well-known defence of Shakespeare's perennial appeal in terms of its agelessness : "What mankind have long possessed they have often examined and compared, and if they persist to value the possession, it is bacause frequent comparisons have comfirmed opinions in its favour. ...The reverence due to writings that have long subsisted arises therefore not from any credulous confidence in the superior wisdom of past ages, or gloomy persuasion of the degeneracy of mankind, but in the consequence of acknowledged and indubitable positions, that what has been longest known has been most considered, or what is most considered is best understood" (1061).

No objective critic of the *Kamasutra* will possibly reclaim today Johnson's eulogy for his text nor will he accept Pannikar's apotheosis of Vatsyayana without a pinch of salt. The real secret of the *Kamasutra's* timeless appeal to readers lies not in its so-called successful harmonization of Piety and Eroticism nor in its theoretical sophistication or academic excellence but in something else. The *Kamasutra* is loved and admired either due to the 'credulous confidence in the superior wisdom of past ages' or to the 'gloomy persuasion of the degeneracy of mankind' but never because of its thematic value or organizational skill. Pannikar is certainly right when he remarks that the *Kamasutra* soon became a canonical text in literature, sculpture and painting, that is, wherever "Love had to be treated. ...No single work has influenced the treatment of love as Vatsyayana's has done" (1963). Archer also agrees that Vatsyayana's work shows "how central and natural to Indian thought was sex. Indian art, poetry and religion had all reflected this basic concern" (1963 : 41). The influence of this work permeated almost all genres of Sanskrit literature, including drama, epic poetry and religious works. Most notable examples of erotic sculpture and painting came to later generations as visual versions of Vatsyayana's aphorisms on sexual union. Pannikar's second reason for praising the *Kamasutra* is that it presents a realistic picture of ancient Hindu society: "A gay and happy people who worshipped their gods, performed their rituals but enjoyed life with all its refinement to the full" (*ibid.*). To quote Archer again: "Vatsyayana is a kind of camera neither praising nor blaming but surveying the whole field of sex" (*ibid.*, p. 41). Finally and most importantly, Pannikar pays rich tributes to Vatsyayana for his proper sociological approach to the problem of sex as well as for his careful description of the social habits and practices of different regions in India. Pannikar therefore considers Vatsyayana as the forerunner of such sociological writers on sex as Havelock Ellis, Malinowski, Craft-Ebbing and others.

Nevertheless, what Pannikar's historical evaluation of *Kamasutra* fails to take note of is the fact that its so-called popularity may have accrued from its being the first manual on sex-relations. But it needs to be emphasized here that a work cannot be said to acquire greatness simply because it happens to precede other works in that field of study. Vatsyayana cannot claim any credit for belonging to an earlier age. As for his sociological approach, it must be noted that his work does not show any valuable awareness of the socio-cultural variables of sex-relations. It is in fact a commonsensical description of what men of different societies do to draw sexual satisfaction from their women. Social customs and practices are bound to differ from place to place and from time to time. Besides, the *Kamasutra* does not show how sex is related or relatable to spiritual development. The concluding section of his text merely tells us that he was engaged in spiritual contemplation while composing this work. Any hack can make that claim. It does not do Vatsyayana any credit to initiate his discussion with a remark like: "Kama is the enjoyment of appropriate objects by the five senses of hearing, feeling, seeing, tasting and smelling, associated by the mind together with the soul" (Archer 1963 : 102-3).

Or conclude his study with a pompous assurance like: "This work is not intended to be used merely as an instrument for satisfying our desires. A person, acquainted with the true principles of this science, and who preserves his Dharma, Artha and Kama, and has regard for the practices of the people, is sure to obtain the mastery over his senses" (*ibid.*, p. 292).

Between the initial generalization and the final claim there is nothing in the text to show that a properly organized sex life is congenial to the harmonization of body and soul, flesh and spirit. The reason for the pervasive influence of the *Kamasutra* on literature, sculpture and painting is not far to seek. Vatsyayana's manual does not come anywhere near Havelock Ellis' *Psychology of Sex* or Freud's *Three Essays on Sexuality*, either in its thematic coverage or in its theoretical sophistication. Unlike the work of Ellis or Freud, the *Kamasutra* is a disappointing dissertation on sexuality from both points of view. Vatsyayana cannot compare with either of these theorists for the simple reason that his generalizations (few though they are) lack validity. As Archer puts it: "Whatever the instructional value the book may have had has since long elapsed" (1963 : 38). Vatsyayana's treatment of the subject is based on all sorts of fantasies about male sexuality. It is amazing that his work, despite such glaring deficiencies should have appealed to generations of religious thinkers and creative artists. The only feasible explanation for its popularity with educated readers is that probably it is the very nature of the subject concerned. Besides, its appeal may also have accrued from the frankness of its presentation. The *Kamasutra* is a lovable book for those thinkers and artists who always think of sex-enjoyment but never have the guts to think aloud. It fascinates those readers who love to visualize sexuality everywhere but do not have the stamina to project their own sexuality. It appeals as much to the general reader as to the learned and the pious mainly because it offers pornography through so-called spiritualism. Traditional Hindu Erotics variously known as Kamashastra, Kokashastra, Vaishikikala and Vaishikupachara is nothing more or less than sheer pornography (cf. Archer 1963 : 91-92 & De 1969 : 45).

Modern readers of the *Kamasutra* may still be grateful to its author. Vatsyayana did what few Maharshis or holy men of his age could have done. It was only a bold idealist like him who could devote himself, risking his whole reputation for generations to come to the unclean work of making available a recorded description of sexual union and its accessories which most educated people cherish but few like to talk about in public. Interestingly, the admirers of the *Kamasutra* also miss the point that Vatsyayana, like Ellis and Freud after him, formulated an ethic of male sexuality from the male point of view, thereby assigning to the female the status of a sex object.

An avowed advocate of free love, Vatsyayana never shrinks from the gross physicality of sex. He defines sex as "the contact between an organ of sense and its object and the consciousness of pleasure of such contact" (Archer 1963 : 103 & 106). He clearly lays down that the pleasure of sexuality is as necessary for the existence and well-being of the body as food. Introducing the reader to the sixty-four coital postures or ways of making love, Vatsyayana also recommends the sexual enjoyment of such women as widows, helpless women, old women, deformed women, sick women, female ascetics, maid servants, dancing girls, public women, married women, poor women and rustic women (cf. *ibid.*, pp. 111, 122, 214-216 & 231-32, De 1969 : 96 & 102). Vatsyayana's view on the enjoyment of women deserves to be analysed with reference to his decree that women who wish to marry must have unimpeachable conduct, physical charms, lucky marks on the body, agreeable name, the proper size and number of teeth, nails, ears, hair, and breasts (Archer 1963 : 173 cf. Chakladar 1976 : 119). He also makes it mandatory for women who wish to be sexually satisfying to their husbands, lovers and enjoyers to learn and master the sixty-four techniques of sexual union (Archer 1963 : 108). He is in full agreement with the orthodox sex ethic which prescribes that women should be enjoyed either for progeny or for pleasure (*ibid.*, p. 119).

A woman who is enjoyed or enjoyable by the *Nagarika* (the man-about-town or the gentleman) is a *Nayika* (cf. *ibid.*, pp. 57, 61 & 119). As the *Kamashatru* makes no allowances for the sexual continence of woman, the term 'Nayika' becomes a synonym for 'woman'. Such implicit semantic equivalence between Nayika and woman suggests, beyond all doubt, that in Vatsyayana's view every woman is sexually enjoyable by men, particularly by 'gentlemen'. A gentleman, he believes, devoid of other knowledge but well versed in the sixty-four ways of making love, is "a leader in any society of men and women" (*ibid.*, p. 170). Vatsyayana is all praise for "roughness and impetuosity" as characteristic of men, and therefore recommends 'oral' and 'anal' sex with women, which he calls "mouth congress" and "lower congress" respectively (cf. pp. 153 & 160-62). His inventory of the sixty-four ways of making love, he says, is not meant to be taken as exhaustive: "An ingenious person should multiply the kinds of congress after the fashion of the different kinds of birds and beasts. For these different kinds of congress, performed according to the usage of each country (that is, region) and the liking of each individual, generate love, friendship and respect in the hearts of women" (p. 153).

Vatsyayana divides Nayikas into four classes: Padmini or Lotus woman, Chitrini or Art woman, Shankhini or Conch woman and Hatsini or Elephant woman. Like the Greek image of Venus, the Lotus woman is represented by Vatsyayana to stand forth as the type of most perfect feminine beauty: "She in whom the following signs and symptoms appear is called a Padmini. Her face is pleasing as the full moon, her body well clothed with flesh, is soft as the mustard flower; her skin is fine, tender and fair as the yellow lotus, never *dark coloured*. Her eyes are bright and beautiful as the orbs of the fawn, well cut, and with reddish corners. Her bosom is hard, full and high; she has a good neck; her nose is *straight* and lovely and three-folds cross her middle—about the umbilical region. Her yoni [the sex organ] resembles the opening lotus bud and her love seed (kamasalila) is perfumed like the lily that has newly burst. She walks with a swan—like gait, and her voice is low and musical, as the note of the Kokila bird (the cuckoo); she delights in white raiment, in jewels, and in rich dresses. She eats little, sleeps lightly, and being as respectful and religious as she is clever and courteous, she is ever anxious to worship the gods, and to enjoy *the conversation of Brahmanas*" (p. 88, my italics). Vatsyayana's description of the Padmini soon became the standard image of the heroine in works of literature, both secular and religious.

As the *Kamasutra* is addressed to the gentleman, it is the undisputed Hindu authority on coital acrobatics which constructs a vantage point for the male in order that he may inflict his sexuality on any and every woman he can lay his hands on with a sense of impunity—both social and religious. A Nayika, after all, is a woman coition with whom is not prohibited by Dharma (cf. p. 61). Vatsyayana fails to separate the wife from the Nayika. Besides, his ethic of marital fidelity on the part of the wife is contradicted by his exhortation to men to seduce married women for adulterous linkages. His prescription that every woman must study and master the sixty-four coital postures and the sixty-four skills in order to be sexually satisfying to men, obliges the female to look upon the male as the reference point for her sexual conduct. The injunction that a woman should never take the initiative in sexual bargaining with a man is a notorious example of the masculinist philosophy which projects men as 'hunters' and the women as the 'hunted'. He says: "Although the girl loves the man ever so much, she should not offer herself, or make the first overtures, for a girl who does so loses her dignity and is liable to be scorned and rejected. But when the man shows his wish to enjoy her, she should be favourable to him and should show no change in her demeanour when he embraces her, and should receive all the manifestations of his love as if she were ignorant of the state of his mind" (pp. 187-88). Contrary to his own maxim that "men want pleasure", while women [courtesans] want money, he admonishes the courtesans: "Even when she be invited by any man to join him, she should not at once consent for a union, because men are apt to despise things which are easily acquired" (p. 249).

As regards physical suitability for coital exercises, Vatsyayana divides both men and women into three respective classes. A man is a hare man, a bull man, or a horse man "according to the size of the lingam". Similarly, a woman is a deer woman, a mare woman or an elephant woman "according to the depth of the yoni" (p. 127). When the male exceeds the female in point of size, the union is called a "high union" but when the female exceeds the male in point of size, the union is called a "low union". Vatsyayana considers a high union superior to a low union because "in the former it is possible for the male to satisfy his own passion without injuring the female, while in the latter it is difficult for the female to be satisfied by any means" (p. 127). However, a little later, he suggests that whether it is a high union or a low union, the female must make such bodily postures as enable the male to obtain maximal satisfaction (p. 150).

Arbuthnot's discovery of the *Kamasutra* in the last quarter of the nineteenth century created quite a stir in the Western world not only because it is the first text on sexuality; it acquires such great historical significance mainly because it has been seen as a uniquely daring exposition of an explosive topic like human sexuality. It took quite sometime for Arbuthnot to realize that far from being "An aberration, it was in fact a crucial part of the Indian tradition" (p. 39). Referring to the Indian tradition of sex scholarship, Sir William Jones had already remarked: "That anything natural can be offensively obscene never seems to have occurred to the Indians or their legislators; a singularity pervading their writings and conversations but no proof of moral depravity" (p. 39). We all know that in a sense we remain naked in spite of our dress and yet we cannot go dressless if we have to continue as decent, civilized people. Our dress or our civilization has not yet given incontrovertible proof of our moral decency or correctness; it still leaves much to be desired. Nevertheless, defects in civilization can be no justification for an organized return to barbarism or even to primitivism. We have already reached a point of no return, where we have an alternative between going ahead or remaining stayput. We have covered our bodies for so long that any programme of denuding ourselves will ultimately amount to barbarism. Nakedness in public therefore has to be viewed as a manifestation of psychic perversity or moral depravity. As it voices a slogan for public nakedness in a civilized society, the *Kamasutra* has to be seen as a recorded code of a moral depravity (or psychic perversity), howsoever, solemn and venerable its depravity or perversity may be thought to be. This view of the *Kamasutra*, as of other texts in this tradition, is validated by how Jones himself reacted to such writings. Archer tells us that in translating the *Gita Govinda* of Jayadeva, Jones shrank from "putting into English the more literal descriptions of Radha and Krishna's love making" (p. 39). Pannikar also agrees that the *Gita Govinda* was written under the influence of Vatsyayana's work. The verses describing the ecstasies of the union between Radha and Krishna in terms of carnal love can be understood fully only "in terms of Vatsyayana's text. Indeed, the standard commentary on this work by Kumbha, the king of Mewar, quotes liberally from the *Kamasutra* to explain the allusions in the text" (Pannikar 1963). For an authentic appraisal of the much glorified Hindu erotic literature, both secular and religious, we need today more than anything else, an objective insight into the thought process that motivated the composition of such literature. We need an *insider* who hates the ugly side of the inside with a venom born of knowledge and yet places the whole thing into its right perspective. We need a Nirad Choudhury to set the record straight: "There lies within the cavernous foundation in India a clayey core and within that clayey core something irredeemably corrupt which is in love with all the obscenities of which mankind is capable" (1987 : 205).

A boundless love of female nudity has been a characteristic of Hindu literature from the earliest times. A representative passage in the *Rig-Veda* describes the lovely goddess of dawn, Usha, as a dancing girl "who clothes herself in best raiments but keeps her bosom bare to attract the eyes of all" (cf. De 1969 : 87). But it was under the direct influence of the *Kamasutra* that Sanskrit erotic literature went beyond all proportions to display and cherish the grossly sensual, the obscenely naked. There is found among ancient writers a general tendency to season their descriptions *can more* with details which are often embarrassing and vulgar. De rightly points out: "The physical charms of men are seldom directly described; but those of women are profusely and frequently depicted with a passionate intensity of detail. Most of these descriptions, no doubt, follow an established literary convention and the stereotyped prescription of the science of erotics and poetics. .... It is remarkable that in describing feminine charms, only such details are selected as have franks sexual appeal" (*ibid.*, p. 38). In depicting female beauty, special attention is focussed on such parts of the body as cheeks, lips, hips, thighs and breasts. As the earliest and most illustrious poetic manifestations of Vatsyayana's magic spell, the works of Kalidasa set a trend which was tenaciously maintained by almost all later writers to the extent that it became a regular practice with epic writers to devote, at least, one Canto to the physical charms of the heroine, as a matter of necessity (cf. Pannikar 1974 : 91).

The *Kamasutra* eulogizes the ancient custom according to which women, except maid servants, had to keep their breasts open. This is evident also from the voluptuous paintings in caves and sculptural designs on the outer walls of temples where the breasts of even royal women are exposed (cf. Archer 1963 : 145 & 206). Vatsyayana recommends that women who want to be loved and enjoyed must keep their breasts open; not only that, they must have their breasts as well as the other sensitive parts of the body nail-marked by their lovers, husbands or enjoyers, for "the love of a woman who sees the marks of nails of the private parts of her body, even when she is old and almost worn out, becomes again fresh and new. If there be no marks of nails to remind a person of the passages of love, then love is lessened in the same way or as when no union takes place for a long time. ... Nothing tends to increase love so much as the effects of marking with the nails and biting" (*ibid.*, pp. 144-45). It is significant to remember in this context that even a great poet-dramatist like Kalidasa endorses this obnoxious custom of biting, nail marking and breast-exposure for lovable women. In a passage already quoted from his famous play, he describes Shakuntala as "a delicate sprout not yet plucked by nails" and "a jewel not yet perforated". In a similar vein he depicts women in the *Ritusamhara* as waiting for their lovers with their "breasts smeared with sandal paste and unguents and their bodies decorated with jewels and ornaments in order to attract men" (cf. Sengupta 1974 : 91). Emphasizing the sexual appeal of woman's hair in the *Raghuvansham* he says: "In the hair of the young damsels, unbraided, perfumed and still wet after a bath, and decorated with the evening jasmine, the god of love regained strength which had been diminished by the departure of the spring" (cf. De 1969 : 39).

The heroine in Kalidasa is a poetic version of Vatsyayana's Lotus woman. The central focus of all such poetic—erotic descriptions is the sexual appeal of woman's body. The woman attracts the attention of the onlooker, lover or husband because she is considered eminently enjoyable. In the *Purvameghaduta* Kalidasa sees a sunken river with cane branches touching its bed as a woman whose loins are stripped naked and whose hips are held by the hands of the lover. The poet therefore poses a rhetorical question: Who can resist the temptation of enjoying such a woman? (cf. Agrawala 1985 : 64). In the *Raghuvansham* pleasure ponds with full blown lotuses and sweet singing passionate birds are compared to women whose smiling faces are so lovely and whose girdles jingle as they are loosened. In another image, the city of Mithila is described on the two occasions of reception and farewell of king Dasaratha's entourage. When king Dasaratha comes, the city resounds with excitement but when he leaves it becomes desolate and sullen. The face of proud Mithila looks like a menstruating woman whose dusky hair looks like hawk's wings and whose blood clothes resemble ominous red evening clouds (cf. *ibid.*, p. 65). For Kalidasa, as for other poets of love, the breasts of woman are the most tempting parts of the female anatomy. In the *Ritusamhara* the thickly clouded sky is likened to a pregnant woman with swollen and dark breasts while in the *Purvameghaduta* the mountain, whose skirt is covered with ripe mango fruits and whose peak is capped by thick clouds, is imagined to be a woman who has large and heavy breasts which are dark at the centre and white in the rest of the expanse (*ibid.*, p. 77). Again, the *Raghuvansham* describes the slender Ashoka tree covered with branches of lovely flowers. This Ashoka tree looks like a slender young pretty woman with lovely and graceful breasts (p. 78). The love-lorn Shakuntala is described as: "Being tormented with love, Shakuntala's cheeks were excessively emaciated, her breasts lost their hardness, her waist became even more slender, her shoulders were extremely sunken and her complexion became pale. Even then the splendour of her loveliness did not leave her" (pp. 276-77). A characteristic passage in the *Kumarasambhavam* depicts the first drops of the first shower as they fall on scantily dressed, near-nude, Parvati's body: "The drops fall on her head and trickle down to her eyelashes where they remain for a moment; then they move down and beat her lips; by the time they come down to her elevated breasts, they get scattered; they take quite some time to cross the three folds of her belly before they reach the deep hole of her navel" (p. 249).

Sanskrit erotic poetry specializes in the systematic sexualization of the female body along the lines suggested by Maharshi Vatsyayana. The poet of the *Shringara-tilaka* exclaims: "Truly, this maiden is a huntress: her brows are like the bow, her glances are like the shafts, while my heart the deer they fall upon" (quoted in De 1969 : 39). A passage, attributed sometimes to Amaru and sometimes to Dharmakriti, depics a love-sick swain cursing himself for his failure to enjoy the beloved: "She is young but it is we who are shy; she is a woman but it is we who are timid; she is weighed down with her ample hips but it is we who can hardly walk; she bears the heaviness of her bosoms, but it is we who feel wearied" (quoted in *ibid.*, p. 52). Harsha's *Nagananda* which dramatizes the Buddhist legend of Jimutavahana depicts the husband's experience of the young and adolescent Malyavati in these words: "Looked at, she casts down her eyes; addressed, she makes no reply; forcibly embraced, she lies averted on the couch and trembles; when her companions leave the chamber, she also seeks to depart. Perverse though she be, my newly wedded love delights me more and more" (*ibid.*, p. 60). A characteristic feature of such erotic poetry is evident from the general tendency of poets to eulogize the adolescent and artless heroine (*mugdha*) as the one just referred to. One can easily collect a compendium of extracts from literary masterpieces which emphasize the sexual and call it erotic.

5.2 The Sacred View

"Lovely her loins, abode of Kamadev,
High and round her hips, hill-shaped her lower region,
Adorned with gold chains,
Sensuous seduction for a saint"!

—*The Mahabharata*

No apotheosis of the symbolism of female nudes sculptured on the walls of temples can ever succeed in convincing a discerning observer that it is out of genuine religiosity rather than of clandestine sexuality that Hindus visualised the sexual act (*maithuna*) as they did. Figures like these deserve to be identified as sculptural representations of Vatsyayana's Aphorisms on sexuality and there is therefore no reason to accept Pannikar's specious generalization: "What the Hindu sculptures endeavour to realize is this mystic union and the figures on the temple walls, voluptuous as they are in their poses, convey an idea of serenity, ever more than that of enjoyment" (1963). The sheer physicality of these figures of sexual union is further confirmed not only by the consistent patronage given by temple authorities to the notorious practice of *temple prostitution*; it is clearly discernible even in scriptural perceptions of the *why* of woman. A verse in the *Brihadaranyaka* Upanishada, for example, offers a teleological justification of the sexual enjoyment of women: "Lord of creatures (Prajapati) bethought himself: Come, let me provide him

[man] a firm basis". So he created woman. When he had created her, he revered her *below*.—Therefore one *should* revere woman below.—He stretched out for himself that *stone* which projects. With which he impregnated her" (Hume 1949 : 168, italics added). Likewise, a lover/husband in the *Atharva-Veda* steals to his wife's room at night and induces her to make love to him with these words: "My love, the disquieter, disquiets thee. With the terrible *arrow* of Kama do I *pierce* thee in thy heart. The arrow, winged with loving, *barbed* with love, whose *shaft* is undeviating desire, with that *well-aimed* Kama shall I pierce thee in the heart .... Consumed by *burning* ardour, with *parched* mouth, do thou (woman), come to me, mine *alone*, speaking sweetly and to me *devoted*" (cf. De 1969 : 3-4, italics added).

The view of sex represented in the extracts just quoted should be sufficient to serve as evidence of the characteristic Hindu view of sex and sexual union because they occur in texts which form the bedrock of Hindu philosophy and theology (cf. Hume 1949 : 2 & Mahadevan 1975). This view of sex involves an inherent contradiction between the high and the low of the Hindu mind—a mind which loves union with God and union with woman at a time or, to put it slightly differently, union with God through union with woman by glossing over the synonymity between the carnal and the divine. The typical Hindu mind is a mind out of joints and hence this extra-emphasis on union. Such a self-contradictory view of celestial sexuality calls to mind Cleopatra's magic over both the secular and the religious:

> "... for vilest things
> Become themselves in her, that the holy priests
> Bless her when she is riggish"
> (Antony & Cleopatra II : II : 242-44).

According to an accepted principle in psychoanalysis, it is possible to explore the psychic history of an artist in terms of the compulsive images which structure his work, that is, a work of art may be read as a psychobiography of the artist. Freud's study of Leonardo is so well known. Freud's contention that a creative work should be seen as a disguised fulfilment of the author's repressed or unsatisfied intra-psychic conflicts and wishes is nowhere as persuasive as in the context of the religious literature of the Hindus. Every single image or fantasy in a creative work, from the Freudian/

psychoanalytic point of view, is the fulfilment of the wish, the resolution of a conflict or the correction of an unsatisfying reality. "The artist", contends Freud, "is originally a man who turns from reality because he cannot come to terms with the demands for the renunciation of his instinctual satisfaction as it is first made, and who then in fantasy-life allows full play to his erotic and ambitious wishes" (cited in Sharma 1986). Defining poetry (i.e., art in general) as: "The record of the best and happiest moments of the best and happiest minds", even Shelley admits that the poet is "a nightingle who sits in darkness and sings to cheer its own solitude with sweet sounds; his auditors are as men entranced by the melody of an unseen musician; who feel that they are moved and softened, yet know not whence and why" (cf. Sharma 1979 : 44). Why does a creative work please the reader or viewer so much? Freud's answer is simple. The real secret of the emotional appeal of a work of art lies in the writer's success in arousing in his audience the same inner satisfaction, the same mental constellation, the same attitude, the sense of relief or the sense of freedom which the composition of the work originally created in his own mind. A work of art is a thing of beauty and enjoyment which comes from a heart and goes to a heart. A reader (or viewer) enjoys a work of art because it enables him to overcome psychic tensions as also because it enables him to obtain full and safe gratification for his libidinal cravings without reproach or shame. Artistic compositions with excessively erotic pictures, portraits, symbols and images acquire immediate as well as lasting acceptability chiefly because of their capacity to forge a secret bridge between the author and the reader (viewer) in such a way that they enjoy pornography under the banner of sublime art.

Every erotic portrait of woman in Hindu poetry, painting and sculpture, irrespective of who is involved, emphasizes those parts and aspects of the female anatomy which provoke and satisfy male sexuality. One can take, without any weakening of this argument, any number of passages for illustration from the *Mahabharata*, perhaps the most puzzling book on male-female equation in the religio-literary corpus of Hinduism. As desired by Satyavati and recommended by Bhishma, the learned and holy sage, Vyas, comes to impregnate the twin-widows of his younger half-brother Vichitravirya with a view to preserving the family line. The epic describes Vyas as a horrible-looking sex-performer with "his frightful face, his matted coppery hair, his livid eyes, black beard and repugnant smell" and

Ambika and Ambalika as tall, slender, young and beautiful women "with skins of the colour of burnt gold, with round heavy breasts and with full hips" (cf. Lal 1980 : 74 & 71). It is only natural that at the site of this monstrous sex-performer Ambika closes her eyes and Ambalika pales with fear, thereby the former giving birth to the perpetually blind Dhritarashtra and the latter to the perpetually jaundiced Pandu.

Born from the centre of a great sacrificial altar, the multi-husbanded, ever-youthful Draupadi is introduced in the first book of the epic as a damsel of rare beauty and charms: "Her eyes were black and lotus-large, her hair fell in waves, and she was dark-skinned; her curved nails shone bright as copper, her eye-brows were fair, her breasts heavy; and her body gave out the fragrance of a blue lotus" (cf. *ibid.*, pp. 98 & 378). Much later, in the fourth book, when Draupadi is wandering in the Kingdom of King Virata as a hair-dressing woman, Queen Sudeshna summons her to say that she cannot be what she claims to be: "You are too beautiful. Your heels are delicate, your navel deep, your thighs touch each other; your breasts and hips are round; you speak as sweetly as a swan, and your body has all the auspicious marks of a Kashmiri mare. Curved eye-lashes, red-brown lips, slender waist, a conchshell neck, a face like the moon—you must be the goddess Shri herself who will be able to resist your charms! Certainly not my husband. Your smile and glance will entrap anyone" (p. 177). Sudeshna's fears come true too soon. Kichaka, the brother of the Queen and the general of the Royal Army, goes mad with love for Draupadi. Lusting after her, he goes to Draupadi to pay an eloquent tribute to her ravishing beauty:

"Who are you, lovely lady?

What a face like the moon, a voice like the Koel's, and eyes like lotuses?

Your full and graceful breasts need garlands of gold,

There is no space for a reed between them.

Desire stirs within me;

Your waist is four-wrinkled and your breasts make you stoop,

Your breasts are like lotus buds-

They inflame me to desire.

Your hips are like river bank;

For you I will abandon my wives,-
Dress you in garlands and robes and jewellery,
Love you as a rain-filled cloud
Loves the earth with its soothing showers" (p. 178).

In a similar passage in the third book, the poet depicts the physical charms of Urvashi, the heavenly dancer:

"In her soft braids were clusters of flowers;
Delicate eye gestures and a moon-rivalling face.
As she walked, her full sandal-scented breasts,
Finally curved, supporting a golden necklace,
Trembled;
The weight of her breasts bent her three-fold waist,
She stooped at every step;
Lovely her loins, abode of Kamadeva,
High and round her hips, hill-shaped her lower region,
Adorned with gold chains,-
Sensuous seduction for a saint;
Her feet flat-soled,
Her toes copper-bright and curved like tortoise shells,
Tinkling with little bells;
Her breath slightly heady with wine and desire;
Her dress a fine and filmy cloth
Through which glowed her body like the moon through the cloud" (pp. 148-49).

As the worshipper and the erotomaniac wrestle with each other in the gymnasium of spiritualism, the latter often dodges the former and succeeds in asserting himself to the utter dismay of the simple onlooker. This sort of wrestling is perhaps nowhere better displayed than in the *Gita-Govinda* of Jayadeva which is generally agreed to be the most picturesque example of Vatsyayana's impact on Sanskrit religious poetry (cf. Pannikar 1963). What baffles an average student of Hindu philosophy is the fact that critical opinions which identify numerous connections between the *Kamasutra* and the *Gita-Govinda* often acclaim the latter as the supreme example of

Hindu religious poetry in spite of their awareness that it shows an obsessive concern with the carnal love between Radha and Krishna.

Born and brought up in a Brahmana family, Jayadeva married, according to divine will, Padmavati, a Brahamana girl who had been dedicated as a dancer to the temple of Jagannatha at Puri. With this marriage Jayadeva terminated his ascetic life and devoted himself along with his wife to the service of the temple deity. It was in the course of their shared devotion to the deity that Jayadeva composed the *Gita-Govinda* to celebrate the legendary amours of Radha and Krishna. It is often suggested that the complex structures in the poem are intended to integrate religious, erotic and aesthetic experiences so that the reader enjoys a unique convergence of human and divine love and that this poem is motivated by works like the *Kamasutra*, the *Meghduta* and the *Kumarasambhava* (cf. *ibid.*). We may, however, take note of the following extracts from the editor's introductory remarks:

"The lyrical techniques of Jayadeva's songs combine with the *conventional* language of Sanskrit erotic poetry to express the intimate power of divine love.

In the *Gita-Govinda* [the author seeks to make] potentially *pornographic* subjectmatter the material of esthetic and religious experience.

Jayadeva's verses nowhere praise *unbodied* joy; they are *explicitly sensual*, and celebrate the sensual joy of divine love.

Like the flower arrows of the God of love, Krishna's magic flute is an adolescent instrument for arousing and sustaining *sexual* desire. Both the arrow and the flute, with their obvious *phallic* significance, function in this way in many societies" (cf. Miller 1977, italics mine).

If the poem is part of 'Sanskrit erotic poetry', deals with a 'pornographic subject matter', celebrates 'explicitly sensual' and 'bodied joy', and contains 'obvious phallic significance' of the 'arrow' and the 'flute', how can it be considered a *religious* poem? If a religious poem does what a chapter in the *Kamasutra* does, how can it deserve the label of a religious poem? The presence or absence of the label *religious* or *divine* does not by itself change the semantics or perspectives of a work. No amount of ambiguation, euphemism or glossary can ever change a carnal poem into a spiritual song.

Philosophization of vulgarity is vulgarization of philosophy. The name does not change the tenor of the poem. A good name cannot convert a bad poem into a good poem: "What's in the name? That which we call a rose. By any other name would smell as sweet" (*Romeo* and *Juliet* II : II : 43-44). Even adolescent Juliet is wiser than the pedantic Hindu who stakes so much for a name. We have no business to say 'divine' and mean `human', to say `spiritual' and mean `carnal' or to say `mystical' and mean `physical'. It is far better and more convenient to say `carnal' and mean `carnal' than to say `spiritual' and mean `carnal'. Anyone who reads the *Gita-Govinda* today, will find it intensely erotic even to the point of being explicitly pornographic. A mere look at extracts like the following should convince any unbiased reader that the *Gita-Govinda* is full of referents which are just sexual.

Recalling the ecstatic experiences of Krishna's love-making to her, Radha confides to a girl friend:

> "I shy from him when we meet;
> he coaxes me with flattering words.
> I smile at him tenderly as he loosens the silken cloth on my hips.
> I fall on the bed on tender forms;
> he lies on my breasts for ever.
> I embrace him, kiss him;
> he clings to me drinking my lips.
> My eyes close languidly as I feel the flesh quiver on his cheek.
> My body is moist with sweat, he is shaking from the wine of love.
> I murmur like a cuckoo;
> he masters love's secret rite.
> My hair is the tangle of wilted flowers,
> My breasts bear his nailmarks.
> Jewel anklets ring at my feet
> as he reaches the height of passion.
> My best, falls noisily;
> he draws back my hair to kiss me" (Part II : Verses : 12-16 pp. 80-81).

Krishna induces Radha to join him in his love-making:

"Punish me, lovely fool!
Bite me with your cruel teeth!
Chain me with your creeper arms!
Crush me with your hard breasts!
Angry goddess, don't weaken with joy!
Let love's despised arrows pierce me to sap my life's power!"
(Part X : Verse : 11 p. 111).

The poet describes Radha's part in the love-game:

"Displaying her passion
In love-play as the battle began,
She launched a bold offensive
Above him
And triumphed over her lover.
Her lips were still,
Her vine-like arm was slack,
Her chest was heaving,
Her eyes were closed.
Why does a mood of manly force
Succeed for women in love" (Part XII : Verse : 10 p 123).

Radha invites Krishna to do her make-up.

"Paint a leaf on my breasts !
Put colour on my cheeks !
Lay a girdle on my hips !
Twine my heavy brand with flowers !
Fix rows of bangles on my hands !
And jewelled ankles on my feet !
Her yellow-robed lover.
Did what Radha said" (Part XII : Verse : 20 p. 125).

Who can separate the religious from the secular in lines as those quoted above? Isn't 'religious' a mere comouflage for the erotic? Literary sexualism, like other forms of sexualism, does not define its limits. As a matter of fact, it infects every aspect of the male perception of the female, no matter who the female is. In the traditional literary corpus, as in other art forms, man-woman relationship is generally viewed as an erotic or even sexual relationship. There is a text which portrays the Rama-Sita relationship as an intensely erotic or sexual relationship. The poet's description of the love game between Rama and Sita in the second act of the *Hanumannatakam*, for instance, often outstrips the ultimate limits of obscenity. The following is an extract from a less obscene part of this poetic presentation:

"Taking overwhelmed and intensely excited Sita in his arms, Rama led her to the couch. Sita agreed to be led to the couch even though she wondered why she was being pierced with countless arrows when the God of love was believed to be only five-arrowed. `Don't touch me, Don't touch me', cried Sita and yet, provoked by Kama, she loosened her body when embraced by Rama lest he should be hurt by her hard breasts. Rama clasped her tight and kissed her. Taking each other in tight embrace and enjoying the cherished bliss, they experienced the world as uniquely new. Then the hero said something very endearing and sweet to her and asked her to lie down but she kept repeating "no, no", just out of shyness. Slowly their grips on each other slackened. A little later, Rama took betel-leaves full of sandal, camphor and nuts and induced Sita to take them from his mouth so that he could get an opportunity to kiss her sweet lips. With closed eyes, Sita took these four betel leaves from mouth to mouth. .... In the process Rama kissed her lips and experienced the highest bliss. Feigning to be weighed down by drowsiness while keeping her hands on her breasts, the lotus-eyed Sita seemed to hold her lord to her breasts so that he did not run away. The nipples of Sita's breasts peeping through her fingers looked like a pair of bees pierced by the arrows of Kamadeva. Gradually, Sita started quivering her thick thighs, loosening her hair, displaying her breasts and armpits while feigning drowsiness, only to further stimulate her lord. Rama kissed again and again but was not satisfied. He kissed her breasts, her armpits, her chest, her navel and her private parts. Extremely stimulated, Rama removed the clothes from her hips and loins; the anklets suddenly clasped with each other as if the god of love had strung his arrows on his bow. Then suddenly ... because it had been quaking with the fear of the noise of earings and anklets. During the coition, Sita would sometimes contract her thighs and say: 'no, no' and yet would enjoy it immensely" (Mishra 1978 : II : 10-12, my translation).

The rarest of rare shocks hits the reader of the *Ramayana* when Valmiki displays Rama and Ravana share an almost identical perception of Sita's voluptuousness. As soon as Ravana saw Sita, he was smitten with lust and he began to eulogize her beauty, thus:

"Ah, my beauty of golden hue, by wearing a lotus wreath you look like the lotus itself ! Perhaps you are Modesty's self, or Beauty, or Honour, or Fortune, or a Nymph, or Rati ranging at will. Your teeth are even, glossy and pointed like jasmine birds. Your eyes are crystal-clear, whose ends are tinged with red and adorned with deep-black pupils. Your hips are heavy and plump, thighs are round like the trunk of an elephant. Your breasts, high and plump with their thick and pointed teats are like two closely placed palms, and adorned with jewels seem to be ever waiting for an embrace. O, my beauty of winning smile, as the current of the river carries off its bank, so you have stolen my heart. Your waist is so slim, hair so dark! To tell the truth, no Goddess, no Gandharvi, no Yakshi, no Kinnari is like thee. In short, I have never seen a damsel like you on earth" (Sen 1976 : 388-89).

This vision of Sita so neatly compares with Rama's vision of her during his lamentation over her abduction by Ravana. Rama goes round the forest, asking everyone: men, women, animals, birds, trees etc., if anyone of them has seen Sita:

"Tell me, O Bilwa, hast thou seen her whose breasts are round like thy fruits, whose body is soft like tender sprouting leaves and who was clad in yellow silk cloth? O Palm, my darling's breasts are like your ripe fruits, please tell me if thou hast seen her! ... O Elephant, she whose thighs are round like your trunk is no doubt known to you, tell me if thou hast seen her. O Tiger, the countenance of my darling is beautiful like the moon, now tell me without any hesitation if thou hast seen her anywhere .... Ah, how lovely was Janaki's nose! How beautiful were her teeth! And how tempting were those lips! ... Alas, when the Rakshas carried her off, how piteously she shrieked in fear and how bitterly she wept ! Her white round breasts, perfumed with yellow sandal-paste, were surely bathed in blood.... Perhaps the blood-thirsty Rakshasas have torn into pieces the sweet neck of my darling adorned with gold chain" (*ibid.*, pp. 415-421).

Isn't it blasphemous to call such portraits religious or mystical? To attribute religious symbolism to such pornographic visions is to indulge in self-deception or to concoct lies, plain and simple. How unfortunate it is that vulgar eroticism is first allowed to permeate such a vast bulk of Hindu literature and art and then innocent people are coerced into looking for religious/mystical symbols, allusions and meanings therin.

Author of three famous plays, more than three dozen poetic masterpieces, and the best known Sanskrit writer, Kalidasa is sometimes known as the Indian Shakespeare. One of his poetic masterpieces, the *Kumarasamabhava* deals with the love-life of Shiva and Parvati, one of the three most revered mythological couples in the Hindu pantheon. A poet like Kalidasa could have written a great poem without borrowing so heavily from the *Kamasutra*. The poem as a whole overflows with vulgar sexuality but the seventh Canto (Kale 1967 : VII), which celebrates the nuptial revelries of the divine couple outstrips all boundaries of decency. Some of the less offensive verses read as follows: "Trembling, she obstructed the hand of Shankara as it was placed near the region of her navel; but her garment of its own accord had its tying knot completely loosened.

In private, with her garments taken off, she closed Shiva's (two) eyes with her two palms; but, as his (third) eye on the forehead continued looking, she had her efforts foiled and became helpless.

Dear to Shiva was the union with his bride, although it obstructed passion, and in which response was difficult to obtain, there being no offering of the lower lip (on her part) while kissing, while her hands hung loose when very firmly embraced.

Parvati could endure only that, and nothing else, on her lover's part, viz., kissing without biting the lower lip, marking with nails without wounding and enjoyment in moderation.

Pressed to his bosom, she embraced her lover. She did not turn away her face when it was desired (to be turned towards him) by him. She became slack in obstructing his hand as it tremblingly searched for her girdle-zone" (Verses 4, 7-9 & 14).

Shiva and Parvati drank heavily and then:

"Immediately that beautiful-faced came under the influence of the two, Shiva and passion, who deprived her of her shyness, who wanted to take her to bed, and whose lust was kindled" (Verse 79).

The poetic description of the revelry goes into minute details from verse to verse, thereby becoming increasingly obscene. What strikes an average student of Sanskrit literature with shock is the discovery that even the greatest of divine couples,—Radha-Krishna, Rama-Sita and Shiva-Parvati, are not left untouched by the fake spiritualists—turned—creative writers. A modern Hindu, surveying religious literature in Sanskrit, gets the shock of his life and loses all sense of literary pride when he gets into passages like the ones quoted above. He is baffled and hurt, stunned and wounded, not so much by the passages as such but by the signboard which they carry over their head. Reading such offensively sexual descriptions, he is not only embarrassed and slandered; he is ashamed of his cultural heritage and swindled out of his sense of morality. He finds in his literature an obsessive concern with the criminalization of theology or the theologization of criminality and comes to the conclusion that it is high time such duplicity was exposed and rejected once for all.

6

HORRORS OF DENIGRATION

6.1 Distorting the Feminine Image

> "A man with a hundred tongues would not be able to describe completely the vices and defects of women."
>
> —*Mahabharata*

Once upon a time, the Chinese used to deform the feet of their girls to shape them as beautiful women. Likewise, other patriarchal societies in their wisdom chose to deform the minds of their girls, their emotions, their creative faculties and their bodies to shape them for happiness in and out of marriage. Married women and public women began to feel 'happy' because they were 'sick' not realizing that they were sick because they had been shaped for marriage or for public service. They were kept in chains for so long and so systematically that most of them began to hug their chains. The male masters had elected to provide for their women and the women learnt in course of time to obey and please their providers. The masters did all they could do to distort, debase and enslave women and then they turned to the ruin with a sense of triumph and declared that the creatures they had so deeply injured were their 'inferiors'.

Why do men do all that they do to women? Who are the most hostile of men to the idea of the independence or equality of women?

It does not require scientific proof or Socratic wisdom to identify the least virile or the most inferior amongst men as the ones who are hell-bent on keeping women in their proper place simply because they have known in their own degradation how painful it is to be un-manly and inferior. As for the charge that women are naturally 'lustful', one has only to reflect that the accuser speaks not from wisdom but from a sense of terror of some weakness in himself, of this secret consciousness of a biological inferiority: the weakness or the inferiority being that he cannot bear children. He has therefore to project his sense of terror, guilt or inferiority upon the type-figure of woman; he has to be continually propped up by woman who can bear children in that he may have a sense of location in the universe. The whole arsenal of misogyny has to be examined with reference to the guilt-consciousness of the misogynist.

It cannot be a matter of simple coincidence that an overwhelming number of grand masterpieces—religious, semi-religious, gnomic, erotic, or pornographic—should operate within the same paradigm whenever they deal with male-female relationships. It cannot be an accident of intellectual adventurism that each of these masterpieces should project woman as 'inferior' to man. The highest common factor which brings these masterpieces together is their shared belief that man is intrinsically 'superior' to woman. Evolved by men for men, this paradigm has always and everywhere remained a paradigm of masculinism. Because it is partial and lop-sided, it is inauthentic and therefore must be condemnable at all times and in all societies. If we simply remember that these masterpieces say what they say only because they are produced by men, we can easily see through the game which is so often and so openly played in the name of God, morality or tradition. It is only proper that each of these masterpieces be viewed as a temporal reminder of the timeless and the local manifestation of the universal philosophy of male-female relationships.

Male history has seldom pricked male conscience. Males have exercised and enjoyed unlimited power over females. Males have indulged in and enjoyed indiscriminate sex. Males have manipulated and enjoyed unlimited exploitation of females. Males have enslaved and violated females. They have loved and hated females. They have admired and condemned females. They have loved to hate and admired to condemn females. They have loved and admired to tighten their grip over females. They have done everything within their power to falsify females. They have invoked divine powers and religious authorities to destroy woman's sense of autonomy, her right to be herself and her consciousness as a being separate from and independent of man. No wonder therefore that woman emerges from Hindu history as a victim of male power and sexuality. The tradition of male-female relationships within the patriarchal paradigm has to be seen as a chain of blatant lies about the nature, function and behaviour of woman.

As head of the family, the Roman *pater familias*, like the Vedic *bharta*, prescribes unexceptionable conformism for all women. The so-called 'weakness' and 'light-mindedness'—*infirmitas sexus* and *levitas animi*—of the female sex are the underlying principles of Roman legal theory that mandates all women to be under the custody of men (cf. Pomeroy 1975 : 150-152). Socrates, the commander-in-chief of Western patriarchal philosophy, confides to Timaeus that the nature of women should be "assimilated and brought into harmony with" that of men (Plato Vol. II : 18). He tells Glaucon in the *Republic*: "All the pursuits of men are the pursuits of women also, but in all of them a woman is inferior to man" (Plato Vol. I : 455). A verse in the *Quoran* decreases: "Men are incharge of women, because Allah hath made the one of them excel the other" (Pickthall 1924 : IV : 34). In the Jewish scripture, God says to Eve: "Thy desire shall be to thy husband and he shall rule over thee" (Genesis 2 : 16). According to the nuptial hymn in the *Rig-Veda*, the bridegroom accepts the bride at the conclusion of the marriage ceremony with a ritual invocation: "The gods have given thee to me that I may be the master of a household" (cf. Shastri 1969 : 15). Besides, there are in the *Rig-Veda* ritual exhortations of elderly guests to the bride so that she may enter her new life with a clear view of her duties and obligations and it is here that the Aryan Hindus surpass any other patriarchal set-up. Perhaps no other community of males has ever formulated such meticulously defined and rigidly systematized maxims and injunctions regarding the duties and obligations of wives and daughters. To be accepted as a wife, a woman is required to accept the values prescribed by the *pater familias* and his cronies.

If a wife is obedient, she becomes virtuous and respectable, and if she is both virtuous and obedient, she becomes a mother of sons. A woman must give sons to her husband, if she hopes to be retained as wife. To be a mother of sons must be considered by every married woman to be the ultimate peak of maternal fulfilment and the combined result of the wife's obedience and devotion to the husband. The son, every wife must realize, is the only passport to heaven. "The mother of a son", exclaims Indrani in the *Rig-Veda*, "deserves honour" (cf. Bader 1964 : 51-52). The sequence in which the three crucial demands are made upon the bride is definitely peculiar to the psychology of the Vedic *pater familias*. The bride is exhorted to "Be amenable; be glorious; be the mother of males" (cf. Shastri 1969 : 15). The new wife is required to be amenable in order to be glorious, to be glorious in order to be the mother of the males and to be the mother of the males in order to retain her wifehood. It is baffling, however, that in spite of her readiness to fulfil these demands, the wife is perpetually censured and scorned. To get the real feel of the cold-blooded and multiplex distortion of woman by man, one may turn to the pompous claims of the Upanishadic seer about the so-called spiritualty of man-woman relationship. Enlightening his scholar wife on the fellowship of the spirit, the eminent Yajnavalkya exclaims: "A husband is loved, not because you love the husband, but because you love in him the divine spirit. ... A wife is loved, not because we love the wife, but because we love in her the divine spirit. ... If we see, hear, perceive and know in him the divine spirit, O Maitreyi, then this whole universe is known to us. ... All is the divine spirit" (*Brihadaranyaka Upanishada* cited in Bader 1964 : 10-11). However, when we turn to survey what these divinely-spirited men have to say about their divinely-spirited women, we suddenly realize (apart from the chronic He in the divine) that the so-called knower and lover of the divinity in the wife habitually tries to seek, possess and condemn the female body and that he has no use for the spirit, human or divine, the moment he runs into a female. As a matter of fact, his attachment to divine knowledge is never as intense as is his full-mouthed attachment to the female body.

"Frailty, thy name is woman" (*Hamlet* : I : II : 147) characterizes the general view of woman in the Hindu canon which treats femininity as synonymous with sexuality, frivolity and fickle-mindedness. Indra's remark in the *Rig-Veda* that the mind of a woman is "ungovernable and her temper is fickle" (cf. De 1969 : 5) is typical of the tradition of thought on the subject. The *Rig-Veda* refers to Indra's *considered* opinion that women "cannot control themselves" (Altekar 1956 : 319-20). In the first love poem in the *Rig-Veda* which happens to be the earliest love-poem in human history, woman is represented as fickle-minded. Puruvas addresses Urvashi as "a fierce-souled spouse", charges her with having disappeared like "the first of dawns" and then implores her to return to him. At this Urvashi says:

"Puruvas, return thou to thy dwelling; I, like the wind, am difficult to capture". A little later Urvashi reveals:

"With women there can be no lasting friendship. Hearts of hyenas are the hearts of women" (cf. De 1969 : 1-2).

The second love poem in the *Rig-Veda* concerns Yama and his sister Yami. Yami is represented as pleading with Yama to have sex with her so that the human race could continue but Yama scorns her lustful overtures saying:

"Not me—go quickly, wanton, with another, whirl round with him like the wheels of a chariot" (cf. *ibid.*, p. 2).

What actually boggles the mind here is not that a sister should try to seduce her brother (perhaps early Aryans did not consider incest a taboo), but the basic question: Why should a sister invite her brother to go in for love-making when other men around? And if other men are around, why should she plead for an incestuous union to preserve the species? How were Yama and Yami created? Were their parents also siblings? It is possible that Rig-Vedic Aryans replaced endogamous or incestuous unions by exogamous marriages. Maybe, it was a period of transition and the leaders of the new social order needed a good deal of slogan—chanting and indoctrination to stop once for all formal or open sexual unions between siblings. But such a possibility does not account for the Rig-Vedic Aryan's denunciation of women as incestuous. Yami's alleged overture must be a deliberate concoction made to ensure that sex and marriage are fully masculinized.

Lustfulness and fickle-mindedness are generally agreed to be the two most prominent charges against women. In days of old, adult Spanish males used to take a ritual vow: "We shall save ourselves from wicked women and should never be captivated by any that have good looks" (quoted in Kidwai 1976 : 8). Socrates believed in a doctrine which condemned the lustfulness of women. He says "Woman is the source of all evil; her love is to be dreaded more than the hatred of man; the poor young men who seek women in matrimony are like fish who go to meet the hook" (cited in Altekar 1956 : 325). The Dialogues of Plato abound in such denunciatory generalizations. Socrates tells Timaeus that women originally owed their existence to their lustfulness and that was the reason why at the time of birth itself the gods "created in us the desire of sexual intercourse, contriving in man one animated substance and in woman another" (Plato : II : 18 & 91). Similarly, the Athenian instructs Cleinias in the *Laws* that women are "accustomed to creep into dark places and, when dragged into the light, they will exert their utmost powers of resistance" (*ibid.*, II : 781). The eternal question of which sex enjoys coition more is vigorously debated in the Olympian kingdom. Zeus holds that the female enjoys coition more than the male while Hera contends that it is just the opposite. To settle this dispute, Zeus invites Tiresias, the blind prophet, who is also a transvestite, that is, one who has been both a female and a male successively, and is a male at the moment, not a hermaphrodite as Eliot portrays him in the *Waste Land*: "An old man with wrinkled female breasts". Like a typical male of his age, Tiresias gives his verdict: "Women enjoy intercourse nine times more than men" (cf. Pomeroy 1975 : 146). There is nothing unusual or original about Tiresias' verdict. Men always condemn women for things which they are always looking for. Lear's condemnation of women as crude embodiments of filthy sexuality is a ready example:

> "Dawn from the waist they are centaurs,
> Though women all above;
> But to the girdle do the gods inherit,
> Beneath is all the fiends;
> There's hell, there's darkness, there is the sulphurous pit"
> (*Lear* IV : VI : 124-131).

How painful it is that even Shakespeare's own view of femininity is no different! In Sonnet 129 (already quoted in full) Shakespeare records his own testament of faith about the basic contradictoriness of the female flesh:

> "All this the world well knows; and yet none knows well
> To shun the heaven that leads men to this hell".

In Hindu literature the lustfulness of women is brought out for condemnation in strongest possible terms. Women's lust knows, no bounds, all great books would say. Like the Socratic pronouncement, a verse in the *Mahabharata* says: "Sexual enjoyment is the sole aim of woman's existence" (Altekar 1956 : 320), while another verse points out: "The fire has never too many logs, the ocean never too many rivers, death never too many living souls, and fair-eyed woman never too many men" (Basham 1967 : 183). Yet another passage in the epic elaborates this point by adding fresh material: "No man can satisfy a libidinous woman's cravings; unless constantly watched, she will consort with every stranger, even with a hunchback, a dwarf or a cripple; and in the last resort will have recourse to lesbian practices with members of her own sex. Her deception is all-embracing as her lust and she is incorrigibly fickle" (*ibid.*, p. 184). The author of the *Mahabharata* cannot visualize any limit to female sexuality. Dilating upon the duties of an ideal wife, Draupadi warns Satyabhama: "Don't be careless and frivolous when other men are present; be silent about what you think; and don't be alone too much *even with your own sons*" (Lal 1980 : 159, italics added). Saint-poet Tulasidasa, the congenital misogynist, takes his cue from Draupadi's remark and makes it more intense: "When a woman sees a comely man"; Kakabhushundi educates Garuda, "be he the *brother*, *father* or *son*, she is excited; nor can she check her passion, as a sunstone melts at the sight of the sun" (Hill 1952 : 306, italics added).

There are texts which visualize woman as the shortest and the surest route to hell. Lascivious and wily as they are, women, these texts constantly warn the reader, tempt and enslave men to perpetual bondage. According to that confused and confusing lover-saint, Bhartrihari, women are the cute agents of the Devil: "Smiles, sentiment, bashfulness, timidity, half-averted and half-tortured glances, side-long looks, loving words, jealously, quarrel and playfulness, all these are the ways by which women bind us" (cf. De 1969 : 34). He figures the love-god as a fisher who casts "woman as a bait on the ocean of the world, catches men by the line of red lips and bakes them on the fire of desire" (*ibid.*, p. 34). Coming on the heels of the Upanishadic Hindu, Jaina thinkers also see woman as a temptress who perpetuates the misery that is life. As women are believed to be eternally fickle-minded and unreliable, it is ordained that a monk of three years' experience has to become the mentor of a nun of thirty years' standing. Wily, evil, inscrutable and unclean as she is, a woman can never be trusted. As one Jain text has it: "The intelligent may know the sands of the earth, the waters of the sea, and the size of the Himalayas, but a woman's heart they may not know" (1964 : 105 & 111). It need not surprise anyone that even the Buddha did not have a good opinion of women (cf. *ibid.*, p. 82).

Given the intellectual milieu of classical Hindu literature, one does not have to think very hard to understand why physiological functions of woman like menstruation, advanced stages of pregnancy, child-birth and early lactation are consistently viewed with disfavour. In orthodox circles they are considered undesirable, impure and disdainful. The *Brihadaranyaka Upanishada* refers to menstrual clothes as "the clothes of impurity" (Hume 1949 : VI : IV : 6). It is not without purpose that menstruating women, like women on the eve of or during child-birth, once used to be, and sometimes still are, are segregated from the rest of the family. It is not for nothing that even great women like Shraddha (Manu's first wife), Sita, Draupadi and Ahalya were abandoned, exiled, denuded and turned into stone respectively, the first two during late pregnancy and the last two during menstruation. It is not a slip of the tongue/pen that women are so frequently spoken of as inherently impure and unclean. The *Kamasutra* reports that the people of Saurasena do indulge in kissing the mouth of women because they believe that, since women are naturally unclean, there is nothing wrong with this apparently indecent practice (cf. Chakladar 1976 : 43). Such notions of impurity appear to be cover terms for something much deeper. Men do not want any impediment to their sexual enjoyment of women. Anything that militates against, interferes with or abrogates the continual enjoyability of the sex object is, therefore, looked upon with disdain and sought to be eliminated.

6.2 Condemning the Innocent Woman

> "Of the woman came the beginning of sin, and through her we all die."
>
> —*cf. Kidwai 1976 : 13*

Greek mythology represents woman as a source of everything that is evil. There is Pandora, a beautiful but foolish and wicked woman, who opens a sealed jar in her husband's house to bring out a swarm of diseases, disabilities and vices like old age, sickness, insanity, spite, passion, plague, famine etc. Then there are three sisters—the furies: horrible, withered, savage, and coal-black women with snakes for their hair, faces like dog's, wings like bat's, and burning eyes, who carry torches and cat-o-nine-tail whips (cf. Graves 1960 : 34 & 38). Taking their cue from the Greeks, the Pagan Arabs saw in their women "the whips of Satan" (cf. Baig 1976 : 55). The peerless Roman scholar-writer, Seneca held: "Where women thinks, she thinks evil" (Baig 1976 : 57). It was widely believed in classical Greece that women were thoroughly untruthful and hence unworthy of trust. As Hesiod wrote: "Who trusts a woman, trusts a thief" (Murry 1910 : 86). These universal denunciations, notwithstanding, it was every where agreed that woman was absolutely enjoyable, though not reliable in the least. A man could accept a woman when he needed one; a man could reject a woman, when he liked to, because the world has been made by God for man and not for woman. Thomas Browne put it so unambiguously: "The whole world was made for man, but the twelfth part of man for woman. Man is the whole world, and the breath of God; woman the rib and the crooked piece of man" (*Religio Medici* 1642 : II : IX). Ancients throughout the patriarchal world found it quite legitimate for man to congratulate himself both when he kissed a woman and when he killed a woman. Phociledes honestly represented the voice of his people when he remarked: "Two days of a woman are very sweet: when you marry her and when you carry her to her grave" (Murry 1910 : 86).

In the autobiography of his soul, Browne clearly admits that he is "amorous of all that is beautiful" and that he is tickled by "the silent note which Cupid strikes" and yet he cannot put up with the idea that man should be created through sex with woman. "I could be content", he suggests, "that we might procreate like trees; without conjunction, or that there were any way to perpetuate the world without this trivial and vulgar way of coition, it is the foolishest act a wise man commits in all his life; nor is there anything that will more deject his cooled imagination, when he shall consider what an odd and unworthy piece of folly he hath committed" (1642 : II : IX). Milton shows complete concurrence with Browne when he motivates Adam in *Paradise Lost* to exclaim:

"O why did God
... not fill the world at once
With men as angels without feminine,
Or find some other way to generate
Mankind? This mischief had not then befallen,
And more shall befall, innumerable
Disturbances on earth through female snares.

Which infinite calamity shall cause
To human life, and household peace confound"
(lines 888-908).

To be born of woman, as Macbeth reads the Witches' prophecy, is to be mortal, while Antony perceives himself as having been feminized by Cleopatra's love (cf. Gohlke 1980). Romeo complains : "O sweet Juliet/Thy beauty hath made me effeminate" (III : I : 115-16). The child in *King Lear* curses his mother for she has violently expelled him into a hostile world: "We came crying hither

Thou knowest, the first time we smell the air
we waul and cry" (IV : VI : 178-80).

Thus we hear a chorus of diverse voices of men—from the new born baby to the dying dotard—hurling stones at women from every side. One of the holiest misogynists in classical India, Bhartrihari even questions the wisdom of God in creating woman: "Who has created woman as a contrivance for the bondage of all living creatures: woman, who is the whirlpool of all doubt, the universe of indiscipline, the abode of all daring, the receptacle of all evil, the deceitful soul of manifold distrust, the box of trickery and illusion, a poison coated with ambrosia, a hindrance to heaven and a way to the depths of hell?" (cf. De 1969 : 35). Do not the Greeks, Romans, Hebrews, Arabs, Spaniards, English *et. al.*, turn into pigmies at the sight of the Hindu giant of destruction? Doesn't their clatter fade into the distance when the Hindu mammoth blows his trumpet? To Browne and Milton the existence of woman seems to threaten the fabric of human society whereas to Bhartrihari woman is an enemy for all living creatures. Browne and Milton merely regret that woman exists; Bhartrihari sounds an alarm because woman is around.

With a boxing champion like Bhartrihari—the unsaintly saint—on his side, the modern Hindu feels assured of a cake-walk victory over his rivals in the area of woman-abuse. There cannot be an indictment of woman more intense and earnest than the one prepared and preserved by orthodox Hinduism over the centuries. The Hindu heritage of woman-scholarship maintains a claustrophobic vision of the female. Seer after seer and text after text seek to reinforce and rationalize the Vedic denigration of woman. The *Taittiriya Samhita* ranks a good woman below a bad man. The *Kathaka Samhita* alludes to woman as scheming and deceitful while the *Maitrayani Samhita* places her on a par with dice and drink, and describes her as one of the major evils in human society (cf. De 1969 : 5 & Shastri 1969 : 78). Panini, the greatest grammarian the world has ever known, denounces woman as mean and jealous while Ashvaghosh, the earliest known writer in the Kavya-style, visualizes woman as the source of all evil. In one of his most passionate poems he says: "Passionate women cause intoxication; women without passion cause fear. Since they bring only fear and trouble, why should one resort to them?" He goes on to add: "In the words of women there is honey. In their heart there is poison" (cited in De 1969 : 13). The *Laws of Manu* tells us: "When creating women, Manu [*i.e.*, the Creator] allotted to women a love of their bed, of their seat and ornaments, impure desire, wrath, dishonesty, malice and bad conduct" (Muller 1964 : IX : 13). Another Hindu law-giver, namely Daksha, is still harsher: "If a wife is allowed to have her way, she becomes uncontrollable like a disease neglected; all wives are like leeches. ... The small leech merely sucks the blood while the other draws the wealth, property, flesh, energy, strength and the happiness of man" (cf. Thomas 1964 : 222). The leech image occurs in the *Devi Bhagavata* as well: "Women constantly suck the blood of man like leeches. ..., rob him of his manhood through sexual indulgence and of his mind, his wealth and all his possessions, for ever new men ... in order to obtain what they want they make a show of chastity. But when they get their beloveds in private, they make as if to devour them" (cf. Baig 1976 : 52 & 54).

Whenever there is a reference to a woman's nature in the *Ramayana*, it is in a spirit of contempt. To take just a few samples. Kausalya's parting sermon to Sita reads as follows: "My daughter, the woman (though she may be the object of everyone's affection) who fails to serve her husband in her adversity is reckoned as unchaste. The nature of such a false woman is that she enjoys happiness at the time of her husband's prosperity, but in adversity she accuses the husband of many things, nay more, even desert him. She is untruthful, and gets irritated even at trivial things, because her mind is not attached to her husband. Fickle-minded women do not care for rank or lineage; they are won over by ornaments or dress; they are ungrateful, and have little regard for righteousness, and they never acknowledge their faults even when pointed out" (Sen 1976 : 187). Unlike Kausalya, Lakshmana does not categorize women into good and bad. He denounces women as a class. When Sita insists on his going to look for Rama following the golden deer, he bursts out:

"Worshipful lady, you are a goddess to me, I dare not reply to your words. It is not at all strange for a woman to use unjust and improper words, it is rather *the* nature of a woman, and it is *everywhere* to be found. They are fickle, irreligious and crooked, and they bring about family dissensions" (*ibid.*, p. 386, my italics). In his lecture on the nature and behaviour of women, the venerable sage Agastya educates Sita with these words: "From the commencement of creation, it has been the nature of woman to seek him who is rich and powerful and forsake him who has fallen on evil days. Women in their instability are like lightening, in their sharpness like weapons, and in their celerity like the wind-god" (cf. Altekar 1956 : 319 & Thomas 1964 : 188).

That women are full of lies, deceit and wickedness is maintained by the stalwarts of the Hindu tradition. The dying Bhishma teaches Yudhishtira that a lie spoken to a woman is not immoral (cf. Lal 1980 : 310). Rama reprimands Lakshmana for having obeyed Sita: "Thou hast taken the words of a woman to be true and leaving off that fair-faced lady hast come here" (cf. Nath 1979 : 79). Kalidasa's Dushyanta charges Shakuntala with concocting lies to cheat him. The old woman accompanying Shakuntala protests saying that as she was brought up in a hermitage, Shakuntala knew nothing of lies or deceit. At this the king makes a more emphatic remark: "Old woman", he retorts, "even in birds and beasts, the female needs no lessons in deceit" (cf. Baig 1976 : 58 & Lal 1964 : 52). It is shocking that even the sublime Buddha should entertain and propagate the doctrine of female-fickleness. In a characteristic passage, he tells Ananda: "Women are soon angered, Ananda; women are full of passion, Ananda; Women are envious, Ananda; women are stupid. That is *the* reason, Ananda, that is *the* cause, why women have no place in public assemblies, do not carry on business, and do not earn their living by any profession" (cf. Baig 1976 : 57). According to the *Mahabharata*, those who are to be excluded from the king's court are "dwarfs, lean men, lame and blind men, idiots, eunuchs and women" (*ibid.*, p. 45). The multi-manned Draupadi shares a secret with Satyabhama: "I've heard of women who commit long-distance murders by sending poisonous gifts to rivals and women are responsible for causing jaundice, leprosy, impotence, lunacy and even blindness in men they hate" (Lal 1980 : 58).

Hindu writers find it politic to use illustrious women like Kausalya, Anusuiya, Sita, Kunti, Shakuntala and Draupadi as props to sustain their passionate and pervasive condemnation of women as a class. They use poison 'to cure the effects of poison', as the adage goes, only to grab credibility to their vituperative campaign against the 'fair-sex'. But, as they cannot trust even these illustrious women to do the job completely and independently (they are women after all), they are obliged to engage the services of some of the greatest men in literature, both secular and sacred, to supervise and glorify their programme of action. One can easily think of a dozen of such names who have contributed to the steady consolidation of male power over the female in the long span of Hindu history. One such name is readily available. In the most didactic book of the *Mahabharata*, that is, in the 'Anushasana Parva', there is, for example, a brief speech attributed to the dying grandpa and addressed to the very embodiment of virtue and righteousness, the Dharmaraja, which refers, among other things, to women. It is of course true that this grand epic, like the *Ramayana*, contains a menacingly large number of scathing descriptions of women but perhaps no single passage in literature is as notoriously virulent as the one being referred to. Coming from the most elderly and revered leader of the epic saga, who has taken a vow of absolute continence for life, this speech focuses on the all-consuming and insatiable lustfulness of women. Bhishma tells Yudhishtira: "Women, even if high-born and blessed with beauty and efficient guardians, love to transgress the codes of society; and rebel against all restraints. None is more inclined to sin than women. Women are the root of all trouble. Even when married to noble, handsome and wealthy men, women are inclined to be faithless when opportunities arise. ... Even those women who are loved by their husbands and treated with respect bestow their favours on hunchbacks, idiots, dwarfs, the cock-eyed and the blind. Beauties lust after cripples and scarecrows. There are in fact, no men, however low or deformed, whom women consider unworthy of companionship. Women remain faithful and loyal to their husbands only when other men are inaccessible or through fear of relatives or dread of punishment—in this world and the next. They are by nature restless and hanker after new experiences. ... Fire is never satisfied with fuel; the ocean is never filled with rivers; death is never satiated with living things, and women with men. ... The destroyer, the deity of the wind, death, the nether regions, the monsters that rove the ocean, the fire-vomiting ceaseless flames, the sharpness of the razor, virulent poison, the serpent—woman is all this in one" (cf. Thomas 1964 : 166).

Perhaps no indictment of women is as comprehensive and intense as this. Agastya's denunciation of women in the *Ramayana*, needless to point out, cannot match Bhishma's condemnation either in scale or in intensity. The nearest equivalent of Bhishma's denigration of women may be found, hopefully, only in the speech that Tulasidasa puts in the mouth of Rama when he addresses Narada in the forest. Easily predictable as it is, Yudhishtira nods assent to Bhishma's decree, adding: "Like kine affecting new pastures, women seek men one after another. ... They make falsehood appear as truth and truth as falsehood" (*ibid.*, p. 167). Besides, here is an interesting anecdote about an old hag, an ascetic, who is said to have tried to seduce the great Ashtavakra and failed. The *Mahabharata* attributes the following confession to this unsuccessful woman ascetic: "Women take the greatest pleasure in congress with men. Among a thousand, maybe hundred thousand women, sometimes one may be found who is devoted and true to her husband. ... Indeed, in the mad pursuit of their lust, they destroy the family they belong to by birth or marriage even as rivers eat away the banks that contain them" (*ibid.*, pp. 168-169).

Sociologically speaking, one of the most denigrating books on women is the *Ramacharitamanasa*, the greatest Hindi epic and the best known literary version of the Rama-Ravana legend. Its plethora of calumnies and tirades against women sometimes verges on the extreme forms of masculinist perversity. It is really unfortunate that Tulasidasa and some of his most venerable characters should make such obnoxious, derogatory and blasphemous observations against the generality of women in an otherwise wonderful epic. Woman, all of them agree, is by nature a universe of lies, distortions, doubts, fickleness, wrong-doing, deceit, lustfulness, cruelty, inscrutability, impurity and stupidity. Indefensible generalizations about women, including great women like Sati and Ahalya are galore in the first Canto itself. The author habitually throws stones at women whenever there is the slightest opportunity for him to do so. He does not seem to have any regard even for the position of the speaker. "Hearken Sati, you are just like a woman"; "now see the consequences of female nature"; "woman by nature is stupid and ignoramous"; "as a woman I am innately stupid and ignoramous" etc., are some of the refrains which occur in a few pages with reference to Shankar's spouse (cf. Hill 1952 : 31-33), only because Sati wants to know if Rama is really an incarnation of Vishnu.

The story of Ahalya's 'pollution' is referred to in the *Mahabharata*, the *Ramayana* and the *Adhyatma Ramayana* as also in the *Ramacharitamanasa*. In spite of the known fact of Ahalya's innocence in the incident of her so-called seduction and pollution by the king of heaven himself, Tulasidasa, without any qualms of conscience, tranforms her into an archetype of female lustfulness. One of Sita's companions describes her as "that great sinner", Janaka and his queen refer to her as "the sage's sinful wife" and so do other characters in the epic (cf. Hill 1952 : 97, 102, 144 etc.).

Every crisis in the plot of the epic is caused by a woman : the need to ascertain Rama's divinity is warranted by the doubts that Sati entertains, the breaking of Shiva's bow becomes inevitable for Sita's marriage, Rama's exile takes place at the instance of Kaikeyi, the joyful kingdom of Ayodhya is abruptly changed into a land torn with strife and chaos by the evil-minded Manthara, Bali has to be disposed of as a punishment for his adulterous attachment to Roma, Ravana's abduction of Sita takes effect because of the partial mutilation of Surpanakha and Sita's unsurpassable beauty, and finally, the golden city of Lanka has to be invaded and destroyed along with its inmates as a retaliation against Ravana's sinful abduction of Sita. Tulasidasa, therefore, comes to the logical conclusion that woman is the sole cause of all troubles in the world. In a mood of divine afflatus, he exclaims: "What is there that fire cannot burn or ocean contain? What deed defies a weak-but-strong woman? What is there in the world that death devours not" (Hill 1952 : 181).

Before her initiation into the sisterhood of the wicked, Kaikeyi, the uniquely privileged darling of a powerful old king, visualizes an ordinary woman as an incarnation of physical deformity and moral depravity: "The one-eyed, the lame and the hunchback are known to be crooked and vicious, especially when they are women, and more especially when they are servants" (*ibid.*, p. 167). "Woman is inherently impure", declares the holy wife of a holy sage (*ibid.*, p. 298). The devout poet fails to maintain any conscious control over his material. He fails to maintain the desired aesthetic distance between the man who lives and suffers and the mind which thinks and creates. The man and the mind are so inextricably mixed up in him that the poet loses track of the artistic situation and starts raving against women in general, even though he is describing an intimate conversation between Anusuiya and Sita. No poet with a modicum of respect even for one woman could have put such sentiments in Anusuiya's mouth while addressing Sita as Tulasidasa has done. It is astonishing that Anusuiya repeatedly describes woman as a veritable devil and yet Sita is "overjoyed". Anusuiya's speech slanders all women, including herself and Sita. To quote her words: "The woman who preserves her chastity merely because it is her duty and because she regards the honour of her family is said in the scriptures to be low; but account that wife lowest of all in the world whom fear alone restrains and want of opportunity. She who deceives her husband and enjoys an intrigue with another is cast for a hundred aeons into the depths of the lowest hell. Who is so vile as she who regards not the torments of innumerable lives for the sake of a moment's pleasure" (*ibid.*, p. 298)? This is Tulasidasa, the man and the poet rolled into one; the mask of the poet is thrown off and the crude reality of the man is here before the reader. He comes out so openly and repeatedly with his tirade against women: "Not even God can fathom the ways of a woman's heart, a very mine of fraud and vice and worthlessness" (p. 227). Satanic revelations like these abound in the epic (cf. pp. 173, 174 & 181 in particular).

In legend Rama and Ravana traditionally represent the end-points of the Hindu ideological spectrum. Polar opposites as they are, they think, speak and act in ways which are mutually exclusive and writers on this legend rightly characterize them as such. But in Tulasidasa's epic, their visions of femaleness share a common ground: they seem to agree (despite their irreconcilable dichotomies in other dimensions) that woman is a box in which evils lie compacted.

Mandodari, Ravana's wife, is traditionally regarded as one of the five greatest women in Hindu history. But Tulasidasa's Ravana does not seem to think so about his wife or about her class. During the crisis of the war, he reprimands his wife for her 'weak-mindedness' and tells her: "Truly do all say of a woman's nature that there are eight defects ever present in her heart—foolhardiness, falsity, fickleness, deceit, timidity, folly, impurity and cruelty" (*ibid.*, p. 373). Ravana's sweeping denunciation of woman is comparable to Rama's devastating decree on woman in the 'Bible of the Hindi-speaking Hindus'.

As the nuclear character of the epic, Tulasi's Rama is called upon to deliver the final judgement on the destiny of woman. Rama's judgement (coupled with Bhishma's decree quoted above) forms the crux of Indo-Aryan thinking on the subject. Rama surpasses his legendary adversary not only in intellectual power and military might, but also in his capacity to have a greater and more sharply focussed clarity of vision about the nature and behaviour of the female. It is logically correct and otherwise proper that Rama should be victorious over Ravana in every dimension of human thought, speech and action.

Sita is kidnapped and taken to an unknown destination. Rama is frantically searching for her with tears in his eyes as if he were a poor mortal lover/husband who has lost his beloved/wife. At such a moment of his desperation there arrives the legendary sage Narada. After the formal obeisance, Narada wants to learn from his omniscient Lord why he had not allowed him to marry when he wanted to. To justify his former decree, Rama makes the following speech, writing in a way the spiritual autobiography of Tulasidasa:

"Lust, wrath, greed, pride and all the other passions from the strong army of infatuation; but amongst them all *the most dangerous and tormenting foe* is woman, illusion incarnate. Hearken, sage; the Puranas and the Vedas and the saints declare that woman is the season of spring to the forest of delusion, and every woman, like the summer heat, *dries up all the pools of prayer* and penance and religious observance. Lust and wrath and pride and jealousy are the frogs and she alone the rains to gladden them. Evil incarnations are a bed of lilies and she the autumn to cherish them. All forms of religion are like lotuses, withered by sensual woman as by the frost of winter. Woman again is the cool season fostered by which the javasa grove of selfishness flourishes. *Woman is a night, impenetrably dark, to bring delight to all the owls of sin;* a hook to catch all the merits of sense and strength and goodness and truth; so say the wise. A young and wanton woman is the root of all evil, a *torment* and a source of every woe. That was what I had in mind, O sage, when I stood in your way" (*ibid.*, p. 22). The poet goes on to add by way of his comment on this rare piece of wisdom: "When he heard Raghupati's kindly words, the sage trembled with emotion and his eyes filled with tears" (p. 322). Reminiscent of Lear's, 'There's hell, there's darkness, there is the suphurous pit', this passage may be seen as a concrete illustration of Tulasidasa's psychic perversity regarding femaleness.

Tulasidasa's zeal for writing invectives against women in general pursues him right into the last parts of the last Canto. Recalling his experiences of a former 'iron age', Kakabhushundi informs Garuda: "Women's only ornament was their hair, they were *never satisfied*; they were poor and wretched and utterly self-centred, they wanted to be happy, poor fools, but ignored religion; their minds were narrow and hard with no tenderness in them" (p. 479 italics in these two paragraphs added). Woman, Tulasidasa feels sure, is a seat of all sorts of vices and cruelties, but sensuality is her all-absorbing passion and her only appeal. He does not get over his obsessive preoccupation with female sensuality. Temptations of the flesh hunt him throughout the epic. It is revealing that he likens Rama (frantically searching for Sita, the greatest of the five greatest Hindu women) to a grossly sensual lover whose beloved has been snatched from him (cf. p. 315), while he compares himself to a sensual lover in relation to his deity. In the concluding couplet of the epic he says: "As a sensual lover loves his mistress and a miser loves his wealth, even so, O Raghunatha, O Rama, mayst thou be loved by me" (p. 499). It sounds unbelievable that a poet who devotes his whole life to the writing of such great poetry, at once, superbly literary and clearly religious, should fail in achieving any degree of transformation of his personal bias against woman. One can therefore only feel sorry for him.

6.3 Characterizing the Ideal Woman : Draupadi and Sita

> "If you cannot live with her, neither can you live without her."
>
> —*Cited in Narasimhaiah (1993)*

A critical survey of the literature of the subject should make it clear to any impartial observer or researcher that Hindu literature is a multi-levelled and multi-dimensional profanation of the name of woman. Far from being a portrait-gallery of womanhood, it is a mine of lies and distortions about femininity. It projects an archetypal woman who has been cajoled, brainwashed, used, abused and condemned, sometimes by the roadside, as a mere lump of flesh to fend for herself. A modern educated Hindu male who elects to scrutinize his ideological heritage with regard to the socio-religious position of woman with some degree of self-criticism can only try to atone for the sins of his ancestors, maybe, by reading aloud one of the confessions of Isaiah:

"Since the beginning of the world *men* have not heard, nor perceived by the ear, neither hath the eye seen, O God, beside thee, what he hath prepared for him that waiteth for him ... behold, thou art wroth, for *we have sinned*. ... We are as an *unclean thing* and our righteousnesses *are* as filthy rags; and we all do fade as a leaf; and our iniquities, like the wind have *taken us away*" (Isaiah 64 : 4-6, italics added).

Or, he could sing in public, on behalf of his prophets, one of the psalms of David:

"O Lord, *rebuke me not in thy wrath*:

neither chasten me in thy hot displeasure

For thy arrows stick fast in me, and

thy hand presseth me sore.

There is no soundness in my flesh because of thy anger;

neither is there any rest in my bones because of my sins.

For my iniquities are gone over my head;

as an heavy burden they are too heavy for me.

My wounds stink and are corrupt because of foolishness.

I am troubled; I am bowed down greatly;

I go mourning all the day long.

For *my loins are filled with a loathsome disease*;

and there is no soundness in my flesh.

I am feeble and sore broken: I have roared by the reason of the disquietness of my heart.

Lord, all my desire is before thee; and my groaning is not hid from thee.

My heart panteth, my strength faileth me: as for the light of mine eyes, it also is gone from me.

For in thee O Lord, do I hope: thou wilt hear, O Lord my God.

For I am ready to halt, and my sorrow is continually before me.

For *I will declare my iniquity; I will be sorry for my sin*" (Psalms 38 : 1-10, 15,17-18, italics added).

Mandodari, Tara, Savitri, Draupadi, and Sita are generally projected by the holy and accepted by the faithful as the five greatest examples of the glorified ideal of womanhood in Hindu history. But there are questions here: Are they really so? Are they really portrayed as authentic ideals of womanhood? Are they projected as adorable women? Are the holy honest and the faithful correct in their references to idealized womanhood? The following view of the characterizations of Draupadi and Sita in the *Mahabharata* and the *Ramayana*, respectively, attempts to show how hypocritical have been the holy and how naive the faithful in their references to ideal womanhood. The very idea of accepting or projecting a woman, howsoever great, as adorable by man or even as equal to man, does not simply fit in with the ideological framework of the Indo-Aryans and therefore, if anyone refers to a woman in history or literature as revered by man, he must be someone who does not either understand what he is talking about or is telling lies on purpose. Traditionally viewed, Draupadi and Sita have, since their first appearance in legend and literature, been images of the archetypal woman who does not change or develop. They have remained stayput for centuries past and may continue to be so for centuries to come, unless there is a miracle which enables them to change and develop.

(a) Draupadi

Draupadi is the most puzzling example in Indo-Aryan history of a wife with a multiplicity of husbands. Her marriage is generally cited as a case of 'polyandry' which it is not, if we confine our evidence to the text of the *Mahabharata*. A polyandrous marriage, by definition, is a marriage in which the woman has the right to have several husbands at a time. As already pointed out, since Draupadi does not have any say in the selection of her husbands, her marriage cannot be considered polyandrous. Moreover, this form of marriage does not agree with the Indo-Aryan definition of marriage and is therefore never included in the eight types of marriage. "The practice", testifies king Drupada, "is against *dharma*, sanctioned neither in the Vedas nor by tradition" and hence his question: "How is it possible for one woman to have many husbands without defiling *dharma*" (Lal 1980 : 102)? The Indo-Aryans, like some other peoples, divide women only in two categories: wives and public women, and there is no scope for a third category. Within the pale of Indo-Aryan socio-religious laws, a woman was never allowed to have several husbands at a time; it was only a man who could have a multiplicity of wives, if he so desired. The Indo-Aryan male was traditionally also free to have sex relations with women other than his wife or wives. Strictly technically speaking, if a woman was not married to one man alone and who allowed several men to have sex with her was to be treated as a 'public woman'. A verse in the *Mahabharata* itself lays down: "A woman who is under the control of many is considered to be a harlot" (Banerji 1976 : 111). This is further confirmed by what Kunti herself states explicitly: "A woman who has intercourse with four men is defiled, and one who has intercourse with five is a prostitute" (Lal 1980 : 82). That Kunti herself has had intercourse with at least four men (or supermen) is another matter. The question here is this: Is Draupadi a wife or a public woman? To try to answer this question is to be aware of the puzzle that is Draupadi.

It seems to be historically true that the early Indo-Aryans, like the early Greeks, had a social custom which obliged married women to be available to other men under certain circumstances and yet allowed them to retain their title as wives. But this custom, however, did not allow a married woman to be another man's wife simultaneously. In all cases of what is known as 'Niyoga' or 'wife-sharing', it was the husband who coerced the wife into having sex with his compatriots. Since the husband 'possessed' the wife as property, he could use her any way he liked. The convention did not allow a wife to have any private deal with another man or a man (married or unmarried) to have a private deal with somebody's wife as a matter of socially acceptable sex ethic. The epic society, (the *Mahabharata* contains so many instances) accepted, even encouraged, wife-sharing on a large scale. The problematic of Draupadi's *anomalous* marriage is basically a problematic of correct representation. Torn between the contrary definitions of wifehood and prostitution, the author of the *Mahabharata* ambiguates (may be on purpose) on the question of Draupadi's union with five men at a time. It would be nonsensical to describe such union as marriage as it would be blasphemous to call it prostitution. So to avoid the devil and the deep sea, the author has to concoct a context to accommodate such a union into the Indo-Aryan frame of reference. Invoking the name of the mother does not solve the puzzle. If the Pandava brothers marry Draupadi because they have been commanded by their mother to share everything among themselves, why don't they share those women who are separately married to Bhima and Arjuna? Critically examined, Draupadi's marriage appears to be a case of wife-sharing—an arrangement mutually agreed upon by all the Pandava Princes and as such something that Drupada and his son are just powerless to resist. Draupadi emerges as the solitary epic woman who is locked in this sort of identity crisis. Call her a wife or call her a public woman, what you choose but you cannot identify a simplistic definition for her simultaneous association with five formidable royal brothers. This was the problem of the epic writer and this remains the problem of the epic reader. Draupadi's tragedy is that she is neither a wife nor a public woman even though she is both at a time. Draupadi wants to marry Arjuna. She is obliged to marry all the five Pandava Princes at the instance of Yudhishtra, the eldest Prince. And yet Yudhishtra never forgives her for her partiality to Arjuna. Climbing the Meru as a member of Yudhishtra's final entourage, Draupadi collapses on the slope. The mighty Bhima asks the truthful Yudhishtra, "She never did anything wrong. Why has she fallen"? "We all loved her equally", replies Yudhishtra, "But she favoured Arjuna. Today she pays the price for her partiality" (Lal 1980 : 358). Draupadi is perpetually locked in an obnoxious situation on account of her obnoxious marriage. Her predicament shows the wonderful woman that she is. She is the only woman in Hindu history who is both 'five-husbanded' (*Panchami*) and 'fire-born' (*Yajnaseni*).

In certain respects Draupadi is like Cleopatra. Both are legendary characters. Both are equally powerful and bold. Both suffer a great deal but both refuse to give in. Both are extraordinarily beautiful, intelligent and assertive. Both are viewed with awe and contempt. Both are described as ever-youthful (*nityauvana*) and charming. Both Vyasa and Shakespeare emphasize the physical attractiveness of their heroines, sometimes to the neglect of their intellectual power. Cleopatra is Greek by culture and heredity, endowed with great intellectual power and rare qualities of imperial leadership and yet portrayed as a gypsy-faced, dark-skinned 'brow of Egypt', playing the exotic companion to Antony's revelries. She has had sex relations with only two men—Caesar and Antony—and yet a hell of debauchery and drunkenness is ascribed to her (cf. *Midsummer Night's Dream* V : I : 11, *Antony and Cleopatra* II : III : 230-245 & Pomeroy 1975 : 185-189). She is a powerful woman and beloved queen and yet she is presented as a desperate woman who is forced to commit suicide as a result of utter helplessness and frustration. Like Cleopatra, Draupadi is portrayed as a bundle of paradoxes. There are references to her great 'intelligence' here and there but on the whole the magical charm of her erotic body is emphasized throughout the epic: "Her eyes were black and lotus-large, her hairs fell in blue waves and she was dark-skinned; her curved nails shone bright as copper, her eyebrows were fair, her breasts heavy; and her body gave out the fragrance of the blue lotus" (Lal 1980 : 89). Draupadi is an Aryan lady and yet she is depicted as the dark-skinned woman: "The delicacy and regularity of her features, characteristic signs of the Aryan family, contrasted with the colour of her complexion, recalling that of the aborigines, were the cause of her being given the surname of Krishna—the dark one" (Bader 1964 : 32-33). Surrounded by five powerful husbands, she is harassed and humiliated in public. In the words of the epic Draupadi is "with husbands, but like a widow"-*nathavati anathavat* (Lal 1980 : 28). As a unique pair of women who have the power to give and the power to demand, Draupadi and Cleopatra are the epitomes of what is hated, loved and feared in woman. They allow themselves to be dominated by men, no doubt, but they can also dominate men when they choose to and it is this doubleness of their personalities that evokes a contradictory response from men to their being.

The story of Draupadi's attempted denudation described with meticulous detail in the 'Sabha Parva' of the *Mahabharata* certainly remains to this day the most incomprehensible, shameful and disgusting outrage against a helpless, lonely and half-naked, menstruating woman in Indo-Aryan history. Wriggling, shrieking and resisting, Draupadi is dragged by the hair into the Assembly Hall by the gesticulating and red-eyed Duhashasana to be stripped in full view of a whole galaxy of philosophers, statesmen, scholars, elders and the joint-stock-company of five heroic husbands simply because she has been gambled away in a game of dice by her eldest husband who is universally recognized as an embodiment of truth and righteousness. Draupadi is simply aghast because an actual attempt is made to strip her of her 'single dress' which is already stained with menstrual blood. Her hair dishevelled and her dress slipping, she turns to the crowd and asks: "How could you consent to my being staked by a man who had already lost himself in the game of dice"? The elders hang their heads in grief and shame. The loser is speechless. There is no answer from any corner to Draupadi's question. After a while, Bhishma reprimands Yudhishtira: "Even abandoned professional gamblers would not stake the harlots who live with them, and you, worse than they, have left the daughter of Drupada to the mercy of these ruffians" (Rajagopalachari 1951 : 93). Similarly, Vikarna, one of Duryodhana's younger brothers, observes: "Hunting, drinking, gambling and whoring are the four vices of kings. Under their influence kings do irresponsible deeds. Yudhishtira staked Draupadi in a gambling fit. She is not his wife only but of four others. He lost himself first before losing her. My conclusion is that she is neither morally nor legally won" (Lal 1980 : 132). At this Karna, gesticulating wildly with his strong arms, rebukes Vikarna, saying, "the Gods have ordained only one husband for one woman. This Draupadi ... hath five husbands. Therefore certain it is that she is an unchaste woman. To bring her, therefore, into this assembly attired though she be in one piece of cloth—even to uncover her is not at all an act that may cause surprise" (Chandra 1970 : 131). A little later Karna exclaims: "Now begins the unchallenged supremacy of Duryodhana. The Pandavas are finished! Draupadi has eunuchs for husbands " (Lal 1980 : 132). At this, Duhashasana seizes one end of Draupadi's dress and begins to pull it off her person. Draupadi raises both her hands in prayer to Krishna. Krishna, hearing her supplication, performs a miracle so that as one dress is pulled off Draupadi's person, another appears in its place, until the entire floor is littered with hundreds and hundreds of dresses and the stripping is given up. Again the question of the ownership of Draupadi is raised. No one speaks till Karna asks Duhashasana to take Draupadi to the inner quarters as a slave. "Wait", says Draupadi as Duhashasana begins to drag her, "I have forgot a noble duty. Revered and wise elders, I pay you my respects. Forgive me for not paying them when I was brought in" (*ibid.*, p. 133). As Draupadi is dragged towards his palace, Duryodhanana uncovers his left thigh (which is shaped like a plantain tree or like an elephant's trunk, and graced with auspicious marks) and shows it to Draupadi (cf. *ibid.*, p. 133). Ultimately, Draupadi and her husbands are set free only to be sent into exile for a period of thirteen years, the last year being a year they have to live incognito. Even here the text says: "Dressed in a blood stained single piece of cloth, hair dishevelled, the weeping Draupadi left her mother-in-law" (*ibid.*, p. 136).

Two crucial aspects of this operation denudation deserve to be noted with care. That a divine intervention saves Draupadi from complete denudation does not in any way absolve the upholders of public morality from the charge of their being a party to this atrocious act which is as barbaric and shameful as obscene. Besides, the text does not explain why Draupadi is sought to be denuded by the winner at the game of dice. He could have taken her as a concubine for life. Why does Duryodhana want Draupadi to be stripped before a hundred per cent male crowd? That Draupadi has insulted Karna and Duryodhana does not sufficiently explain why they should choose to have her stripped in public. Why do the powerful elders not stop this barbaric exercise? The real motive for such attempted disrobing seems to emanate from much deeper levels than those mentioned in the epic. Since no answer to the question can ever be definitive, one is reduced only to conjecture and the conjecture leads to a number of counter questions. Some of these counter questions could be: Must Draupadi be stripped because she consented to be a wife, and a wife of several husbands? Could she not have remained an Aspasia or Ambapali? Could she not have chosen to be a courtesan so as to be accessible to many? Is the stripping an unconscious protest against her menstruation? Do women of Draupadi's excellent charms have a physiological right to observe no-sex days periodically? Or, finally do women, howsoever talented, have a right to assert their independence of men? No one seems to know for sure, but the episode of the attempted disrobing mentioned in the epic definitely points to something more than what meets the eye.

The second aspect of the stripping episode is related to Draupadi's question about her status after the game and her ironic greeting to the elders. When she is dragged into the Assembly Hall, she raises a fundamental question about the husband's right over his wife. A husband even according to orthodox beliefs, is supposed to protect and provide for his wife and children. What sort of husband is Yudhishtira who wilfully surrenders his great wife to a pack of rascals? Does he have the moral or legal right to stake his wife once he has gambled himself away? Draupadi has dared to ask a question that cuts at "the very roots of the Hindu social tradition, especially in relation to its attitude to the position and rights of women" (Lal 1980 : 27). Even the learned Bhishma sidesteps this question and openly admits that he is baffled. As a symbol of the *status-quo* doctrine in matters of social customs and laws, he can only repeat the cliche: "Morality is too subtle even to the sages". Draupadi does not get any satisfactory answer to her question but her question continues to ring in every ear that can hear. Again, Draupadi has a devasting dig at the assembled elders while being dragged out of the Hall. Her sarcastic greetings thunder these elders and superiors drowning them in the sea of shame and humiliation. She scoffs at these stupid eunuchs who ordinarily pass for learned and masculine men but fail to protect a woman against a veritable scoundrel. Are they men? Are they wise and valiant? Are they respectable? Questions like these echo from the walls of the Hall even after Draupadi has been dragged out. A biting irony leaves every hero speechless and stunned.

These two aspects of Draupadi's invincible heroism even in the face of the most degrading circumstances distinguish her from the general run of Hindu women. Her question and her dig raise her far above the greatest of women in Hindu history, including women like Sita and Savitri. As a scholar puts it: "She is no silent, suffering and compliant Sita, no docile Damayanti, no self-sacrificing Savitri. She is not awed by the authority of self-appointed gentlemen" (Lal 1980 : 27).

Draupadi suffers humiliation and harassment as most women do. But what distinguishes her from other women is her refusal to submit to the forces of evil. She can not only ask questions and have a dig at the elders, she vows revenge against those who harass and humiliate her. She is the solitary unforgiving and revengeful Hindu woman. It is only Draupadi who can wash her hair in the blood of her humiliator. She can never forget the macabre scene in the Assembly Hall nor can she ever forgive her enemies. She continually refers to her humiliation and harassment with a sense of outrage. Quite many years after the shameful incident, she tells Krishna, during her life in the forest, how cruelly she was treated by the sons of the blind king:

"O Krishna, they dragged me, the sister of Dhrishtadyumna, the wife of the Pandavas, during my period, stained with blood, dressed in a single cloth—they dragged me in front of all the kings—and the sons of Dhritarashtra laughed at me! They wanted to make me their slave by force! And my husbands sat through it, unmoving! Arjuna! Doesn't dharma say a husband should protect his wife's honour? Others they protect—me they couldn't!

Have I not given them five sons? And don't I deserve protection at least on that account? Shame on Arjuna's magic bow, that slept while I was dragged in my period through the Hall! Shame on Bhima's strength! Poison he could drink, serpents he could kill, Kunti he could save from the burning lacquer house, but me he couldn't protect! I was seized by my hair, Krishna, while the Pandavas watched, the brave Indra, my own husbands" (Lal 1980 : 142)!

When Duhshasana's belly is ripped open in the battlefield on the sixteenth day of the war and blood flows out of it, Draupadi washes her hair in this blood. Draupadi's action deserves to be seen in its proper context. It is not only blood for blood; it is something much deeper. Duhshasana had dragged her in spite of her flow of blood. He had pulled her blood-stained cloth. He had dragged her by the hair with his eyes red. It is therefore only logical that she washes her hair in Duhshasana's flowing blood. Apart from it, there is another reason for her action. According to the contemporary Hindu belief, a woman in child-birth or menstruation was held to be 'impure' (*ashaucha*) and therefore was not to be touched or outraged by anyone, particularly by a male, under any circumstances (cf. Baig 1976 : 84-85 & Lal 1980 : 26). It was inconceivable for such a woman to appear before men or to be brought before men. For Draupadi to say that she was in her period should have been enough to deter Duhshasana from touching her body. But he did not listen to her. When Draupadi tried to run for help, he intercepted her and dragged her to the Assembly Hall. It is only natural and appropriate for a woman of Draupadi's stature and determination to seek her redemptive revenge or purification by washing her hair in Duhshasana's warm blood in an age which has such rigid laws of pollution and purification.

In ancient Greece, as in ancient India, there prevailed very orthodox notions of purity and impurity, of purification and pollution. The Greeks identified four major causes of pollution : menstruation and childbirth, contact with a dead body, murder and undesirable sex acts like adultery, incest and rape. They also identified four major processes of purification : washing in water or in the blood of the sacrificial victim, fumigation of a room or house with sulphur, ritual offering to the gods and goddesses, and burial of the dead body and expulsion from society of the polluted object, person or thing (cf. Vickers 1973 :140). It is plausible to view Duhshasana's dragging of Draupadi and Draupadi's hair-washing in Duhshasana's blood as a variant of the pollution-purification sequence. To understand Draupadi's uniqueness as a heroic woman, it may be pertinent to contrast the stripping episode with the violation and condemnation of Ahalya reported in the *Mahabharata* itself.

According to a legend in the *Mahabharata*, Indra, the God of heaven, once thought of making love to Ahalya, the pretty but chaste wife of the sage Agastya. He chalked out a plan in collusion with

Chandrama, the moon-god. The moon-god appeared in disguise before the house of Agastya and started crowing like a cock. Mistaking the cock-crow as the herald of dawn, the sage hurriedly left for the bank of the Ganga to have his daily ablutions and morning meditations. When he reached the bank of the river, he found to his surprise that the river was unusually serene. Suddenly doubts entered his mind. He used his extraordinary Yogic powers to see for himself what was really happening. To his utter dismay, the sage discovered that his menstruating wife had already been polluted by Indra who had appeared in the form of Agastya himself and that the polluter and his accomplice were about to run away from the scene of the crime. Immediately he returned home to catch the culprits. He cursed the moon-god to carry dark spots on his face for ever and the god of heaven to have a thousand vaginal sores on his body. These sores were later changed into eyes. Indra thus earned the epithets of *Sayoni*, the vagina-marked, and *Sahasraksha*, the thousand-eyed. But Agastya awarded the cruellest punishment on the innocent and devoted Ahalya. He changed her to stone symbolizing shameless lustfulness (cf. Lal 1980 : 380, Sen 1976 : 70-71 & Nath 1979 : 14-15). The Ahalya episode should demonstrate the ideological significance of Draupadi's action. Draupadi is not an Ahalya and therefore Draupadi cannot be abandoned, cursed or turned into stone, by anyone. To outrage Draupadi should be enough for the vilest of men to merit death and destruction. It is no accident that Draupadi is never outraged again. Draupadi is no stereotype of a timid and silently suffering woman.

If the *Mahabharata*, making due allowances for its divergent and intractable material, is viewed as an organic whole, Draupadi definitely stands out as its nuclear ingredient. It would have been impossible for Vyasa to conceive of or compose the epic without her. She is just indispensable to the very structure of the epic. The soul of the *Mahabharata*, Draupadi coalesces within her unique personality the literal and the poetic, the depressing and the buoyant, the grotesque and the sublime, the pitiable and the fearful, and the docilely feminine and the aggresively masculine, which makes her so enigmatic and yet so fascinating an epic character. She is the Mona Lisa of the *Mahabharata*. She is the lifeblood of the *Mahabharata*. She is the *Mahabharata*.

The microcosm of the greatest epic in the world, Draupadi emerges as a matchless woman in the whole history of Indo-Aryan literature. With her supreme intellectual stature, moral stamina, emotional resilience and unique determination, Draupadi invites comparison with the boldest heroine of Greek tragedy. Humiliated and persecuted, she becomes a Medea. Exactly like Medea, she refuses to give in or to reconcile with her humiliators and persecutors. Like Medea, she fights back. As a powerful mouthpiece of rebellious womanhood, Draupadi like Medea, seems to address herself to all women in the world when she asks her questions and scoffs at the elders. The following speech of Medea can easily be read as Draupadi's key-note address to women everywhere:

> Of all things upon earth that *bleed* and grow
> A herb most *bruised* is woman. We must pay
> Our *store of gold*, hoarded for that one day,
> To buy us some man's love; and lo, they bring
> A *master of our flesh* ! There comes the string of *the whole Shame*.
> And then the jeopardy,
> For good or ill, what shall the master be;
> Reject she cannot; and if he but stays
> His suit, 'tis shame on the woman's days.
> So thrown among new laws, new places, why
> 'Tis magic she must have, or prophecy—
> Home never taught her that—how best to guide
> Toward peace, this thing that sleepeth at her side.
> And she, who *labouring* long, shall find some way
> Whereby her lord may *bear* with her, nor fray
> *His yoke* too fiercely, blessed is the breath
> That woman draws ! Else, let her pray for death
> Within doors, gets him forth, some merrier place
> Will ease her heart : but she waits on, her whole
> Vision *enchained* on a single soul
> And then, forsooth, 'tis that they face the call
> Of war, while we sit sheltered, *hid from all*
> Peril!—False mocking! sooner would I stand
> Three times to face their battles, and shield in hand

Than *bear* one child. (Murry 1910 : 232-252, italics added).

Knox's prose rendering of Medea's speech reads:

"Of all creatures that have breath and intelligence, we women are the most afflicted. We buy our husbands with dowry—not knowing if they will be good or bad, go into a new home unprepared for the new life. If we work hard and make a success of it, we're lucky; if not, death would be better. The man, when he tires of our company can go out for distractions; we are forced to keep our eyes steadily on one single human being. They say we live at home in safety, while they fight the wars—what fools? I'd rather stand in the battle line three times than go through child-bearing once" (1983).

Another wronged but rebellious Greek wife named Procne reminisces about the travails of her married life in the following passage from Sophocle's *Tereus*:

"Now seperated (from my family), I am nothing. Many a time I have observed that in this case our sex, the female sex, is nothing. When we are children, in our father's home, our life is the most pleasant in the world; young girls grow up in thoughtless delight. But when we reach maturity and intelligence, we are expelled, bought and sold, far away from the gods of our fathers and from our parents, some to barbarians, some to houses where everything is alien, others to houses where they meet with hostility. But all this, when one has joined us to our husband, we must acquiesce in, and pretend that all is well" (cited in *ibid.*).

To have a better grasp of the emotional intensity, the honest scepticism and the ruthless irony of these speeches as applied to Draupadi, one has to recall certain facts and traits of her life and character which set her apart from Indo-Aryan heroines in general. Draupadi is a unique heroine in the very literal sense of the term. One has to think of the story of her birth: she is sacrifice-born or fire-born, the only daughter in the whole of Hindu history who is obtained by her father through appropriation to the gods (cf. Lal 1980 : 99 & 378). A darling of her father and brother, Draupadi is brought up and educated lavishly and lovingly and then suddenly she is surrendered to an atrocious marriage (unwillingly though) by her father and brother. The lone example of the Aryan wife with five husbands, she enjoys her conjugal life majestically. To quote the words of the epic: "Just as the river Sarasvati enjoys elephants playing in her waters and the elephants enjoy her, Draupadi delighted in her five husbands and they delighted in her" (*ibid.*, p. 106). Won through `lottery' (or *svayamvara*, if you like), her marriage to the Pandava brothers is a lavishly dowered marriage (*ibid.*, p. 103). Though dark-skinned, she is a paragon of Aryan feminine beauty and is ever-youthful and yet Bhima and Arjuna indulge in extra-martial amorous dalliance. She bears at one-year intervals a son to each of her five husbands: Partivindhya to Yudhishtira, Shrutasoma to Bhima, Shrukarmana to Arjuna, Shatanika to Nakul and Shrutasena to Sahadeva (*ibid.*, p. 109) and yet she is a unique example of an Aryan wife who is gambled away to scoundrels by her own husbands. Persecuted and harassed she is, but she rises from her ashes, as it were, like the proverbial phoenix. At the appropriate moment she revenges herself on her persecutor not only by washing her hair in his blood; she pulls out his intestines and plaits her hair with them, thereby achieving the final catharsis of her feelings of hurt. "And almost all things", says the scripture, "are by the law purged with blood; and without shedding of blood is no remission" (Hebrews 9 : 22). Draupadi is invincible, taintless and immortal.

(b) Sita

'Sita'—the semantic variability of the term—gives rise to a volley of questions: Is she human, superhuman or divine? Is she a real individual? Is she an abstract idea? Is she a power or a symbol? Is she a function or a structure? Is she the cosmic illusion by which the Divine One appears to be the material many? Is she the cosmic magic of God (Brahma) by which the phenomenal world appears to be real? Is she co-extensive with the Godhead? Is she the female principle which complements Brahma, the male principal, to create the universe? Is she equal or subservient to the supreme self? Is she the embodied soul? Is she the cause or the effect of illusion? Is she both illusive and abiding, apparent and real, ideal and individual, human and divine, temporal and timeless or particular and universal at a time? The moment one thinks of the image of Sita for the purposes of critical analysis, questions like these crop up and agitate the mind. It is not only that the semantics of this name varies from text to text; the problem is complicated by the fact that such semantics at times seems to vary from context to context within the same text.

Most words, particularly the words used in literature, as we all know, do have multiple meanings. But opposed to such general or open-class words, only a handful of proper names have multiple referents. It is possible that a name refers to a person or persons and/ or objects. In spite of such possibilities, proper names are distinguishable from polysemic words in general in the sense that their referents are fixed and limited in number. A name may refer to more than one person. 'Ashvatthama', for example, refers to the valiant son of Dronacharya as well as to the ferocious elephant in the *Mahabharata* (cf. Lal 1980 : 241). Whether it refers to the man or to the elephant, the nature of the relationship between the name and its referents, however, does not change. The trouble with the name 'Sita' is that even when it refers to the same character in the legend, it acquires different connotations in different works dealing with the legend. The co-existence of such variable connotations or referents, therefore, calls for a careful analysis of the epic character known by this name. Questions, like those listed above, only point to the difficulties that arise in course of the critical analysis.

In Indo-Aryan literature, 'Sita' has several connotations (cf. Sen 1976 : 460, Nath 1979 : 20, Roy and Gidwani 1985 : 23 & 1986 : 94-95). According to the *Brahmanda Purana* (chapter 51) and the *Matsya-Purana* (chapter 121), 'Sita' is the name of one of the three streams of the Ganga, which comes out of the Vindu-sara and flows into the Western Ocean. Geographically speaking, 'Sita' is perhaps the Tagdumbush branch of the Arkand river in Central Asia. In the *Rig-Veda* (IV : 75) 'Sita' is described as a goddess personifying the "furrow" (*kshetra*) and allied to the " Lord of the field" (*kshetrapati*). The *Ramayana* of Valmiki, however describes Sita as a woman who comes from the earth. Borrowing its etymology from the *Rig-Veda*, Valmiki hypostatizes the "furrow" into a "woman" and unites her with the hero of this epic, though the story of her birth and death retains its primordial links with the earth. Originally arising from and ultimately disappearing into the earth, 'Sita' in her new form appears to be an allegorical representation of the Indo-Aryan acceptance of agriculture as their main occupation in life. Revealing the mystery of Sita's birth, her foster father, King Janaka explains to Vashishtha and Vishwamitra on the eve of her marriage with Rama: "As I was ploughing the ground for the purpose of purifying it for sacrifice, Sita ... appeared in the furrows. I saw her with loving eyes and took her for my own daughter" (Sen 1976 : 66 & Nath 1979 : 20).

Towards the end of the *Ramayana*, Sita's final entry into the earth is described as follows: "If I have never thought of any person but Rama, then let mother Earth be divided and let me enter into it. If I have adored Rama with my body and soul, let mother Earth be divided and let me enter into it. If it be true that I do not know anybody besides Rama, let mother Earth be divided and let me enter into it" (Sen 1976 : 479). As soon as the invocations are over, the earth opens up and Sita disappears into it.

As an allegory or a symbol in literature, 'Sita' does not pose a serious problem for critical analysis. The problem starts as soon as we begin to analyse her identity as an epic character, that is, as a woman. In the following paragraphs she is discussed as an epic character with special reference to the *Ramayana* of Valmiki. The *Ramayana* of Valmiki is the earliest recorded literary version of the Rama-Ravana legend wherein the author presents a vision of the Hindu dream of perfection. The *Ramayana* is the biography of a supremely intelligent, knowledgeable, handsome, eloquent and mighty hero who is the defender of religion and of the caste-system, the protector of friends and the destroyer of enemies. The legend passes through several hands in several languages but it is not too difficult from the critical point of view to identify three stages in its religio-literary evolution from Valmiki to Tulasidasa. Valmiki's work constitutes the original stage, Kamba's work may be taken as the intermediate stage, while the *Adhyatma Ramayana* must be taken as the final stage of this evolution. Valmiki projects an ideal hero, the best of men, who still has some human failings. The *Kamba Ramayana* idealizes the legend to an extent that the author has to equivocate on some of the unsavoury parts of the legend so as to transform the best of men into a divine hero. Taking the deifying thought—process to its logical conclusion, the *Adhyatma Ramayana* transforms a heroic legend into a divine saga with the result that it becomes a completely devotional poem. Tulasidasa's classic is a further refined and enlarged version of the *Adhyatma Ramayana* as far as its plot is concerned. He not only changes a heroic legend into a divine saga, he skips over all the unpleasant or embarrassing parts of the story in order that the *Ramacharitamanasa* becomes an epic of glory and perfection. This study attempts to analyse Sita as an epic character with special reference to Valmiki's *Ramayana* for the simple reason that it is the least diluted of the available literary versions of the Rama-Ravana legend.

A rare combination of beauty, loyalty and patience, Sita stands alone throughout history as the most telling example of the timid, obedient, suffering and pitiable woman. The basic problem of the unique epic character is her matchless beauty coupled with her boundless love for her husband. This unfortunate combination makes her vulnerable, both physically and emotionally. It is no ordinary tribute to her physical charms that her husband, even after years of her company, should find it impossible to believe that she was able to resist Ravana's overtures during her year-long confinement in the golden city. In point of fact, Rama seems to be continually dazzled by her beauty and he fails to understand how anyone who has access to Sita's presence can overcome the irresistible temptation to make love to her. It is this ingredient in his psychology that haunts him again and again to such an extent that he ultimately decides to give her up for good. Perhaps the best account of Sita's unique beauty is contained in Surpanakha's report to her brother: "Her eyes are drawn up to her ears, her face is like the full moon and her hue is like that of polished gold. She is a perfect beauty. Her nose is beautiful, her hair glossy and her nails are well-shaped and of reddish tinge, her waist lean, hips heavy, breasts high and plump. She looks like the beauty of the forest and the goddess of wealth. No goddess, no Gandharvi, no Kinnari, no Yakshi is like her. In a word, I have not seen such a woman on earth" (Sen 1976 : Vol. I : 365).

Sita herself is conscious of her supreme beauty as well as of her commitment to Rama. She hears Rama's cry for help during the chase of the golden deer, asks Lakshamana to rush to his brother, Lakshamana refuses to leave her and she bursts out: "You are not going to Rama's help under these circumstances. You are his enemy in the guise of a friend. You wish for his death in order to secure me. It is clear to me that just for your lust for me you have refrained from going to your brother ... you wicked villain, it is either at the instigation of Bharata, or at your own initiative that you are deceitfully following Rama just for me. But your desire will never be fulfilled ... I shall give up my life even in your presence. I shall not live even for a moment without Rama" (*ibid.*, pp. 385-386).

Ravana's first encounter with Sita spontaneously turns into an eloquent tribute to her beauty: "I have never seen a damsel like you on earth. ... Such superb beauty, such exquisite grace, this prime of youth and this living in seclusion has made me quite anxious on thy account" (*ibid.*, p. 389).

The war is over. Sita is brought to her husband's camp. Rama speaks to her in sheer cold blood: "Gentle lady! know it for certain that it is not for you that I have come to the termination of the war with the help of my friends. I have done this for my dignity, for removing the stain of a scandal, and for the prestige and honour of my renowned family. I have done the deed just to prove that I do not belong to a mean family. I do now doubt your character for you stayed in the stranger's house. You are standing before me but your sight is unbearable to me, as light to a man suffering from eye-disease, so I tell you to go wherever you like, I do not want you. Who being born of a noble family can take back his wife who lived in another's house. ... You were molested on Ravana's lap, his sinful eyes gloated over your person, now how can I receive you back, thinking of the noble family from which I come ... I say unto you without any hesitation whatsoever, that you can pay your attentions upon Lakshamana, Bharata, Shatrughna, and Sugriva, or if you like, you may follow Vibhishana. Finding you charming and beautiful and having got you in his house, Ravana could not have refrained long" (*ibid.*, Vol. III pp. 341-342).

Rama charges her with congenital infidelity:

"In noble lineage you were not born,
But like the spineless worm, born from the earth
You have but played your part too well" (cf. Aiyar 1970 : 312).

Sita is stunned by such accusations:

"And grieving like a wound by probe exclaimed,
Blood and tears suffused her downcast eyes;
With senses dazed she heaved a sigh" (*ibid.*, p. 312).

Recovering from the shock a little, she pleads with him:

"I may be the chastest to the world entire,
And of heart unfaltering, beyond even Brahma
To shake. Ah, foolish me! If you, who are
The focus of the world deny, would God
Acknowledge me"(*ibid.*, p. 312).

Sita has had forebodings of Rama's charges on way to the camp:

"Ah wretched me! ...
And freed from my prison, how shall I prove
My virtue uncorrupt, if he should say,

Away, thou art not worthy of my love" (*ibid.*, p. 314)?

Sita recollects her forebodings and compares them with her husband's accusations. Composing herself, she explains her position and raises a few questions in view of these accusations in words like these:

"As a low person abuses a low woman, why do you use all such unutterably rude expressions against me?... I can swear about my character; have faith in my honour. Having seen the conduct of low women, you suspect all women as a class, but that is not proper. If you have any experience of me, then give up that unfounded suspicion. ... (That) Ravana touched my body .... How could I help it? ... When you sent Hanumana for my information, why did you not send me word that you had renounced me? ... You do not take into consideration why you married me" (Sen 1976 : Vol. III : 343-44)?

By way of reacting to Rama's suggestion that she could now go with anyone she liked, Sita reminds him: "I am not a dancing girl that you should make a gift of me to others" (cf. Mazumdar 1974 : 434).

Whatever it may be, Sita's explanations and entreaties fail to convince her husband of her incorruptibility and he orders her to face the fire-ordeal then and there. Lakshmana prepares the pyre. Sita enters into the fire with the following invocation, while Rama fixes his gaze on the pyre, looking grim like death:

"If I am thoroughly devoted to Rama, then let fire protect me in every possible way" (*ibid.*, p. 344). Fire does not burn her. She comes out fire-tested, shining like pure gold. The God of fire assures Rama: "Rama, this is your Janaki. She is stainless. She has not committed any sin by word, action or thought. ... Her heart is pure and she is absolutely sinless. Accept her now ... Do not suspect her even for a moment" (*ibid.*, p. 347). The generous and all-forgiving Rama', `the best of men', accepts his `fire-tested' wife with a public declaration: "Now, I cannot renounce her on account of residing in a stranger's house. She is the purest in the three worlds. ... Now, I shall protect her for ever" (*ibid.*, p. 348).

At the happy conclusion of the fire-ordeal and the public declaration, triumphant Rama returns to Ayodhya, accompanied by his wife and brother and the heterogeneous retinue of men, monkeys, bears and others. Rama ascends the throne. A new era of hope, prosperity, liberty, equality, fraternity and love is ushered in for the people of Ayodhya. With Rama as a peerless king and a mighty defender of the good and the virtuous, Sita is the happiest woman in the whole kingdom. Sita is the queen and the object of love and respect from all. Rama and Sita live happily together, surrounded by boundless power and prosperity.

In course of time Sita becomes pregnant. When she reaches a very advanced stage in her pregnancy, she looks for some distractions out of the bustle of the busy kingdom. With a gentle smile on her face, Sita seeks her husband's permission to have a brief outing: "My lord! I wish to revisit the sacred hermitages of the Rishis and want to go to those holy men. I wish to spend at least one night in their hermitage. This is my heart's desire" (*ibid.*, p. 419). To her great pleasure, Rama immediately responds: "Your desire will be satisfied, you will start even tomorrow for the hermitages" (p. 419). Saying this he leaves for the Audience Hall to listen to people's grievances.

At the Audience Hall, while people are engaged in jokes and lively conversations, Rama takes one of his spies, Bhadra to a corner and asks him if people gossip about Sita. Bhadra reports that people are all praise for his great victory and for his love of justice and piety but they have strong reservations about his accepting Sita in spite of her abduction by Ravana and her confinement in Ravana's city for fourteen months. Rama is extremely pained. He has a private counsel with his brothers to share with them, once again, the story of Sita's successful fire-ordeal and Indra's guarantee of her inviolability. He is shocked that in spite of all these tests and guarantees having been matters of public knowledge, his people still point fingers at Sita's character. He tells his brothers: "This infamous report has greatly pained me. He lives in hell about whom evil reports are spread. Everybody hates ill-fame and worships fame" (p. 422). And therefore, making up his mind on this crucial question, Rama tells Lakshmana: "On the other side of the Ganga stands the sacred hermitage of Valmiki on the bank of the Tamasa. Go and leave Janaki there in some secluded place .... she wanted to visit the hermitages .... now fulfil that desire of hers" (p. 423).

Next morning, Sita is driven to the other side of the Ganga. She is overwhelmed with joy that her kind lord has fulfilled her desire for an outing. Lakshamana abruptly informs her that as her husband has abandoned her for good, she has to spend the rest of her life in these holy forests. Sita is stunned and speechless. She has suddenly lost the world. Even after some time, she cannot formulate a proper answer to a question like why she has been abandoned by her just and virtuous husband. Embarrassment or no embarrassment, Sita has no choice left for her now: she has to find a shelter for herself in a hermitage. Reconciling herself to her predicament, she says to Lakshamana: "Leave this miserable woman and obey the royal command .... Convey my respects to my mothers-in-law, then after due greetings tell my royal lord that I am thoroughly devoted to him and my character is stainless .... I shall not grieve even for a moment even if I lose my life .... Her husband to a woman is her highest lord, friend and preceptor. A woman should even sacrifice her insignificant life for the good of her husband" (pp. 427-28 cf. Sharma 1962 : 242).

Sita takes shelter at the hermitage of Valmiki. She gives birth to twins: Kusha and Lava. A few years pass. Then Valmiki, accompanied by Kusha and Lava, visits Ayodhya to conduct sacred rights during the performance of the historic horse-sacrifice (*Ashvamedha*) to celebrate the final supremacy of king Rama. Kusha and Lava sing sweet songs during the festival. The king is exceedingly pleased. He orders a large amount of money to be paid to them. The boys refuse to accept the reward money. Rama is surprised. In course of time Rama comes to know that they are his own sons. Impressed by the boys, Rama agrees to take Sita back again. Sita is brought to the kingdom. Valmiki testifies under oath that Sita is chaste and pure before a large congregation of people. But Rama is not convinced. He says to Valmiki: "O worshipful master! I take Janaki as chaste and pure on your words, but let her prove herself so" (p. 459).

Sita is formally asked to make a public declaration on oath that she is chaste and pure in spite of her abduction and captivity and that she has never entertained any thought about any man other than her husband. Sita makes the required public declaration before the large crowd with three invocations to the mother Earth and suddenly disappears in a gorge created by the Earth: "Goddess Earth took Sita in her embrace .... Flowers were showered from above and the gods sang her [Sita's] praise " (p. 460). The twins are retained by Rama who never takes a second wife.

Critically examined as a character in an epic, Sita seems to bear an antithetic resemblence to Helen. Sita is and is not like Helen. The

Trojan war is fought for Helen. The war destroys the Trojans but Helen is unbruised. She is restored to her husband and kingdom with love and respect, even though she had eloped with the Trojan Prince, Paris. The Lankan war is technically, but not genuinely, fought for Sita. The war destroys the Lankans and it also destroys Sita in the long run, even though Sita had been abducted by a mighty foreigner from an unguarded hermitage and kept in captivity for more than a year.

The Desdemona of Hindu literature, Sita is continually persecuted and ultimately destroyed on account of her indescribable beauty as well as on account of her single-minded devotion to her husband and her boundless patience for non-resistance. She suffers indignities and atrocities one after another mainly because she does not resist, protest or rebuff. She cries and obeys when she should shout and rebel. If she has to die anyway, why doesn't she choose to die the first time she is insulted in public? Why is she chronically apologetic for things she is never guilty of? Why does she comply with the outrageous requirement of the fire-test in Lanka or of the public declaration in Ayodhya? Why does she care for a man who does not care for her? She is whipped with suspicion and treated with cruelty because she can never turn round and say 'hell with you'. Jealousy or suspicion requires no proof "Alas the day", bemoans Desdemona, "I never gave him cause"! Rightly says Emila: "But jealous [*i.e.*, suspicious] souls will not be answered so;/ They are not ever jealous/'Tis a monster/Begot upon itself, born on itself". In yet another passage, the notorious Iago defines 'jealousy' (that is, suspicion) as: "It is the green-eyed monster which doth mock/The meat it feeds on" (cf. *Othello* III : IV : 158-162 & III : III : 170-71). Sita suffers endlessly because she fails to realize that no explanation can appease a suspicious mind. Sita's tragedy, agrees Rajagopalchari, is symbolic of "the voiceless and endless suffering of our womenfolk" (1951 : 311). One does not necessarily have to go the whole hog with Ambedkar (1987) to denounce Rama's conduct in relation to Sita but it is definitely valid to view Sita's fire-ordeal, banishment and self-destruction as the most shameful chapters in the Indo-Aryan treatment of women. Glosses and euphemisms cannot transmute evil into good, suicide into sacrifice or crudity into poetry. No apotheosis of Sita's death can ever turn it into a symbol of holy sacrifice. Even Rajagopalachari reacts to Sita's tragedy in this way: "I must say my heart rebels against it. It is painful to read the story" (1951 : 311). In Bhavabhuti's *Uttara Ramacharita*, Sita's maid Vasanti, denouncing Rama's banishment of Sita, asks him: "O thou hard-hearted one, is it honour that thou dost profess to hold dear? What dishonour, I ask, is more dreadful than this" (cf. De 1969 : 72)? Lakshmana's comment on Rama's decision to banish Sita in the *Hanumannatakam* reads: "While the female deer is giving birth to her child, the male deer does not desert her even if it hears a lion's roar. But Janaki has been abondoned by her husband, Raghuraja, when she is about to give birth to her child" (Mishra 1978 : XIV : 92)! While examining Sita's final rejection by Rama, one has only to bear in mind that the Indo-Aryan social system does not allow a violated or abducted woman to return to the Aryan fold. Such women are ultimately obliged to choose between reconciliation with their new fate or suicide (cf. Altekar 1956 : 310).

Sharply opposed to the multi-faceted, continually evolving, ever dynamic, free, lively, human, assertive, 'round', powerful, independent and rebellious heroine of the *Mahabharata*, Sita is the static, monotonous, unidimensional, timid, constrained, glum and 'flat' character of the *Ramayana*. Denied the freedom of thought, movement and action, she remains a stereotype or even an automation throughout her long and horrendous journey from Valmiki to Tulasidasa. She is everywhere an archetypal image of the self-sacrificing, suffering, patient, mute and compliant Hindu wife who takes every word as a command and every curse as a blessing. Sita does not grow, change or resent. There is no perceptible difference between Sita in the first Canto and Sita in the final Canto of Valmiki's epic. The story of her origin is an awkward myth while the episode of her terminal diappearance is an agonizing tale. In between the beginning and the end, Sita's life is a long chain of shocks, indignities and persecutions. A poor shadow of her awe-inspiring, ever-demanding and all-powerful husband, Sita, as an epic character, fails to command spontaneous respect or appreciation from discerning readers. The critical reader can only sympathise with her, pity her or shed tears for her. The reader cannot do otherwise because she refuses to stand up or speak out.

The image of Sita as a stereotype of taken-for-granted wifehood logically emerges from the central thrust of the *Ramayana*. The *Ramayana* and the *Mahabharata* are very rightly acknowledged as two of the fifteen greatest masterpieces of world literature (cf. Chatterji 1978 : 5-6), although the two are so radically different from each other. The *Ramayana* comes to the modern reader as the *ancient* manifesto of a consciously organised and severely inhibited people. As the eloquent prophet of such a people, Valmiki cannot brook any interference in his working out the utopian superstructure of an ideal community of men and women who can and must transcend their mutual rivalries, meannesses, squabbles and distrusts in order to achieve a high level of political stability and moral piety. His hero has to be a man who commands unfailing obedience and boundless adoration from his subjects, including his life-mate.

Contrasted with Valmiki's dated epic, the *Mahabharata* is a modern masterpiece which invites the reader to share a timeless fraternity with its men and women. Vyasa's stark honesty and ruthless frankness draw today's reader to reciprocate the embrassing-but-genuine overtures of his characters. How appropriate is his claim:

"What is found in this epic may be elsewhere;

What is not in this epic is nowhere else"!

A labyrynthine-yet-fast-moving narrative, full of great poetry, beauty, delicacy and poignance, the *Mahabharata* still deserves to be read as the national biography of the early Hindus. It is the monumental record of their collective unconscious as much as of their socio-political behaviour and it is this unique combination of the inner and the outer in their shared fullnesses that makes this classic an eternally readable and immensely enjoyable literary text. Vyasa's matchless masterpiece must not form part of our national museums because it is a living document whose characters still live and flourish in our towns and villages with all their uncouthness, cruelty, filth, power and grandeur. It is therefore only appropriate that its great Draupadi is as fresh and adorable today as she was thousands of years ago.

To get a better view of Sita's over-all epic personality, it may be interesting to compare her with Eve. Seen in the light of the Rama-Sita relationship, the relationship between Adam and Eve as a fellowship of the body and the spirit appears, to the critical reader, to be a more genuinely shared relationship as described in Milton's epic. After the crucial eating of the fruit of knowledge at the instance of Eve, Adam is tense and nervous. In sheer terror of imminent expulsion from Paradise, he asks Eve to get out of his sight. Apologetic Eve begs him not to abandon her:

"Forsake me not thus, Adam, witness heaven
What love sincere and reverence in my heart
I bear thee ... thy suppliant
I beg, and clasp thy knees, bereave me not,
Whereon I live, thy gentle looks, thy aid,
Thy counsel in this uttermost distress,
My only strength and stay, forlorn of thee
Whither shall I betake me, where subsist" (*PL* X : 914-22).

Adam is moved. He relents and then he has to make up his mind about what to do next. Faced with an irreversible choice between Eve and Paradise, he decides in favour of the former for he cannot visualize a life without her. He is expelled from Paradise. So is Eve. They walk hand in hand out of Paradise and Eve exclaims:

"... thou to me
Art all things under Heaven, all places thou,
Who for my wilful crime art banisht hence
This further consolation yet secure
I carry hence" (*ibid.*, XII : 617-21).

Adam's reconciliation with Eve may not be the best solution of conjugal problems and polarities, yet it is far superior to a wife's rejection by her husband. At the end of her story, Sita carries no 'consolation' and Valmiki's portrait of her conjugal status therefore leaves much to be desired for.

Seen as a character in literature, Sita can very well be compared with Shakespeare's Desdemona. Young, beautiful, innocent, and devoted to marital fidelity, Desdemona suddenly finds Othello indifferent and withdrawn. Puzzled by his coldness, she asks him:

"Tell me Othello—I wonder in my soul
what you would ask me that I should deny" (III : III : 89-90).

And then one day he charges her with infidelity. She is stunned.

The following conversation between them may give an insight into their psychic polarities:

Othello: Had it pleased heaven

To try me with affliction; had they rained
All kind of sores and shame on my bare head,
Steeped me in poverty to the lips,
Given to captivity me and my utmost hopes.
I should have found some place of my soul
A drop of patience; but alas, to make me
The fixed figure for the time of scorn
To point his slow unmoving finger at !—O, O!
Yet I could bear that too; well, very well;
But there; where I have garnered up my heart,
Where either I must live or bear no life,
The fountain from the which my current runs,
Or else dries up—to be discarded thence!
Or keep it as a cistern foul toads
To knot and gender in ! Turn thy complexion there,
Patience, thou young and rose-lipped cherubin—
Ay, here, look grim as hell.

Desdemona: I hope my noble lord esteems me honest.

Othello: O, ay; as summer flies are in the shambles,
That quiken even with blowing. O thou weed
Who art so lovely fair and smell'st so sweet
That the sense aches at thee!
Wouldst thou had'st never been born!

Desdemona: Alas, what ignorant sin have I committed?

Othello: Was this fair paper, this most goodly book,
Made to write 'whore' upon? what committed!
Committed ! O thou public commoner!
I should make very forges of my cheeks
That would to cinders burn up modesty,
Did I but speak thy deeds. What committed!
Heaven stops the nose at it, and the moon winks;
The bawdy winds, that kisses all it meets,

Is hushed within the hollow mine of earth,

And will not hear it. What committed!

Impudent strumpet" (IV : II : 49-82).

Othello finally makes up his mind to murder her. But when he enters Desdemona's room to smother her to death, he realizes how painful and trying an experience it is to dispose of such a lovely and loving wife. Repeatedly kissing while she is fast asleep, Othello cries out:

"O balmy breath, that doth almost persuade

Justice to break her sword! One more, one more.

Be thus when thou art dead, and I will kill thee,

And love thee after. One more, and that's the last.

So sweet was never so fatal. I must weep

But they are cruel tears" (V : II : 16-21).

Desdemona suddenly wakes to find that her husband is preparing to kill her. The brief conversation between the killer and the victim reads:

Desdemona: Kill me tomorrow, let me live tonight.

Othello: Nay, and you strive—

Desdemona: But half an hour !

Othello: Being done, there is no pause.

Desdemona: But while I say one prayer!

Othello: It is too late" (V : II : 84-89).

Othello smothers Desdemona to death. But before she succumbs to death, she has a word with Emilia:

Desdemona: A guiltless death I die.

Emilia: O, who hath done this deed?

Desdemona: Nobody. I myself. farewell.

Commend me to my kind lord" (V : II : 125-127).

The silent sufferer is finally silenced in the physical sense too. The deadly combination of beauty and devotion ultimately becomes literally 'deadly' for both Sita and Desdemona.

7

Meaning Of Liberation

7.1 Responsibilities of Woman

"Every woman is the image of the Goddess."

—*Mahanirvana Tantra*

Articles 14, 15 and 16 of the *Constitution of India* guarantee, in unequivocal terms, equality before law, equal protection of the law and equality of opportunity to all Indian citizens. Article 14 reads: "The State shall not deny to any person equality before the law or the equal protection of the law within the territory of India". Article 15 prohibits discrimination against any citizen on grounds of religion, race, caste, sex or place of birth. It clearly lays down that no citizen shall, on grounds of religion, race, caste, sex, place of birth or any of them "be subject to any disability". Article 16 provides for equality of opportunity to all Indian citizens, irrespective of their religion, race, caste, sex or place of birth (cf. Varma 1978 : 45-47). These constitutional guarantees ensure that all Indian citizens are treated as equal in the eyes of law, are given equal protection of the law and equal opportunities and that no one is discriminated against by the State or an individual or a group of individuals on grounds of his or her religion, race, caste, sex or place of birth.

We have been a constitutional country for more than four decades now. But questions like the following stare us in the face even today : Are men and women equal? Do women know their rights and privileges as guaranteed by the constitution? Do they realize that they are equal to men in every respect and that no one can take away their constitutional rights and privileges? If they do not, who is responsible for their ignorance or failure? Are women themselves responsible for their 'inferior' status in the society? It is true that a vast majority of women, Hindu women in particular, are quite innocent of their constitutional rights and privileges. But there are women who know or should know about such rights and privileges. Do such 'knowledgeable' women make conscious or systematic efforts to increase the general awareness among women of their rights and privileges?

If there is a struggle for existence, only the *fittest* survive, argues the archangel of 'evolution'. If women have to survive and exist as authentic individuals, they will have to think and rebel. "I think, therefore, I exist", writes Descrates while Camus testifies, "I rebel, therefore I exist" (cf. Sengupta 1974 : 252). Since only those who think and rebel do exist, women have got to think and rebel in order that they exist in the true sense of the term. How unfortunate and incomprehensible it is that even those who can, do not usually think and rebel! Such women cannot shirk their responsibility for their predicament as well as for that of other women. It hardly needs to be pointed out that a large number of women do in fact abet men in committing crimes against women, at times, against themselves. Men have indeed been cruel and vicious in their entire approach to women and their place in society but it is equally true that a large number of women are themselves to blame for a large part of male cruelty and vice either by their act of abetment or by taking vices and cruelties lying down. No society or class does win independence or autonomy unless it is ready to make sacrifices. Women make sacrifices, no doubt, but in most cases they make sacrifices for helping or defending men and not for their own rights and privileges. The few who do, succeed but often only as individuals. Medea and Draupadi acquire greatness as independent and authentic individuals but they do not do much for the generality of women. Medea and Draupadi fail as leaders or liberators of women. They have not been many Medeas and Draupadis, not only because men have not allowed many women to become Medeas or Draupadis but also because women in general have not so far been roused to fight for their rights by women leaders. An oasis, howsoever fertile and lively, cannot by itself transform a whole desert into a lush growth of vegetation. If women have to be liberated, they will have to be taught or led in most cases and for most of the time, by women leaders and achievers to refuse and reject the images of femininity inflicted on their class by men.

A Hindu girl is married to a man by her father (or male guardian) who performs the marriage rites as part of a religious obligation. Marry she must, and that too, the man selected by her father (or male guardian). The Hindu girl has no option either to refuse to marry that particular man or not to marry at all. Should it be a reason powerful enough for the Hindu girl to consent to doing what she may not like to do? Shouldn't the girl exercise her option whether to marry the man she likes or not to marry at all? Is Hindu marriage a sacrament? If it is, is it a sacrament only for the bride? Once married, the Hindu wife has to be devoted to her husband in thought, word and deed even if her husband is a moral wreck. Kanva warns Shakuntala : " Never be angry with your husband, no matter what happens. In everything be humble. These qualities make a woman; those without them are black sheep in their families" (Lal 1964 : 44-45). Are humility and devotion only wifely virtues? Why can't wives, educated wives at least, insist that they will be good only to husbands who are good to them? Why can't they remind their husbands that as wives they are their equal under the law of the land as also according to the definition of marriage? A husband who is not truthful and affectionate to his wife does not deserve a wife to be truthful and affectionate to him. A wife has to remind her husband in unequivocal terms that marriage by definition is a participatory institution, a long-term contract, between two equals and that it is viable only so long as both partners trust and respect each other on a one-to-one basis. Why should a married woman be devoted to her husband (*pativrata*) when she knows that her husband is not devoted to her (*patnivrata*)? Why can't married women relate their marital roles to mutual understanding rather than to religious or domestic obligations? Why should such obligations be peculiar to women alone? Can't women decide on their own to accept, modify or annul traditional functions of a wife (cf. Mehta 1970 : 206)?

Denouncing social stereotypes and archetypes of womanhood, a woman writer in a recent paper complains that the image of woman as reader or achiever is "either non-existent or rare" (Bhat 1993). But it is intriguing that the same writer as editor of the volume *The Image of Woman in Indian Literature* includes a paper by a male writer who has the cheek to make sweeping generalizations like the following:

"All the abuses piled upon ancient credoes and practices by modern feminists and leaders of women's liberation become irrelevant if we confine ourselves to understanding the vision of great poets or thinkers of the past."

Again, "A woman finds her fulfilment only as a wife or life-partner of a loving husband for whose sake she deems no service or sacrifice too great. This is the ideal of *pativrata* set before woman! And every woman therefore seeks eagerly to marry in order to get the status of a *pativrata* and *grhini* (Krishnamoorthy 1993).

With all respect to his age and scholarship, I would like to ask Professor Krishnamoorthy a few questions : What is 'great' about the 'vision' of his "great poets and thinkers of the past"? Why should a woman *alone* find "her fulfilment only as a wife or life-partner of a loving husband"? Why shouldn't a man find *his* fulfilment only as a husband or life-partner of a loving wife? Why should a woman "eagerly" seek "to get the status of a *pativrata* and *grhini*? Why shouldn't a man "eagerly" seek to marry in order to get the status of a *patnivrata* and a *grhi*? Why shouldn't a husband deem "no service or sacrifice too great" to please his wife? What is so sacrosanct about the "Brahmanical culture"? And finally, what exactly does "constitute the ideal of womanhood" or the ideal of manhood?

A change in social conditions should normally be accompanied by a change in people's attitude. New situations call for a recasting of attitudes and a revised system of values. Commonsensically speaking, this is the meaning of human evolution, civilization or progress. Human beings march forward and improve their lot when they are ready to change both on behavioural and attitudinal levels. If they fail to undergo changes in their behavioural patterns and attitudinal textures, they fail to march forward. If they refuse to undergo such changes, they fail to bring about changes in their situations or social conditions. The basic problem with the modern Hindu woman is attitudinal. She is now doing something which her mother never did nor could ever conceive of doing but her attitude to life remains the same as her mother's. Many educated women are now working in professions which remove them from their traditional domestic chores. But most of such women, whether in politics, social work, business or in other professions do not seem to have been able to develop a new ideology or a new attitudinal texture which should facilitate their conduct outside home. These women, unfortunately, all too often want to have their cake and eat it too. They want new opportunities but old security; new freedoms but old protection (cf. Cormack 1961 : 105). It is of course true that these new opportunities and freedoms are often partial, tentative and socially disapproved, but it must also be borne in mind that unless women take risks and prepare themselves to make sacrifices (for themselves as well as their class), these opportunities and freedoms cannot be fully utilized nor can they be made instruments of stable social change favourable to the coming generations of women.

If a woman works in an organization where there are many smart and friendly men around, the husband (or guardian) starts having agonies of suspicion and jealousy. Can't a woman, at least a professional woman, articulate similar agonies of suspicion and jealousy if her husband or boy-friend is found working with lots of smart and friendly women around? A husband likes his wife to look pretty and smart and then suspects her if she is nice to other men. Can't a woman announce her suspicion of her handsome and smart husband if he is nice to other women? There is still a big hiatus between constitutional guarantees and actual situations in regard to woman's position in society because the normative system continues to be conservative (cf. Kapoor 1974 : 162). Why can't working wives persuade or oblige their husbands to shake off their patriarchal and obscurantist attitude towards them because they have to work and move about with male colleagues in order to meet the exigencies of their professional career? Why are husbands allowed to believe that their wives deserve only to be ordered about or to be kept waiting for them? Why are husbands allowed to stick to their sole prerogative to indulge in love-making with their wives whenever and as often as they want to? The biological nature and function of woman is fundamental to her differentiation from man. Conception and child-bearing are peculiar to woman. Should it not be a woman's prerogative, therefore, to decide of her own whether she would like to go in for love-making, conception, contraception, abortion or child-bearing? That woman alone undergoes such experiences does not and must not mean that every thing about her is 'feminine'. Does a woman perceive as a woman, see as a woman, think as a woman, speak or act as a woman as a general rule of her psychosomatic behaviour? How much of the 'feminine role' is gender-based? Why can't women stop the media and the males from bothering about or glorifying the virtues of femininity? Why do young and beautiful women run away with or marry flirts, divorcees or elderly widowers with several children? Why do pretty and smart women expose their anatomy to the agencies of modelling, film-making or sexist advertising (cf. Cormack 1961 : 117, Figes 1971 & Stott 1971)? If 'bachelorhood' is a matter of pride for men, why should 'spinsterhood' be an anathema to women? Can't women choose between career and marriage or balance the two to their own advantage? Are not emotion and sensibility as much a privilege of women as of men? Why can't career women oblige their husbands to appreciate that cooking, cleaning, washing, knitting and baby-minding are as much masculine chores as feminine? What is so specifically feminine about these chores or functions? If men can perceive their gender as primary and referential, why can't educated women perceive their gender as more primary and referential?

Conjugal statistics about contemporary American society show that 53.8 per cent men while 88 per cent women are disturbed by the sexual infidelity of their spouses while only 37.9 per cent men and 23 per cent women are content with their marital relationships (cf. Durden-Smith and De Simone 1983 : 207). These figures clearly suggest that men are more untrustworthy than women as marriage partners and also that many more women than men are unhappy in marriage. Why do so many wives put up with husbands who are not true to their marriage vows? Why can't women use their unique capacity to bear children as some sort of a lever to get whatever they want from their husbands? Men claim that women who fight for gender equality are easier to have sex with and cheaper to court and date than tradition-bound women. If it is so, then why is it so (cf. *ibid.*, p. 214)? What women usually do in the family should be based on an equitable distribution of work. Why should a division of labour in the family entail a larger amount of work and a lower status for women? Maternity is certainly an inconvenience for woman but that is no reason why it should be used as a handle against the expectant mother. Can't working women, at least educated working women, wrest firm and irrevocable assurances from their husbands before they go in for maternity exercises? In India girls still account for more than three-fourths of non-school-going children while only a handful of selected pockets possess a satisfactory level of female education. Rapes, dowry-deaths and other forms of violence and exploitation against women still continue to increase from year to year. What are women activists, particularly those in centres of power, doing to stop or reduce the annual increase in crimes against women? How is it that the mother-in-law is almost invariably involved in cases of bride-burning? Sometimes even the sister-in-law is involved. What stimulates women, both old and young, to connive with men in burning members of their own class? Widow-burning was legally stopped in India in 1829 and yet the highest legislative body and the highest court in the country are still concerned about widow-burning so as to prevent recurrences of the Deorala outrage. Why should it be so? Has any woman leader or activist ever threatened to undertake a fast-unto-death unless the executive machinery and the judicial system of the country are obliged to guarantee against death by fire? How can a country which does not burn married men and bereaved husbands be allowed to burn brides and widows? If a country allows such burnings to take place, how can it swear by a constitution which guarantees equality between men and women?

Social status is a matter of having power over others. The pursuit of status is only a power game. The more powerful you are, the higher status you have. It is this outlook that makes administrative/executive services and politics the most sought after professions in independent India. If women wish to secure higher social status, they will have to acquire more power. To gain power, they will have to stir out of traditional homes and orthodox definitions of womanhood. Since they have had not much power in the past, they will have to run a hurdle race to acquire power in order to acquire stable and genuine respectability. It is only natural that if a woman comes out of the charmed circle to take up an administrative/executive career or political position, she is faced with disturbing problems. In her efforts to do her job effectively, she offends the family and public opinion while in her efforts to satisfy the family and conform to public opinion, she lets down her job and herself. The career woman does not, therefore, find it easy to transcend the barbed fencing of family possessiveness and social ostracism (cf. Baig 1976 : 206-207). Popular notions of femininity intensify her mental strains day and night. If she is young and attractive, she is caught in a puzzling dilemma. Aloofness from her male colleagues might isolate her in her profession and affect her efficiency while her natural warmth towards them might be misconstrued as overtures towards them and these misconstrued overtures might ultimately mar her chances of a happy marriage or strain her conjugal harmony if she is already married. Similarly, if she is natural and polite, she might be dismissed as too weak-kneed a creature to be fit for exacting jobs but if she is tough and demanding, she might be branded as uppish and disagreeable. In view of such formidable hazards as these, a career woman is called upon not only to throw away all social and ideological fetters and free herself in order to achieve her desired goal, she is duty bound to pave the way so thoroughly that the next generation of career women walk into their profession as naturally as leaves come to a tree. The contemporary career woman has to look after herself as well as to ensure a safe passage for her future successors. How many career women are aware of their onerous responsibilities?

No one can possibly deny that women have so far been conditioned by their mentors, both men and women, to look at everything from a male point of view. The Hindu woman, more than her cousins elsewhere, has been tied to an endless chain of do's and don'ts in her life. She cannot deviate from the prescribed norm because it is a divine decree, a religious obligation and a social or domestic duty. When a man ridicules, chastises or destroys a woman for deviating from the ethic of social or family behaviour, one does not have to take it as something unpredictable or incomprehensible. But when a woman taunts, punishes or finishes another woman for violating the law, the mind really boggles. Everything that women do cannot be accounted for or defended simply with reference to centuries of male domination, manipulation or indoctrination. Women cannot shirk their own responsibilities. Even Beauvoir admits: "The daughter is for the mother at once her double and another person, the mother is at once overwhelmingly affectionate and hostile towards her daughter; she saddles her child with her own destiny: a way of proudly laying claim to her own femininity and also a way of revenging herself for it. The same process is to be found in pederasts, gamblers, drug-addicts, in all who at once take pride in belonging to a certain confraternity and feel humiliated by the association" (1953 : 20 cf. Baig 1976 : 250).

Despite the near-universal and rapidly increasing masculinization of history, there have been a few assertive and powerful women. Their femininity has never hindered them in discharging their onerous duties in any way. Joan of Arc, Razia Sultan and Rani Lakshmi Bai showed beyond all doubt that they could oblige even powerful men to dance to their tune. Bhandarnayake, Golda Meir, Margaret Thatcher and Indira Gandhi made history. Benazir Bhutto, Khalida Zia and Chandrika Kumartunge do easily order he-men about. Today it is not unnatural to find women in corridors of power. These women like their illustrious predecessors, are continually demonstrating that they can carry the burden of responsibility as well as, sometimes even better than, men. And yet they remain great as women. But the question is: Have these powerful women changed the generality of women into a progressive, challenging and assertive community? Besides, isn't it true that in spite of them, the 'average' or 'ordinary' woman is too timid even today? Does an ordinary woman have the ambition to wield her influence in society? Is the average educated woman a New woman? Or doesn't an average career woman still subscribe to the deliberate concoction that as a woman she has not the ability to compete with or outrun men as a class? In either case, she is to blame (cf. Trench 1971). There are today women in academia, judiciary, business, police, aviation, defence forces and professions but, how many women are appointed to headships in co-educational institutions? How many women get through to the top position in industry, commerce or journalism? How many women join the legal profession, the police, the defence services or religious administration? How many women control positions in political parties or trade unions? If women are conspicuous by their absence in areas like these, who is to blame? Apart from questions like these, there are other problems. A 'masculine' woman should be as bad a phrase as a 'feminine' man and yet women, enlightened women, like to be eulogized as 'hero-like'. Will a gentle and meek male like to be admired as 'heroine-like'? If men spurn feminine epithets, why do women cherish masculine titles? Baroness Burdett married her former secretary and Queen Victoria commented that she was an 'old silly woman'. Yet many important or affluent women of our own time have "achieved their present status as former secretaries to their husbands whom no one would describe as silly old men" (Sticks 1971).

Men are free to look up, around and down to pick up wives but women are supposed to look up to become wives. Are only men responsible for such inherited attitudes to heterosexual equations? In many cases, young and educated women themselves develop a sense of their worth only as females. They refuse to tell their men that sex is a communication between two individuals, not a male prerogative, and that conjugal harmony depends on both man and woman, not on woman alone. How many modern women realize that a New woman has to emerge from a human society, not to drop from above or to spring up from a conchshell (cf. *ibid.*)? Well placed women are free to wear and look what they like. They can follow their own taste and consult their own comfort. Then, why do they submit to the dictatorship of fashion? Why do they make up to please their men while their men are indifferent to what they like or dislike? Why does an educated wife have to say "All right, Sir" to her stupid husband (cf. Narasimhaiah 1993)? It is a fact that a vast majority of women are not yet free to dictate terms to their fathers, brothers or husbands but there are women who can do this. If such women do not stand up to assert themselves, the fault is certainly theirs.

7.2 Attainment of Liberation

"The basic freedom of the world is woman's freedom."

—*Margaret Sanger cited in McPhee (1979 : 239)*

It was in 431 B.C. that Euripides created *Medea*, a terrible tragedy, out of a popular Greek myth. Almost everything that Medea says about the position of women in society is still relevant, although the universal appeal of Euripides' play does not seem to have occurred to anyone except Chaucer in the *Wife of Bath* until Simone de Beauvoir wrote *The Second Sex* in 1949. If women, remarks Chaucer, had written stories about men, they would definitely have written much more about man's wickedness than men have written about woman's wickedness. Men fear and hate superior power or intelligence in women. But the Chorus in the *Medea* celebrates the beginning made by their invincible leader:

"Legends now shall change direction,
Woman's life have glory,
Honour comes to the female sex,

Woman shall be a theme for slanderous tales no more"(cf. Murry 1910 & Knox 1983).

Euripides' Medea is a woman who has given up everything—her home, country, parents and power—for her love for Jason. She has born him two sons. She accompanies him wherever he goes and helps him in whatever he does. But Jason comes to treat her, in course of time, as a liability which he is desperate to get rid of. He arrives in a foreign country where he meets a beautiful princess. He decides to discard Medea and to marry the princess in order to become king. The father of the princess decrees that Medea must be banished so that life becomes smooth for his daughter and would-be son-in-law. Jason supports the king and asks Medea to get out of the kingdom to fend for herself, leaving the sons behind. Medea is an abandoned and helpless woman in an alien land. Threatened with imminent banishment, Medea decides to revenge herself by killing the sons and the bride while leaving Jason alone amid the ruin of all his hopes for his sons, his marriage and his kingship. Having carried out her plans successfully, she leaves the city untouched in a celestial chariot for a safe stay in Athens.

The playwright's characterization of Medea is simply marvellous. Medea is no passive sufferer, no ordinary woman wronged. Like a typical Greek 'hero', she fears more than anything else the mockery of her enemies. She is a hero who inflicts death and destruction to punish those who wrong and mock her. With the determined resolve of the Sophoclean hero, she says: "The deed must be done", "I must dare", "I shall kill". How aptly the nurse describes her ! Medea takes no food, listens to no comfort, no advice; she only weeps and rages. She is full of anger, wrath and the determination to destroy. She is terrible and wild like a beast, obsessed with her revenge and glory. A bull, a wolf and a lion, Medea combines within herself the naked violence of Achilles with the cold craft of Odysseus. "Let no one", she cries out, "think me contemptible and weak, nor inactive either, but quite the opposite—dangerous to my enemies and helpful to my friends. Such are the qualities that bring life glory" (cf. *ibid.*). This is the creed by which Homeric and Sophoclean heroes live and die. Medea sees herself as an ally of the Gods and achieves divine approval for her action.

Historically speaking, human civilization or masculinist civilization, to put it more correctly, has so far depended upon various forms of breaking, including the breaking of glass and the breaking of woman's body. How frightful would it be for men if powerful women now turn round and begin to define feminist civilization by breaking man's body, by reminding old-time male leaders that 'Resistance to tyranny is obedience to God' (cf. McPhee 1979 : 160 & 162)! A man does not feel the hurt that he causes to woman by breaking her body unless someone begins to hurt him by breaking his body. If woman turns violent towards man to assert herself or to pay for his traditional tyranny against her race, the whole course of history will take a catastrophic round-about-turn. The Choral hymn in the *Medea* should forewarn men against a resurgence of feminine insurgency:

> "Back streams the wave on the ever-running river:
> Life is changed about the laws if it overtrod.
> Man shall be the slave, the affrighted, the low-liver!
> Man hath forgotten God.
> And woman; yea, woman, shall be terrible in her story:
> The tales too, meseemeth, shall be other than of yore.
> For a fear there is that cometh out of woman and a glory
> And that hard hating voices shall encompass her no more"
> (Murry 11910 : 411-18).

Men can no longer lie about their so-called pious intentions about women. Their ancestors have lied too long, cheated too long, exploited too long. They must now look back and take stock of what their ancestors have done to the *better half* of humanity. "I think", writes Jawaharlal Nehru, "it would be true to say that the position and status of women in India for many hundreds of years has not been a good one in law or in public life" (cf. Baig 1976 : 1). "By sheer force of a vicious custom", contends the Mahatma, "even the most ignorant and worthless men have been enjoying superiority over women which they do not deserve and ought not to have" (cf. Sachchinanda & Sinha 1984 : 3). Gandhi wrote in *Young India* in 1918 : "Woman is the companion of man, gifted with equal mental capacities, she has the right to participate in the minutest details of the activities of man and the same right of freedom and liberty as he" (cf. *ibid.*, p. 3). Madame de Stael rightly remarks: "Genius has no sex" (cf. Baig 1976 : 38). Academic studies have now convincingly demonstrated that women are no less intelligent and talented than men (cf Amundsen 1971 : 29). One can therefore, legitimately conclude that a society which does not respect women as equal to men must be a pack of liars. The socio-political status of women reflects the cultural attainment of a people. A society is as advanced as its women. The image of woman projected in the Hindu tradition of thought is proof of the Hindu male's lack of basic humanity. The Hindu male does not accept woman as his equal even today. The orthodox Hindu view of woman may be described in the words of D.H. Lawrence: "A man is willing to accept her ... as a man in skirts, as an angel, as a devil, as a body face, a machine, an instrument, a pair of legs, a servant, and encyclopedia, an ideal or an obscenity: the only thing he won't accept her as is a human being, a real human being" (cf. *ibid.*, p. 38).

For the emergence of a new social order, it is essential that the old cultural agents and the transmission belts of the past are replaced or modified. Lazy and tradition-bound Hindus find it difficult, often impossible, to adapt a new philosophy which would demand a radical departure from a repressive past to a liberal future. It is no wonder that even educated families operate today according to orthodox ideologies rather than accept new values and patterns. Why is there so much violence or so much uncertainty in contemporary Hindu society? The Hindu society is currently passing through a chain of emotional convulsions and a number of 'conversion experiences' due to continually widening cracks between the old and the new because the Hindu culture has proved to be a non-functional culture. Few people in sober thought would maintain that progress is always civilizing or that civilization is always humanizing. The Hindu society does not succeed in switching over to a radical philosophy or a radical mode of life because there are built-in resistances in its secular theology or theological secularism: "The spiritual crisis of contemporary Indian society is basically due to the initial encounter of a .... traditional society with the problems of a technological civilization. ... The problems of a modern technological society cannot be faced by traditional institutions and values: it can be faced by absorbing the spirit of the modern age which expresses itself in scientific terms and faith in human potentialities" (cf. Cormack 1961 : 226, 227 & 229). Orthodox Hinduism deters progress and change. If we want to change from a cramping past to an expanding future, we must replace obscurantism with a liberal humanistic vision of society in which ignorance is bondage and knowledge is freedom.

Both man and woman take from life; both man and woman give to life; both man and woman need to live happily. But then there is a big gap between what society expects from man and what it expects from woman. Society's expectations derive from a bunch of murky notions of what man and woman ought to be doing. There is no rule, no analysis or no rationale for such expectations. Such expectations still continue to be there simply because they have always been there. An average Hindu does not want his wife to go out, work and earn money while he remains at home, unless he has important work to do outside, to cook food and mind the children simply because he has not yet been bullied into seeing reason, into realizing that household duties are as much his as his wife's. It has, therefore, become imperative for educated women to note once for all that most of what is expected of them is expedient on the core of imputed and arbitrarily formulated feminine attributes. We have now reached a stage in human evolution where women must critically review and upset, if necessary, their, *expectancy* roles and *assigned* functions (cf. Amundsen 1971 : 107 & Trench 1971). The male society must be taught to look at life from the woman's point of view as well. It is high time men were obliged, if necessary through emotional coercion, domestic supervision or political power to realize that the image of woman created by their ancestors was a sheer concoction designed to mislead and cheat women, that it has already misled and cheated women long enough and that therefore it now deserves to be exposed and discarded. The image of women has to be created afresh and to be created by woman herself. As a great woman put it, more than a hundred years ago: "Leave to my own perception what is proper for me as a lady, to my own discretion what is wise for me as a woman, to my own conscience what is my duty to my race and to my God" (cf. McPhee 1979 : 236). Only this woman-created-image-of-woman will be genuine and authentic. Every other image is a lie or distortion. It is time men were reminded that spinsterhood is less depressive than wifehood and that working wives are physically and physiologically far healthier than housewives. Not too long ago, reliable scientific investigations showed that wives were sixty times more likely to feel depressed than single women and that housewives were far more likely than working wives to complain of psycho-somatic ailments and complications (cf. Amundsen 1971 : 123). It must not be out of season for educated Hindu women to avail of such scientific hometruths.

To attain liberation women have to understand and expose the traditional hypocrisy of their male counterparts. Men always do in private what they condemn in public. They coerce women as a matter of habit to fashion themselves on a pattern that pleases them because they have economic and political power. They keep women in seclusion and control because they buy sex with women and yet condemn sex as something evil. Respectable men do not talk about sex or about contexts in which sex is practised but they must have women for their sex game. The cultural standards of such respectable and moral men should be gauged by the culture of their prostitutes. "Morality", wrote Attiah Habibullah in 1935, "cannot exist by falsehoods and through negative beliefs. It must be born of positive convictions. The only external safeguards must be material so that the existence may be made possible of a generation of men who never in their life chanced to buy a woman's surrender by money or any other instrument of power; and a generation of women who never happened to give themselves to a man for any consideration other than love" (cf. Thomas 1964 : 359). Sexual independence is as important for woman as economic independence but no woman can attain the former without first attaining the latter. When a woman is financially dependent on a man, even for an hour, "she puts herself, to some extent, in his power" (cf. McPhee 1979 : 100). As Kamaladevi Chattopadhyaya points out: "Indivisibly linked up with her economic independence is woman's sexual independence. One without the other would be innocuous; it [the combination of sexual independence with economic independence] alone will make sex equality a true reality for ever. Man's fight against woman's struggle to free herself from undesired motherhood is one of the bitterest wars waged by him, for he knows that her victory will deal a death blow to his vested interests and devastate for ever that atrocious structure of the female character" (cf. Thomas 1964 : 360). She goes on to argue: "No woman can herself be free who cannot own and control her body, and who can be subdued and enslaved through that very equality of fertility which once raised her to the altar as the deity" (*ibid.*, p. 360). Recommending the desirability of adopting full-proof birth control measures, Kamaladevi observes: "Motherhood is one of the most sacred and unique functions of womanhood and should not be left to the mercy of exigencies of accidental circumstances or allowed to be determined by ignorance. It must be a conscious task undertaken with joy and a full sense of its responsibilities, controlled and regulated according to the emotional urge and physical capacity of the woman" (*ibid.*, p. 361). Gandhi goes even further to suggest that no woman should allow her husband to have sex with her unless she wants a child; "Man has no right to touch his wife, as long as she does not wish to have a child, and the woman should have the will-power to resist even her own husband.... Sex urge is a fine and noble thing. There is nothing to be ashamed of it. But it is meant only for the act of creation. Any other use of it is a sin against God and humanity" (cf. *ibid.*, p. 375). Whether we agree with Kamaladevi and Gandhi or not, it is crucial for the liberation of women that they have economic independence and/or political power before they can hope for physiological and sexual independence. It is therefore imperative for economically independent and politically secure women to create conditions in which other and more and more women acquire independence on all levels: economic, political, ideological and sexual.

Sex, love, partnership, marriage or any other act related to heterosexual transactions has got to be, it is being pointed out so often in the present study, a conscious and participatory process, if women's liberation movements have to make any meaningful progress. The centrality of ideological independence for women must be recognized by all those who really want women to be free, equal and respectable. No other form of independence is going to stay with women unless they are ideologically free, even though it is true that unless they have achieved other forms of independence, it is pointless to try for ideological independence. Slaves and beggars have no use for God, morality, progress or self-respect unless they are physically full and free. Sexual slavery of the wife must be recognized as a fact by educated wives before they can hope to try to achieve sexual freedom. Those who fight for women's liberation must note that women's roles and functions have so far been and still continue to be stereotyped and artificially or arbitrarily imposed upon women. The highest aim of a women's liberation movement must be, as it is, freedom from oppressive ideological constraints in order that women in general hope to become human "in a world which declares them only female" (Lenz *et. al.*, 1980). Besides, leaders of such movements have got to be far more thick-skinned and daring than they have so far been so that they reject patent male strategies like name-calling and scandal-mongering. They can as well ignore and scandalize men who resort to such anti-woman tricks. Every woman fighter has to take note of the recent conclusions of Shere

Hite, the Americal social historian. Basing her conclusions on a survey of 7000 men, Shere Hite says that if women fight with men to achieve equality with them, they are labelled" aggressive and bitchy" (cf. Statesman, October 25, 1986). Women fighters can either ignore such labellings or return their antonyms to men and go forward in their struggle. They have to create conditions which oblige men to realize genuinely that women are not inferior men and that they are different but equal and respectable. "We do not", says Indira Gandhi, "wish to imitate men. ... What we want is true equality of opportunity to develop our latent talents and the ending of discrimination" (1974).

The nuclear part of man-woman relationship, sex deserves to be understood and practised as a conscious and humanizing interaction between two equally valuable heterosexual participants and never as an invasion and conquest of the one by the other. "Sex must be rescued", argues Germaine Greer, "from the traffic between powerful and powerless, masterful and mastered, sexual and neutral, to become a form of communication between potent, gentle, tender people" (cf. McPhee 1979 : 229). Or, as Erikson puts it: "There must clearly be an important evolutionary function on the selectivity of sexual love: I think it is the mutual search for a shared identity, for the mutual verification through an experience of finding oneself, as one loses oneself, in another" (1961). Contrary to masculine misconceptions that gender equality would feminize men and masculinize women, psychologist Abraham Maslow suggests after several studies that the more "dominant" the woman, the greater is the enjoyment of sex, the greater is her ability to give herself freely in love. Alice A Rossi observes: "Women with dominance feeling were free to be completely themselves, and this was crucial for their full expression in sex. They enjoy sexual fulfilment to a much greater degree than conventionally feminine women" (cf. Amundsen 1971: 127). For a woman to feel genuine pleasure in sex, it is imperative for her to be wholly free from inhibitions, complexes and wrong notions about human sexuality and eroticism. Sex is not merely a biological activity; it is more importantly a psychological performance. To perform it better physically, it is essential to achieve psychological health and ideological freedom. To be a really lovable experience, an erotic participation must be a spontaneous coming-together of free and full partners. It deserves to be noted by sex educationists that the sex education of children begins in the conjugal harmony and co-operation between the parents. Sex is not just a matter of biology, or morals or even resposibilities in human relations—although this might go a long way towards it, but of "something that spills over from a living marriage: joy. When a couple feel sheer pleasure in each other, the children learn something about the value of adult sexuality and its wholeness which is sufficient to balance all the ugly forms of sex that they may encounter. And girls, identifying themselves with their mothers, develop a sense of their worth as women" (Kitzinger 1971).

Love is the most distinctive aspect of human behaviour and human behaviour is the product of an interacting complex of forces "ranging from the individual blood-sugar level to the ethos of his civilization" (Hunt 1961). If we wish to usher in a new era of man-woman relationship, we must transform love from a masculine monopoly to a mutual participation where there is no withdrawal, no tension, no struggle, no victory, no defeat. We must make it an enjoyable reciprocity in which each participant is at once a subject and an object so that duality becomes mutuality. In an ideal love situation there is a simultaneity of selfishness and generosity, possessiveness and sacrifice (cf. Beauvoir 1953 : 138-139). Unless the participants merge into each other to become a single identity, love for women will continue to be a deception and a horror. To qoute Beauvoir: "One day when it will be possible for women to love not in her weakness but in her strength, not to escape herself but to find herself—on that day love will become for her, as for men, a source of life and not of mortal danger" (cf. *ibid.*, p. 361).

Few educated men realize today that it was because of the mindless masculinization of heterosexual relationships for centuries that created such a gnawing gap between love and sex, on the one hand, and between desirable and undesirable forms of sex, on the other. Marital sex was taken for granted while erotic sex was confined to pre-marital or extra-marital interactions. Sex was used to denote the former while love was reserved for the latter. Love was associated with the invasion and conquest of the sexual object who was a woman other than the invader's/conqueror's wife. Whenever a man saw a woman, he decided to pursue, conquer and possess her for a time and then to reject her as an object condemned. This sex/love philosophy gave rise to notorious institutions like concubinage and prostitution. The wife was never considered an object of love, though she always remained an object of sex. Within marital bounds there was no quest or conquest and therefore there was no love. To be in love with one's wife was scandalous for ancient men. "Oxoriousness" was a term of derision for men in India and Greece. In Xenophone's *Symposium* Socrates speaks with astonishment about a man who is deeply in love with his wife (cf. Hunt 1961). For most Hindu males love is still incompatible with marriage. After all, we are the products of our history and culture.

When we examine the concept of sex as a matter of real-life experience, we begin to see how nefarious and incomprehensible can male hypocrisy be, what vicious consequences can it lead people to. We arbitrarily divide sex into desirable and obnoxious and then expect our children to have healthy perceptions or experiences of sex. Sexual desire is considered evil in the child, naughty in the adolescent and normal in the adult and then it is expected that this deep-seated contradiction should be overcome by the mere ceremony of marriage. We fail to anticipate that our attitudinal contradictions towards sex might engender in our children, particularly in girls, an incorrigible dissociation of sensibility. Boys are boys; they soon discover that their elders bluff them and thereby they easily overcome their ambivalence towards sex and love. Much sooner than expected, they come to understand that they can use wives as objects of routine sexuality and turn to other women for erotic adventures. But girls are so different. Innocent and gullible as they turn out to be, they faithfully separate sex from love so that for them where there is sex, there is no love, and where there is love, there is no sex. For young women, despite education and exposure, sex is marital and loveless, while love is extra-marital and asexual. When they fall in love, they do not expect any sexual overtures from their lovers. When they marry, they do not expect any love from their husbands. Marriage is for them is an era of loveless sex which their husbands can foist on them whenever and as frequently as they choose to. A modern educated woman generally tends to be a Miriam or a Clara Dawes (cf. D.H. Lawrence's *Sons and Lovers*). Marriage for most women is loveless but full of sex. Marriage however is not a simple experience. Even here, women face an acute emotional crisis. Brought up in cultural contexts where sex is constantly condemned as something evil and degrading and now suddenly thrown into a situation where they have to surrender themselves to indiscriminate and unilateral sexuality at the hands of their husbands, new wives find it very difficult to shift overnight their allegiance from an inhibitive past to a licentious present. It is for this reason that tensions, inhibitions, apprehensions and fears continue to haunt, as powerful pathological forces, the sex-life of a great majority of married women. No programme of women's liberation from a repressive culture and a crippling social structure can ever succeed in making a marriage a fulfilling experience for women unless they see through the traditional masculine game and reconcile love with sex. Since few males would have females equated and liberated, women would have to liberate themselves, in spite of men.

A genuine programme of women's liberation will have to break down the fictionalized images of femininity. Those fighting for women's rights to freedom and equality will have to define and establish femininity afresh. They will have to create and project the correct image of the authentic woman based on scientific evidence and honest insight. No false theories of woman's nature, no ideology of the so-called proper roles of woman, no artificial gender norms must be allowed to characterize and determine the New Woman. The female has to develop into the human. Every woman must be assured of equalify of education, opportunity, income and status on a par with a respectable man. What is most needed is a community where arrangements are made to "ensure the realization and utilization of the potential of every human being, for there are too many men among us whose talents remain undeveloped, whose skills are not used, whose spirits are still twisted. The liberation of women will mean—must mean—the liberation of men as well" (Amundsen 1971 : 156). To be a democracy in the true sense of the term, it is essential that every human being, woman or man, must be free from ignorance, fear and exploitation. Political independence will have no meaning unless it is backed up by economic, social, sexual and intellectual independence. The true aim of the movement must be to change the whole texture of consciousness so that women and undeveloped men feel, think and act as they like. Women's liberation should not, need not, always mean a sex war against men. Liberation should ultimately be a positive pursuit, not a negative or destructive game. An advocate of women's liberation points out that "anti-family, hate-male campaigns are strictly non-productive both on the political, and in the long run, on the personal level" (*ibid.*, p. 173).

Institutionalized oppressions of women as a class still characterize the mainstream of Hindu society. Systematic violence, organized denigration and ideological vilification of women do not yet show any noticeable symptoms of abatement. As a matter of fact, incidence of sexual assaults, wife-beating and wife-burning is on the increase. One possible reason for such increase is relatable to the growing demands of women's liberation movements for changing the existing social equations in order to accord women rights to genuine equality with men. Men tend to be more aggressive and violent to silence opposition to their traditional rule over women. The situation in India is comparable (ironically though) to that of Hindu women overseas, 'diasporic' women in particular. In a learned paper on the predicament of diasporic Indians, Bhikhu Parekh (1993) points out that while Indians in the Diaspora, particularly Hindus, have the lowest rate of violence against outsiders, they have the highest rate of domestic violence against women. Male violence erupts due to women's demands for equality and the abolition of parental control over marriage: "The knowledge that women can obtain outside help themselves threatens male domination and worsens the situation. Even when there is no violence, there is much aggression, hostility and subtle or crude attempt at domination" (Parekh 1993).

Nevertheless, there is a growing awareness among educated Hindu women, both native and diasporic, younger women in particular, that this is an inevitable phase of transition from the old to the new and that such violence and hostility will not silence organized protests of conscious and vigilant fighters. Leaders of women's liberation movements are now confident that they can raise their voice, organize protest rallies and go to courts of law against tyranny and exploitation of individual women or of groups of women. They know that they can now openly stand by their rights and privileges as guaranteed by the constitution of India. They can loudly demand amendments of laws and modification of social customs and definitions. They can stand on their own and, in spite of men, seek divorce and demand compensation. With heartening signs of change such as these, women can now certainly look forward to a genuine recognition by men of their rights and privileges as equal and free citizens within a democratic and secular set-up in the near future. It is certain that the future is going to be far better than what the past and the present have been. History will not be allowed to repeat itself if women leaders bear in mind the popular maxim: 'Eternal vigilance is the price of liberty'. Besides, to hasten the process of change on all levels, fighters for the women's cause will have to be far more active than they have so far been. To bring about a stable harmony between a demanding present and an unmastered past, they will have to rouse every woman from her dogmatic slumber. To secure the future, they will have to reverse the past and restructure the present. Encouraging it is to note that sufficient attention has already been drawn to women's problems. Never before in history were women and their problems discussed in as many books and journals, in as many educational institutions and legislatures, on as many public platforms in India and abroad, as has been done in recent years. The ever increasing number of works and organizations dealing exclusively with women's rights and problems in itself is an indication of the degree of consciousness, both in women and men, that has been brought about. But all this is not enough. Women will have to create history which places them as respectable citizens of a civilized society and ensures that this process of change for the better is going to remain irreversible until the goal is realized. Having achieved some such awareness of the present and a right perspective of the future, students of women's studies may now look back to survey the whole field of Hindu thinking about women and may not discover a wholly empty garner. Even post-Aryan history itself has preserved a few scattered memoirs of men who could see and appreciate women in their own right and for their own sake. Unfortunate it was that such thoughtful men could never acquire the status of a determinative significance for mainstream Hinduism. They could never achieve a number that could not be ignored or sidetracked by the intellectual majority. Nonetheless, it gives a modern Hindu male a sense of consolation that, some of his ancestors, though very few, were men who could feel and document their appreciation of and regard for the essential worth of women. They were no mere do-gooders. They were those rare honest men who could see the light that was woman and talk about her with absolute sincerity and clarity. It is to their credit that despite the persuasive and continuous campaign and clamour against women masterminded by conservative thinkers and law-givers, they were able to establish a line of thinking as well as to preserve a tradition of scholarship about women which placed Hindu womanhood in its right perspective. This tradition of scholarship is variously known as the Shakta Cult

Shaktism and Tantrism.

Two characteristic doctrines of Shaktism distinguish it from Vedism (Aryanism, Brahmanism or mainstream Hinduism). These two characteristic doctrines are: (I) That the male principle in the universe is inert and so all active virtues are inspired by the female principle which is the main object of worship and (II) That every woman is an image of the Great Goddess (Mahadevi or Mahashakti or Shakti) who is the Absolute and who does not allow any social hierarchy or caste system in a human society (cf. Thomas 1964 : 276, Roy and Gidwani 1984 : 38-39 & 1986 : 14, 15 & 167-68).

Shaktism has existed in India since the earliest times and side by side orthodox Hinduism. But it has never been swamped by the latter. It glorifies woman and posits an egalitarian social structure in which everyone is free to pursue his or her own ends in order to achieve salvation in life itself. There is no room for a theory of God, of the other world or of a soul outside the body. One can go up or sink down with the body: "That which is not in the body is not in the universe" (cf. Roy and Gidwani 1986 : 168). The mother is uniquely generous, limitlessly resourceful and supremely adorable because she creates and preserves the body. It is through the body that one can know the world and distinguish good from evil. It is through the body that one can raise or demean oneself. It is, above all, through the body that one can synthesize sex with superconsciousness. There is nothing naughty, profane or evil about sex, provided one can see through and transcend one's sexuality.

As pointed out at the beginning of this study, Shaktism must not be confused with the Indo-Aryan casual apotheosis of the Goddess (Devi). The Indo-Aryan view of the Devi must be separated from the pre-Aryan and non-Aryan philosophy of Shaktism (cf. Chanda 1976 : 122-161). The Indo-Aryan or Vedic Devi is just an appendix to the Deva (God). The Devi-Sukta of the *Rig-Veda* does not represent any independent significant female deity. Among goddesses, the *Rig-Veda* eulogizes the Mother Earth but even she is worshipped as the spouse of the Father Sky (cf. Roy and Gidwani 1984 : 38-39, 1986 : 14). **Indo-Aryan theology does not visualize any** autonomous goddess; every goddess happens to be the wife or female partner of a god. Durga or Parvati is the Shakti of Shiva, Lakshmi is the Shakti of Vishnu while Sachi is the Shakti of Indra.

Similarly, in post-Vedic Indo-Aryan literature Radha is associated with Krishna and Sita with Rama. Belief in the ultimate supremacy of the female principle, egalitarian social structure and liberation within life itself separate Shaktism from Vedism. The non-Vedic form of Shaktism does not enunciate a polytheistic divine order headed by a He-God or a supra-mundane metaphysics created and sustained by utopian male seers and prophets. Its ideal is not Moksha (liberation after death) but Jivana-Mukti (liberation within the span of life itself). It does not visualize the Holy Trinity of the Creator, the Preserver and the Destroyer. It enunciates instead a monotheistic philosophy that revolves round the Devi. It believes in the Devi as both the ultimate source and the final destination of all created beings. The Devi is full of kindness, light, beauty and splendour—the mother and preserver of the world. She is also the Terrible one who can destroy all those who transgress the laws of life. All Yogic practices are therefore so channelized as to awaken the *Kundalini* in order that one can concentrate on the Mother and organize life in consonance with her wishes. The Mother is the Adya Shakti, the Primodial Cosmic energy, the Supreme being (cf. Chanda 1976 : 143). Every woman is the image of the Mother and must be revered as such. Shaktism is thus the opposite of Vedism and must be seen as such. If we look back, we should consider it a miracle that despite concerted Indo-Aryan attempts to amalgamate it within the Vedic doctrine, Shaktism has survived through the ages as a self-sufficient theology parallel to mainstream Hinduism. The ideological framework of Shaktism does not allow any pejorative reference to women. The *Mahanirvana Tantra* declares that even rudeness to women should be appropriately expiated. It lays down: "He who unjustly forsakes his wife shall put on ass' skin and beg in seven houses with the words: "give alms to one who has left his wife" (cf. Thomas 1964 : 278).

Again,

"A man who ravishes a woman, even if she is a Chandala (outcast), should be punished with death and should never be pardoned:" (*ibid.*, p. 278).

The author of the *Brihada Samhita* observes: "There are no greater jewels created by God than the jewel that is woman, that is capable of giving delight to man by sight, by hearing, by speech. ... Women are superior to men in their capacity for virtue, men are pure in their feet, the cow on her back, the goat and dog in the mouth, but women are pure in the whole body. Women are incomparably pure; they are never defiled ... Man is born of woman; O ungrateful ones who slander women, to whom you owe your very existence, how can you ever be happy? ... Man's sex desire is not abated even when he is a hundred years old ... whereas in women it is controlled by their will" (*ibid.*, p. 280).

The view taken in this study is that Shaktism is a unique extant gift of the Afro-Dravidian Matriarchy that probably existed in India till it was replaced by Indo-Aryan patriarchy. It was a quirk of fate that the matriarchal order could not have its way in spite of the Aryan invasion and conquest of India. The view held in this study may be disputed and therefore it is important that the whole question of the Pre-Aryan social structure is examined through a systematic and careful research. Unless a definitive view on this question is available, leaders of women's liberation movements may turn to these ancient Tantric Hindu texts to trace the historical genuineness of their cause and draw inspiration to steer their campaign through a constructive and organized ideology.

Works Cited

Agarwala, Vinod (1985) : **The Imagery of Kalidasa**, Delhi, Eastern Book Linkers.

Aiyar, V.V.S. (1970) : **Kamba Ramayana—AStudy**, Bombay, Bharatiya Vidya Bhavan.

Allchin, Bridget and Raymond, (1968) : **The Birth of Indian Civilization**, Harmondsworth, Penguin Books.

Altekar, A.S. (1956) : **The Position of Women in Hindu Civilization**, Delhi, Motilal Banarsidass, First Published in 1938.

Ambedkar, B.R. (1987) : 'Riddles of Rama and Krishna' Appendix to **Riddles in Hinduism**, Bangalore, Dalit Sahitya Acedemy.

Amundsen, Kirsten (1971) : **The Silenced Majority—Woman and American Democracy** Englewood Cliffs, New Jersey, Prentice Hall.

Archer, W.G. (1963) ed : **The Kamasutra of Vatsyayana** London, George Allen & Unwin.

Bader, Clarisse (1964) : **Women in Ancient India**, Varanasi, The Chawkhambha Sanskrit Series Office Translated by Mary E.R. Martin, (1925) Originally Published in French in 1867.

Baig, Tara Ali (1976) : **India's Woman Power**, New Delhi, S. Chand & Company.

Banerji, S.C. (1976) : **Indian Society in the Mahabharata**, (An English translation of selected verses from the **Mahabharata**), Varanasi, Bharata Manisha.

Barker, Ernest (1946) ed. : **The Politics of Aristotle**, Oxford, At the Clarendon Press.

Barse, Sheela (1985) : 'Selling Body and Soul' in **The Statesman, Miscellany**, Calcutta, 17 November, 1987.

Basham, A.L. (1967) : **The Wonder that was India**, Calcutta, Rupa & Co., Fontana Books.

Beauvoir, Simone de (1953) : **The Second Sex**, Translated by H.M. Parshley London, Landsborough Publications, Originally published in French in 1949.

Berggren, Paula S. *et. al.*, (1980) : 'The Woman's Part' in **The Woman's Part : Feminist Criticism of Shakespeare**, edited by Carolyn Ruth Swift Lenz *et. al.*, pp. 17-34.

Bhandarkar, R.G. (1965) : **Vaishnavism, Shaivism and Minor Religious Systems**, Varanasi, Indological Book House, First Published in 1913.

Bhat, Yashoda (1993) : 'The Changing Image of Woman' in **The Image of Woman in Indian Literature**, edited by Yashoda Bhat and Yamuna Raja Rao, Delhi, B.R. Publishing Corporation, pp. IX-XXIV.

Bodkin, Maud (1963) : **Archetypal Patterns in Poetry**, Oxford, Oxford University Press, First Published in 1934.

Bose, N.K. (1975) : **The Structure of Hindu Society**, New Delhi, Orient Longman, Translated by Andre Beteille Originally published in Bengali in 1949.

Browne, Sir Thomas (1642) : **Religio Medici**, English classics for Indian Students, Bombay, Karnataka Publishing House.

Chakladar, H.C. (1976) : **Social Life in Ancient India : Studies in Vatsayayana's Kamasutra**, Delhi, Bharatiya Publishing House.

Chanda, R.P. (1976) : **The Indo-Aryan Races**, New Delhi, Indological Book Corporation.

Chandra, Pratap (1970) : **The Mahabharata**, an abridged English transalation, New Delhi, Munshiram Manoharlal.

Islam, Bahrul (1986) : 'Religion and State' in **The Statesman**, Calcutta, 18 & 19 August 1986.

Janeway, Elizabeth (1981) : 'Women's Literature' in **Harvard Guide to Contemporary American Writing**, ed., Daniel Hoffman Bombay, Oxford University Press.

Johnson, Samuel (1961) : 'Preface to Shakespeare' (1765) in **Shakespeare Criticism**, (1623-1840) ed., D.N. Smith, pp. 77-116, Oxford, Oxford University Press.

Jowett, B. (1937) ed. : **The Dialouges of Plato**, Vols. I, II & III Newyork, Random House.

Kale, M.R. (1967) : **The Kumarasambhava of Kalidasa**, An English translation Delhi, Motial Banarsidass, First Published in 1923.

Kalidas, S. (1993) : 'Conversations with B.N. Pande' in **The Times of India**, New Delhi, 22 August, 1993.

Kanchan, R.K. (1987) : ' New Light on Ancient India' in **The Hindustan Times**, New Delhi, 19 March, 1987.

Kapur, Promila (1974) : **The Changing Status of the Working Woman in India** Delhi, Vikas Publishing Fouse.

Kidwai, S.M.H. (1976) : **Woman Under Different Social and Religious Laws**, Delhi, Seema Publications.

Kitzinger, Shiela (1971) : 'The woman on the Delivery Table' in **Woman on Woman**, ed. Margaret Laing pp. 272-293.

Knox, B.M.W. (1983) : 'The **Medea** of Euripides' in **Greek Tragedy : Modern Essays in Criticism**, ed Erick Segal, pp. 272-273, New York, Harper & Row Publishers.

Krishnamoorthy, K. (1993) : 'The Image of Woman in Sanskrit Literature', in **The Image of Woman in Indian Literature**, ed. Yashoda Bhat and Yamuna Raja Rao, pp. 109-117.

Laing, Margaret (1971) ed. : **Woman on Woman**, London, Sidgwick and Jackson.

Lal, P. (1964) : **Great Sanskrit Plays**, New English Translation, Norfolk, New Directions Books, First Published in 1957.

Lal, P. (1980): **The Mahabharata of Vyasa**, An Abridged Translation, Delhi, Vikas Publishing House.

Lenz, Carolyn Ruth Swift *et. al.*, (1980) : 'Introduction' to **The Woman's Part : Feminist Criticism of Shakespeare**, pp. 3-16, Urbana, University of Illinois Press.

Mahadevan, T.M.P. (1975) : 'Introduction' to **Upanishads**, ed. T.M.P Mahadevan, New Delhi, Arnold Heinemann, pp. 7-44.

Mahajan, V.D. (1990) : **History of India**, New Delhi, S. Chand and Company, First Published in 1970.

Majumdar, R.C. *et. al.*, (1978) : **An Advanced History of India**, Madras, Macmillan India Limited, First Published in 1946.

Mangalvadi, Vishal (1987) : 'Exorcising the Evil of Sati', in **Indian Express**, 23 September, 1987.

Mazumdar, Sudha (1974) : **Ramayana**, An English Translation of Krittivasa **Ramayana** in Bengali, Calcutta, Orient Longman.

McFarlane, James (1970) ed. : **Henrik Ibsen—A Critical Anthology**, Harmondsworth, Penguin Books.

McPhee, C. and Fitzgerald, A. (1979) ed. : **Feminist Quotations**, New York, Thomas Y. Crowell.

Mehta, Rama (1970) : **The Western Educated Hindu Woman**, Bombay, Asia Publishing House.

Miller, Barbara Stoter (1977) ed. : **Jayadeva's Gitagovinda**, An English Translation, Delhi, Oxford University Press.

Miller, Peter (1987) : 'Sex Behind the Curtain', in **The Hindustan Times**, New Delhi, 15 March, 1987.

Mishra, Pt. Jagdish (1978) ed. : **Hanumannatakam**, Sanskrit Text with Hindi Translation, Varanasi, Chawkhambha Sanskrit Series.

Muller, Max (1964) ed. : **The Sacred Books of the East**, Vol. XXV, **The Laws of Manu**, Delhi, Motilal Banarsidass, Originally Published in 1886, This Volume Translated by G. Buhler.

Murry, Gilbert (1910) ed. : **Medea**, London, George Allen & Unwin.

Narasimhaiah, C.D. (1993) : 'Foreword' to **The Image of Woman in Indian Literature**, ed. Yashoda Bhat and Yamuna Raja Rao, pp III-IV.

Nath, L.B. (1979) ed. : **The Adhyatma Ramayana**, An English Translation, Delhi, Bharatiya Publishing House.

Neely, Carol Thomas *et. al.*, (1980) : 'Women and men in Othello', in **Woman's Part : Feminist Criticism of Shakespeare**, ed. Carolyn Ruth Swift Lenz, *et. al.*, pp. 211-239.

Pannikar, K.M. (1963) : 'Introduction', to **The Kamasutra of Vatsyayana**, ed. W.G. Archer, pp. 43-77.

Parekh, Bhikhu (1993): 'Some Reflections on the Indian Diaspora', in the **Journal of Contemporary Thought**, ed., P.C. Kar, *et. al.*, Baroda & Sherveport, M.S. University of Baroda and College of Liberal Arts, Lousiana State University, pp. 105-151.

Pickthall, M.M. (1975) : **The Meaning of Glorious Koran**, New York, Mentor Books.

Pomeroy, Sarah B. (1975) : **Goddesses, Whores, Wives, and Slaves—Women in Classical Antiquity**, New York, Schoken Books.

Quirk, Randolph *et. al.*, (1972) : **A Grammar of Contemporary English**, London, Longman.

Radhakrishnan, S (1993) : **The Bhagavatagita**, An English Translation, New Delhi, Indus, First Published in 1948 by George Allen & Unwin, London.

Rajagopalachari, C. (1951) : **Mahabharata**, Bombay, Bharatiya Vidya Bhavan.

————, (1951 a) : **Ramayana**, Bombay, Bharatiya Vidya Bhavan.

Rao, Nagesh (1988) : 'The Shankaracharya of Puri', in **Indian Express**, 13 April, 1988.

Ratnesh, R.S.S. (1987) : 'Brahmavada', in **Hindu Samaj ke Pathabhrashtaka Tulasidasa**, ed., Vishvanath, New Delhi, Vishvavijaya Prakashan, pp 149-156.

Richards, I.A. (1960) : **Principles of Literary Criticism**, London, Routledge and Kegan Paul, First Published in 1924, First Published as a Paperback, 1960.

Roy, A.K. and Gidwani, N.N. (1983) : **Dictionary of Indology**, Vol I.

————, (1984) : **Dictionary of Indology**,Vol. II.

————, (1985) : **Dictionary of Indology**,Vol. III.

————, (1986) : **Dictionary of Indology**, Vol. IV, New Delhi, Oxford & IBH Publishing Co.

Sachchidananda and Sinha, R.P. (1984) : **Women's Rights : Myth & Reality**, Jaipur, Printwell Publishers.

Safran, Claire (1987) : 'Why Men Hunt Women They Love', in **Reader's Digest**, Bombay, R & I Printing & Publishing (P.) Ltd. March 1987, pp. 135-140.

Sahai, S.N. (1985) : **Women in Changing Society**, Delhi, Mittal Publications.

Sen, M.L. (1976) : **The Ramayana of Valmiki**, An English Translation, Abridged, Calcutta, Firma K.L.M.

Sengupta, Padmini (1974) : **The Story of Women of India**, New Delhi, Indian Book Company.

Sharma, Ramananda (1962) : **Manasa kee Mahilayen**, Madras, Kanyakumari Prakashan.

Sharma, Ramashraya (1971) : **A Socio—Political Study of the Valmiki Ramayana**, Delhi, Motilal Banarsidass.

Sharma, R.P. (1979) : **I A Richards' Theory of Language**, New Delhi, S. Chand and Comapany.

Sharma, R.P. (1986) : 'The Freudian Paradigm of Literature' in **NEHU Journal of Social Sciences and Humanities**, Vol. IV, No. 4 October-December 1986 pp. 1-36.

Shakespeare, W. (1951) : **The Complete Works**, London, Collins, ed., Peter Alexander.

Shastri, Shakuntala Rao (1969) : **Women in Vedic Age**, Bombay, Bharatiya Vidya Bhavan First Published in 1952.

Singh, Nalini (1987) : 'Sati versus Sathin' in **Indian Express**, New Delhi, 13 December, 1987.

Smith, Vincent A. (1981) : **The Oxford History of India** ed., Percival Spear Delhi, Oxford University Press First Published in 1919.

Sophocles (1962) : **Antigone** in **Three Plays**, translated by H.D.F. Kitto Oxford, Oxford University Press.

Spenser, H.S. (1965) : **The Aryan Ecliptic Cycle**, with a 'Foreword' by Ramaswami Aiyer, Poona, Rajkamal.

Stimpson, Carolyn R *et. al.*, (1980) : 'Shakespeare and the Soil of Rape' in **The Woman's Part : Feminist Criticism of Shakespeare**, ed

Carolyn Ruth Swift Lenz *et. al.*

Stocks, Lady (1971) : 'Eighty years on' in **Woman on Woman**, ed., Maragaret Laing, pp. 11-26.

Storr, Anthony (1973) : **Jung**, London, Fontana Collins.

Stott, Mary (1971) : 'The Female Ghetto' in **Woman on Woman**, ed., Margaret Laing, pp. 155-169.

Subramanian, Nirupama (1988) : 'Dowry Deaths' in **Indian Express**, New Delhi, 13-14 April, 1988.

Summerskill, Lady (1971) : 'Ideal Husband, Imperfect Law' in **Woman on Woman**, ed., Margaret Laing, pp. 133-52.

Tandon, P.D. and Wolseley, R.E. (1975) : **Three Women to Remember**, Allahbad, St. Paul Society.

Thapar, Romila (1966) : **A History of India**, Harmondsworth, Penguin Books.

————, **The Hindu**, New Delhi, 18 December, 1986.

————, **The Hindustan Times**, New Delhi, 2 April, 1987.

————, **The Holy Bible**, King James Version.

————, **The Statesman**, Clacutta, 22 & 25 October, 14 November, 15 November, 1986, 30 March, 1987.

Thomas, Paul (1964) : **Indian Women Through the Ages**, Bombay, Asia Publishing House.

Trench, Sally (1971) : 'One Woman Band', in **Woman on Woman**, ed Margaret Laing, pp. 191-205.

Varma, S.P. (1978) : **Indian Constitution and Government**, New Delhi, NCERT.

Vickers, Brian (1973) : **Towards Greek Tragedy**, London, Longman.

Volger, Christopher (1988) : A Practical Guide to **The Hero with a Thousand Faces**, Glendale, The Story Company.

Waddington, C.H. (1961) : 'The Human Animal', in **The Humanist Frame**, ed., Sir Julian Huxley, pp. 67-80.

Wiser, William H. and Wiser, Charlotte V. (1963) : **Behind Mud**

Walls, Berkley & Los Angeles, University of California Press, First Published in 1930.

Wright, B.A. (1962) ed. : **Milton's Poems**, London, J.M. Dent & Sons Ltd., Everyman's Library.

Wurm, Alois (1976) : **Character Portrayals in the Ramayana of Valmiki**, Delhi, Ajanta Publications.

Index